Reading Autobiography

Reading Autobiography

A Guide for Interpreting Life Narratives

Sidonie Smith and Julia Watson

University of Minnesota Press
Minneapolis • London

MIN NE SO TA

Published with assistance from the Margaret S. Harding Memorial Endowment honoring the first director of the University of Minnesota Press.

Published by the University of Minnesota Press
111 Third Avenue South, Suite 290
Minneapolis, MN 55401–2520
http://www.upress.umn.edu

Printed in the United States of America on acid-free paper

Library of Congress Cataloging-in-Publication Data

Smith, Sidonie.
    Reading autobiography : a guide for interpreting life narratives /
Sidonie Smith and Julia Watson.
        p. cm.
Includes bibliographical references and index.
    ISBN 0-8166-2882-3 (HC) — ISBN 0-8166-2883-1 (PB)
    1. Autobiography. I. Watson, Julia. II. Title.
    CT25 .S595 2001
    808′ .06692—dc21

                                        2001005278

12 11 10 09 08 07 06 05 04 03 02 01   10 9 8 7 6 5 4 3 2 1

To our inspirational colleagues in the AutoBiography Society

Autobiography is the highest and most instructive form in which
the understanding of life comes before us.
Wilhelm Dilthey, *Meaning in History*

Autobiographies . . . may reveal as much about the author's
assumed audience as they do about him or her, and this is a further
reason why they need to be read as *cultural documents*, not just as
personal ones.
Robert F. Sayre, *American Lives: An Anthology of*
Autobiographical Writing

In spite of the fact that autobiography is impossible, this in no way
prevents it from existing.
Philippe Lejeune, "The Autobiographical Pact (bis)"

I . . . found myself constructing Gayatri Spivaks who "represented"
various historical and geographical cases. How to distinguish this
from a request to speak of the singularity of one's life?
Gayatri Spivak, "Lives"

Contents

PREFACE

This book aims to be at once a comprehensive critical introduction and a retrospective study of autobiography. We hope that it will be useful to advanced undergraduate and graduate students and to scholars in the humanities, the social sciences, and the arts who are interested in the burgeoning field of life writing. We also intend the organization of this guide to be user-friendly for the general reader.

Reading Autobiography is divided into seven substantive chapters that explore the building blocks and components of autobiographical acts, review the histories of autobiography and autobiography criticism, and offer a "tool kit" of pertinent questions for twenty key concepts. Each chapter has several clearly labeled subsections. There are also several appendixes—an overview of the genres of life writing, classroom exercises, Internet resources, and bibliographies of primary and secondary texts. The book is laid out in such a way that instructors can use chapters independently or out of sequence, and tailor the information to their course needs.

Instructors in departments of literature, American studies, women's studies, African American and ethnic studies, history, and other fields in which the study of autobiography comprises a significant subject of inquiry will find *Reading Autobiography* a helpful guide. At the graduate level, this text offers a comprehensive introduction for students engaging primary texts or doing intensive theoretical work in life writing. At the undergraduate level this text is a handbook to accompany survey, period, or multicultural courses on autobiography, memoir, personal narrative, or literary history more broadly. It may also be of interest to general readers engaging the "memoir boom."

ACKNOWLEDGMENTS

This book is the distillation of over two decades of our individual work and fifteen years of spirited conversation about autobiography during our collaboration on three coedited books and several conference papers. Our conversations, however, have always been permeated by the voices of others, those colleagues whose proposing, prodding, and questioning have shaped our thinking about life narrative and practices of interpretation. We want to acknowledge debts of many sorts.

We thank Biodun Iginla, formerly of the University of Minnesota Press, for inviting us to contribute to a series of contemporary critical interventions. His concept of that project encouraged us to think through our own relationship to autobiography studies and to frame a wide-ranging investigation into life narrative. First William Murphy and now Richard Morrison of the Press guided us through successive stages of this project. And our copy editor, Therese Boyd, graciously accommodated our editorial needs.

We are grateful to Susanna Egan, trenchant critic of autobiographical theory and resourceful organizer of enterprises in autobiography studies, for her detailed, incisive, and insightful reading of a draft of this manuscript. As we made our revisions, we were greatly aided by both her probing questions and her sense of the breadth and diversity of North American life narrative.

We thank Mary Louise Pratt for prodding us to confront the implications of our own collaborative work in relation to the range of life-narrative practices around the globe. In coming to articulate the critical enterprise of autobiography as just one mode of life writing, while acknowledging its authority as a master narrative and institution-alizing force, we acknowledge the importance of Pratt's comparative theorizing about autoethnographic practice, as well as that of other postcolonial critics such as Françoise Lionnet. Their work has exercised an influence both collegial and cautionary in frequently reminding us how diverse the meanings and consequences of telling one's life are.

We are indebted to Timothy Dow Adams not only for his ready wit and critical accomplishments but also for inviting us to conduct the West Virginia University Department of English Summer Seminar in Literary and Cultural Studies on "Getting a Life: Autobiographical Genders, Bodies, Borders" in 1998. For four heady days we presented early drafts of several parts of this book to an extraordinary group of over fifty scholars from around the country whose enthusiasm for the autobio-graphical in all its forms renewed our own determination to give shape to this project.

Independently, each of us presented parts of this book to hos-pitable audiences at the University of Kansas, Texas Tech University, the University of British Columbia, the annual meeting of the Michigan College English Association held at Michigan State University, and the Massachusetts Historical Society. We have also engaged nonacademic groups and audiences at libraries, cultural centers, and even the Montana Bureau of Land Management. In these venues the questions of audiences about the work life narratives do in the world stimulated our own think-ing about the democratic and enabling process of narrating a life.

We thank the American Antiquarian Society for the exciting seminar in June 1999 on "Telling Lives, Telling Lies?" directed by Ann Fabian. As our group of scholars intensively engaged the history of the book, the AAS's rich collections led us to see life narratives as embedded in the material histories of the books and editions in which they were published. That process inaugurated our understanding of the relation of a particular narrative to both its cultural moment and the history of reading, the signs of which will be abundantly evident throughout this book.

We are grateful to our home universities, and especially their libraries, for support of our research. In particular, Julia thanks the Institute for Collaborative Research and Public Humanities at Ohio State University for appointing her a fellow in its collaborative project on memory in 1999–2000. And she acknowledges the support of the National Endowment for the Humanities, which enabled her to participate in its summer seminar on Issues in Rhetorical Theory of Narrative, directed by Jim Phelan of Ohio State University in 1995. While Jim and other members of the Society for the Study of Narrative Literature may not always recognize their nuanced distinctions about autodiegesis in this book, we have learned from both their careful attention to the rhetoric of address and their energetic annual conferences. Julia is also grateful to members of the University of California Humanities Research Institute on Autobiography in the Americas for stimulating conversations about the presentation of lives in visual, media, and literary formats.

Sidonie thanks the University of Michigan, especially the Women's Studies Program, for its support of research assistance in the preparation of this manuscript. More particularly, both of us thank Caryn Elizabeth Burtt for her excellence as a research assistant in tracking down bibliographic information about the many narratives included in this volume and for her unfailing good humor and generosity. Portions of chapters 5 and 6 have been excerpted, with revision, from chapter 1 of Sidonie's *The Poetics of Women's Autobiography: Marginality and the Fictions of Self-Representation* and from chapter 3 of her *Subjectivity, Identity, and the Body: Women's Autobiographical Practices in the Twentieth Century*, both published by Indiana University Press.

Some debts are of a more diffuse but deeply felt sort.

We acknowledge the enduring community of our colleagues in the AutoBiography Society. An intrepid band of scholars with whom we have worked to bring academic legitimacy to the study of life narrative, they have challenged, cajoled, and consoled one another for fifteen years. In that process, which saw the recovery of an extraordinary wealth of life narratives and the consolidation of a critical tradition of autobiography studies, their insight and vigorous scholarship have constantly enriched our own work. In more ways than we can count, their voices are intermingled here. Similarly we are indebted to the energetic conversations generated at conferences on autobiography organized over nearly two decades, which ranged from the Gender Text and ConText Conference on Women's Autobiography at Stanford University in 1984, where we first met, through the superb Autobiography and Changing Identities conference at the University of British Columbia in 2000.

We owe a particular debt of gratitude to James Olney. Independently, each of us benefited from his support of our work at an early stage, and found his generosity sustaining and inspiring. James's profound engagement with questions at the heart of self-referential discourse, his commitment to the field of autobiography studies, and his generosity to younger scholars were and continue to be inspirational.

And, as always, we acknowledge the understanding and good-humored tolerance of the usual suspects. They know who they are.

Finally we acknowledge the schooling in wisdom of life narrators themselves. Studying self-referential writing is, if nothing else, an enduring lesson in humility. As Montaigne observed: "There is no use our mounting on stilts, for on stilts we must still walk on our own legs. And on the loftiest throne in the world we are still sitting only on our own rump" (III: 13, "Of experience," 857).

CHAPTER 1

Life Narrative: Definitions and Distinctions

My life is history, politics, geography. It is religion and
metaphysics. It is music and language.

Paula Gunn Allen, "The Autobiography of a Confluence"

Defining Kinds of Life Writing

What could be simpler to understand than the act of people writing
about what they know best, their own lives? But this apparently simple
act is anything but simple, for the writer becomes, in the act of writing,
both the observing subject and the object of investigation, remembrance, and contemplation. This book intends to complicate our ordinary understanding of the concept and the practice of self-referential
writing. By way of introduction, we define terms and draw distinctions
between autobiographical writing and other closely related kinds of life
writing.

In Greek, *autos* signifies "self," *bios* "life," and *graphe* "writing."[1]
Taken together in this order, the words denote "self life writing," a brief
definition of "autobiography." The British poet-critic Stephen Spender
cites the dictionary definition of *autobiography* as "the story of one's life
written by himself" but notes its inadequacy to the "world that each is to
himself" (115). More recently, French theorist Philippe Lejeune has
expanded that definition: "We call autobiography the retrospective narrative in prose that someone makes of his own existence when he puts
the principal accent upon his life, especially upon the story of his own
personality."[2] When "life" is expanded to include *how* one has become
who he or she is at a given moment in an ongoing process of reflection,

clearly the autobiographical story requires more explaining. Let us first situate the term historically.

The term *autobiography* was first coined in the preface to a collection of poems by the eighteenth-century English working-class writer Ann Yearsley, although most critics still cite Robert Southey's anglicizing of the three Greek words in 1809 as the first use of the term in English. In his extensive history of the term *autobiography*, Robert Folkenflik specifies the exact dates of the word's emergence in the West: "The term *autobiography* and its synonym *self-biography*," Folkenflik notes, "having never been used in earlier periods, appeared in the late eighteenth century in several forms, in isolated instances in the seventies, eighties, and nineties in both England and Germany with no sign that one use influenced another" (5). Folkenflik also notes that until the twentieth century the word *memoirs* (the French *les mémoirs*) was commonly used to designate "self life writing."

"Autobiography," now the most commonly used term for such life writing, thus described writing being produced at a particular historical juncture, the early modern period in the West with its concept of the self-interested individual intent on assessing the status of the soul or the meaning of public achievement. By the eighteenth century notions of self-interest, self-consciousness, and self-knowledge informed the figure of the "Enlightened individual" described by philosophers and social and political theorists. And "autobiographies" as studies in self-interest were sought by a growing reading public with access to affordable printed books (see Krailsheimer, Weintraub, and Sturrock).

But the relatively recent coinage of the term *autobiography* does not mean that the practice of self-referential writing began only at the end of the eighteenth century. In earlier centuries, terms such as "memoir" (Madame de Staël, Glückel of Hameln) or "the life" (Teresa of Avila) or "the book of my life" (Cardano) or "confessions" (Augustine, Rousseau) or "essays of myself" (Montaigne) were used to mark the writer's refraction of self-reference through speculations about history, politics, religion, science, and culture. Moreover, since the end of the eighteenth century many other terms, among them *testimonio, autoethnography, psychobiography*, have been coined to designate new kinds and contexts of self-referential writing. Because of this rich and diverse history of self-referential modes, we need to make some crucial distinctions among a set of terms—*life writing, life narrative, autobiography*—that may seem to imply the same thing.

Throughout this book, we try to make clear distinctions among life writing, life narrative, and autobiography. We understand *life writing* as a general term for writing of diverse kinds that takes a life as its subject. Such writing can be biographical, novelistic, historical, or an explicit self-reference to the writer. We understand *life narrative* as a somewhat narrower term that includes many kinds of self-referential writing, including autobiography.[3] Chapter 2 explores in detail the components of autobiographical acts in life narrative: memory, experience, identity, embodiment, and agency. Chapter 3 elaborates the narrative features of particular autobiographical acts in their complex contexts. These two chapters suggest the processes, formal options, and rhetorical addresses that, taken together, comprise the diverse acts by which a life narrative may be composed. Chapter 4 offers a brief historical survey of the many kinds of life narrative that have emerged in the West over the last two thousand years, many of them by subordinated subjects, and a glimpse at practices of life narration outside the West. Life narrative, then, might best be approached as a moving target, a set of ever-shifting self-referential practices that engage the past in order to reflect on identity in the present.

Autobiography, by contrast, is a term for a particular practice of life narrative that emerged in the Enlightenment and has become canonical in the West. While *autobiography* is the most widely used and most generally understood term for life narrative, it is also a term that has been vigorously challenged in the wake of postmodern and postcolonial critiques of the Enlightenment subject. Privileged as the definitive achievement of a mode of life narrative, "autobiography" celebrates the autonomous individual and the universalizing life story. Its theorists have installed this master narrative of "the sovereign self" as an institution of literature and culture, and identified, in the course of the twentieth century, a canon of representative life narratives. But implicit in this canonization is the assignment of lesser value to many other kinds of life narratives produced at the same time and, indeed, a refusal to recognize them as "true" autobiography. Thus, a growing number of postmodern and postcolonial theorists contend that the term *autobiography* is inadequate to describe the extensive historical range and the diverse genres and practices of life narratives and life narrators in the West and elsewhere around the globe. Indeed, they point out that autobiography, celebrated by an earlier generation of scholars such as Georges Gusdorf and Karl Joachim Weintraub as a master narrative of civilization in the West, has been defined *against* many coexistent forms of life narrative. We track the historical emergence of this concept of autobiography as the preeminent version of life narrative and the subsequent critique of its limitations throughout chapters 5 and 6. And we situate it throughout in terms of many other genres and practices of life narrative to suggest the terms in which a new, globalized history of the field might be imagined.

Life Narrative in Relation to Biography, the Novel, and History Writing

Some further distinctions need to be made between autobiographical writing and the practices of other closely related kinds of life writing, notably biography, the novel, and history writing.

Life Narrative and Biography

Although life narrative and biography are both modes of narrating lives, they are not interchangeable, no matter how often people subsume both under biography and think of autobiography as the biography someone writes about him- or herself. In fact, although both forms narrate a life, they do so quite differently.[4] In biography, scholars of other people's lives document and interpret those lives from a point of view external to the subject. In life narrative people write about their own lives (even when they write about themselves in the second or third person, or as a member of a community) and do so simultaneously from externalized and internal points of view.

Why are these kinds of life writing so different from each other, and what is the significance of that difference? Spender suggested that the life narrator confronts not one life, but two. One is the self that others see—the social, historical person, with achievements, personal appearance, social relationships. These are "real" attributes of a person living in the world. But there is also the self experienced only by that person, the self felt from the inside that the writer can never get "outside of."

The "inside," or personally experienced, self has a history. While it may not be meaningful to an objective "history of the times," it is a history of self-observation, not a history observed by others.

> We are seen from the outside by our neighbors; but we remain always at the back of our eyes and our senses, situated in our bodies, like a driver in the front seat of a car seeing the other cars coming toward him. A single person ... is one consciousness within one machine, confronting all the other traffic. (Spender, 116)

To continue Spender's metaphor of driving the "auto," the biographer can circle the car with the driver in it to record the history, character, and motivations of the driver, the traffic, the vehicle, and the facts of transportation. But only the life narrator knows the experience of traffic rushing toward her and makes an interpretation of that situation, that is, writes her subjectivity.

Matters of time and timing also differentiate biography and life narrative. For a biographer the death of the subject is not definitive. A biography can be written either during the life or after the death of the person being written about. In fact, biographies offering different interpretations of particular historical figures may appear periodically over many centuries, as have biographies of Byron, Caesar, Galileo, and Michelangelo. For the life narrator, on the other hand, death is the end of the matter. While a life narrative can be, and often is, written over a long span of time, as is the case with the multiple narratives of Edward Gibbon and Maya Angelou, it must be written during the writer's life span—or be published posthumously "as is."

In writing a life, the life narrator and the biographer also engage different kinds of evidence. Most biographers incorporate multiple forms of evidence, including historical documents, interviews, and family archives, which they evaluate for validity. Relatively few biographers use their personal memories of their subject as reliable evidence, unless they had a personal relationship to the subject of the biography (as a relative, child, friend, or colleague). For life narrators, by contrast, personal memories are the primary archival source. They may have recourse to other kinds of sources—letters, journals, photographs, conversations— and to their knowledge of a historical moment. But the usefulness of such evidence for their stories lies in the ways in which they employ that evidence to support, supplement, or offer commentary on their idiosyncratic acts of remembering. In autobiographical narratives, imaginative acts of remembering always intersect with such rhetorical acts as assertion, justification, judgment, conviction, and interrogation. That is, life narrators address readers whom they want to persuade of their version of experience. And, as we will see in chapter 2, memory is a subjective form of evidence, not externally verifiable; rather, it is asserted on the subject's authority.

The biographer almost invariably writes about the object of his or her study in the third person, while the life narrator usually employs the first person. Certainly, there are autobiographical narrators that present their subjects in the second and/or third person. In *The Education of Henry Adams: An Autobiography*, Henry Adams refers to himself as "Henry Adams," "he," and "him." But readers understand that this is Adams's convention for presenting himself and that the teller and protagonist of the narrative are one and the same. "Henry Adams" appears as both the subject and author on the title page. The biographer, however, cannot present his or her subject in the first person—except when quoting statements or letters or books written by that person.

Of course, there are texts that combine biographical and autobiographical modes of narration. As early as the second century B.C.E., Plutarch wove his own ethical observations and judgments into his parallel *Lives of the Noble Grecians and Romans*. In the seventeenth century, aristocratic women in England such as Anne Lady Halkett and Margaret Cavendish, Duchess of Newcastle, often appended brief narratives of their lives to the adulatory biographies they wrote of their husbands. More recently, life narrators have blurred the boundary separating autobiographical and biographical modes by embedding their versions of the life of a family member in their own personal narratives, as does Kim Chernin in *In My Mother's House: A Daughter's Story*, John Edgar Wideman in *Brothers and Keepers*, and Drucilla Modjeska in *Poppy*; or they entwine the case history of a patient with the writer's own self-analysis, as Annie G. Rogers does in *A Shining Affliction: A Story of Harm and Healing in Psychotherapy*. As much as we have argued for distinguishing life narrative and biography, contemporary practices often blend them into a hybrid, suggesting that life narrative is indeed a moving target of ever-changing practices without absolute rules.

Life Narrative and the Novel

People often confuse life narrative and fiction. Typically, they call autobiographical texts "novels" though they rarely call novels "autobiographies." A life narrative is not a novel, although calling life narrative "nonfiction," which is often done, confuses rather than resolves the issue. Both the life narrative and the novel share features we ascribe to fictional writing: plot, dialogue, setting, characterization, and so on. Further complicating matters, many contemporary writers are interested in blurring the boundary between life narrative and narration in the first-person novel. Yet differences that have historically arisen between them are crucial to understanding how autobiographical writing is a self-referential mode.

In the nineteenth century many novels were presented as autobiographical narratives, the life stories of fictional characters. Think of Charles Dickens's *David Copperfield*, Charlotte Brontë's *Jane Eyre*, and

Fyodor Dostoyevsky's *Notes from Underground.* The narrators of these texts employ the intimate first-person voice as protagonists confiding their personal histories and trying to understand how their past lives have made them who they are. Many twentieth-century novels are also narrated as first-person autobiographies, for example, Rainer Maria Rilke's *The Notebook of Malte Laurids Brigge* J. D. Salinger's *Catcher in the Rye*, Thomas Wolfe's *Look Homeward, Angel,* and Jamaica Kincaid's *Autobiography of My Mother.* And the great modernist novels of Thomas Mann, Marcel Proust, and Robert Musil invoke tropes of autobiographical narration. In such cases, one signal to readers that they are reading a novel and not an autobiographical narrative is that the authorial name on the title page differs from the name of the character narrating the tale. That is, Malte is the named narrator of *The Notebook* and Holden Caulfield the named narrator of *Catcher.* Readers of such narratives are challenged to observe the biases and fantasies of these young protagonists and discover discrepancies between how each views himself at various moments and how we, as readers, regard the limitations or the blind spots of their knowledge.

The convergence of authorial signature and narrator, by contrast, is a distinguishing mark of life narrative, argues Philippe Lejeune in "The Autobiographical Pact." Lejeune defines the relationship between author and reader in autobiographical writing as a contract: "What defines autobiography for the one who is reading is above all a contract of identity that is sealed by the proper name. And this is true also for the one who is writing the text" (19).[5] For Lejeune, two things indisputably distinguish autobiography and, by implication, a wide range of life narratives, from the novel: the "vital statistics" of the author, such as date and place of birth and education, are identical to those of the narrator; and an implied contract or "pact" exists between author and publisher attesting to the truth of the signature (21). When we recognize the person who claims authorship of the narrative as the protagonist or central figure in the narrative—that is, we believe them to be the same person— we read the text written by the author to whom it refers as reflexive or autobiographical. With this recognition of the autobiographical pact,

Lejeune argues, we read differently and assess the narrative as making truth claims of a sort that are suspended in fictional forms such as the novel.

There is also a temporal distinction between a novel and an autobiographical text. Novelists are not bound by historical time. They can situate their narratives at any time in the past, present, or future. This does not mean that life narrators always and simply offer a retrospective narrative in chronological order of the life lived to the point of its writing. They can range far into the past, even the cultural past before the writer's birth, and they may offer an imaginative journey into the future. The narrator of Thomas DeQuincey's *Confessions of an English Opium Eater*, for example, is stimulated by opium to transport his life to other centuries and continents; yet corporeally he remains located in nineteenth-century London. Unlike novelists, life narrators have to anchor their narratives in their own temporal, geographical, and cultural milieux.

In summary, novelists are bound only by the reader's expectation of internal consistency in the world of verisimilitude created within the novel. They are not bound by rules of evidence that link the world of the narrative with a historical world outside the narrative. In contrast, life narrators inevitably refer to the world beyond the text, the world that is the ground of the narrator's lived experience, even if that ground is comprised in part of cultural myths, dreams, fantasies, and subjective memories. Audre Lorde may subtitle *Zami: A New Spelling of My Name* a "biomythography," thereby emphasizing the mythic resonance of her story of growing up as an African American child of a woman from Carriacou, Grenada; but the struggles of her young self are embedded in the New York of the 1950s, no matter how the myth of Carriacou women's friendship lets her valorize the differences of lesbian identity. Moreover, autobiographical narrators are expected to remain faithful to their personal memory archives while novelists need not make this claim (Eakin, *Touching the World*, 28).

Of course, the boundary between the autobiographical and the novelistic is, like the boundary between biography and life narrative, sometimes exceedingly hard to fix. Many writers take the liberties of the novelistic mode in order to mine their own struggles with the past and with the complexities of identities forged in the present. This fluid boundary has particularly characterized narratives by writers exploring the decolonization of subjectivity forged in the aftermath of colonial oppression. Such writers as Michelle Cliff in *Abeng: A Novel* (Jamaica), Tsitsi Dangarembga in *Nervous Conditions* (Zimbabwe), Maryse Condé in *Hérémakhonon* (Guadeloupe), Myriam Warner-Vieyra in *Juletane* (Guadeloupe-Senegal), and Laye Camara in *The Dark Child* (Guinea) create hybrid forms tied to local histories of struggle. As Françoise Lionnet says of her decision to treat such narratives as self-referential texts, they function to illuminate the processes of identity formation through a subjectively rendered consciousness ("Of Mangoes and Maroons," 321–23).

Life Narrative and History

Sometimes people read autobiographical narratives as historical documents, a source of evidence for the analysis of historical movements or events or persons. From this perspective, autobiographical narrating and history writing might seem to be synonymous. Although it can be read as a history of the writing/speaking subject, however, life narrative cannot be reduced to or understood only as historical record. While autobiographical narratives may contain "facts," they are not factual history about a particular time, person, or event. Rather they offer subjective "truth" rather than "fact."

When life narrators write to chronicle an event, to explore a certain time period, or to enshrine a community, they are making "history" in a sense. But they are also performing several rhetorical acts: justifying their own perceptions, upholding their reputations, disputing the accounts of others, settling scores, conveying cultural information, and inventing desirable futures among others. The complexity of autobiographical texts requires reading practices that reflect on the narrative tropes, sociocultural contexts, rhetorical aims, and narrative shifts within the historical or chronological trajectory of the text. Jeremy D. Popkin, a historian interested in both the parallels and the differences between writing life narrative and history, notes another distinction about temporality. Autobiographical writings, Popkin suggests, "privilege a temporal framework based on the individual author's lifespan, whereas historical narrative takes place in collective time." The "arbitrary and concrete" personal time of experience in a life narrative does not have to engage the moments of shared experience that historians identify as significant in the collective time of a society (727).[6]

Historical and autobiographical narratives are also distinguishable in how they use personal narrative. The professional norms of their discipline require historians to be faithful to the evidence available and to seek out multiple sources of evidence, including personal narratives. Excellence in history writing demands scrupulous objectivity. Historians preserve this objectivity and the truthfulness it pledges by maintaining distance from their material and removing or qualifying any reference to themselves in the narrative. Thus, while historians, like life narrators, are writers assembling a story about the past from archives available to them, they must place themselves outside or at the margin of the historical picture. But autobiographical narrators are at the center of the historical pictures they assemble and are interested in the meaning of larger forces, or conditions, or events for their *own* stories.

The power of Sally Morgan's *My Place*, at once the narrative of a young woman coming to claim her identity as an Aboriginal Australian and an exposé of the effects on the older generations of her family of the colonial practices of forceful removal and assimilation, resides in its acknowledgment of an official history of the Australian nation and its insistence on inserting the history of indigenous Australians into the national dialogue. The power of William Apess's "A Son of the Forest" and "The Experience of Five Christian Indians of the Pequot Tribe" derives from the way in which Apess situates himself as an agent of American history, negotiating his status as Native American in his relationships to a series of white people and to literacy in the new republic. In the details and the immediacy of the lived lives of such autobiographical narrators, the political and cultural contexts of the historical past become vivid and memorable.

In summary, autobiographical narrators establish for their readers a different set of expectations, a different pact, than the expectations established in the verisimilitude or suspension of disbelief of the novel or the verifiable evidence of biography and history writing.

Autobiographical Truth

When we try to differentiate autobiographical narrative from biography, the novel, and history writing, we encounter a fundamental question: What is the truth status of autobiographical disclosure? How do we know whether and when a narrator is telling the truth or lying? And what difference would that difference make? These questions often perplex readers of autobiographical texts. For example, a life narrator may narrate his history as a young person full of illusions subsequently lost by the adult narrator, as does the young American immigrant Edward William Bok in *The Americanization of Edward Bok: The Autobiography of a Dutch Boy Fifty Years After*. Life narrators may present inconsistent or shifting views of themselves. They may even perpetrate acts of deliberate deceit to test the reader or to suggest the paradoxical "truth" of experience itself, as Timothy Dow Adams suggests of strategic decisions to deceive in literary life narrative (*Telling Lies*, 14–16).

What is it that we expect life narrators to tell the truth about? Are we expecting fidelity to the facts of their biographies, to experience, to themselves, to the historical moment, to social community, to prevailing beliefs about diverse identities, to the norms of autobiography as a literary genre itself? And truth for whom and for what? Other readers, the life narrator, or ourselves?

John Sturrock has pithily noted, "It is impossible for an autobiographer not to be autobiographical" (52). More recently, Stanley Fish has observed that "[a]utobiographers cannot lie because anything they say, however mendacious, is the truth about themselves, whether they know it or not" (A19). Any utterance in an autobiographical text, even if inaccurate or distorted, characterizes its writer. Thus, when one is both the narrator and the protagonist of the narrative, as in life stories, the truth of the narrative becomes undecidable. We need, then, to adjust our expectations of the truth told in self-referential narrative. Of course, autobiographical claims such as date of birth can be verified or falsified by recourse to documentation or fact outside the text. But autobiographical truth is a different matter; it is an intersubjective exchange between narrator and reader aimed at producing a shared understanding of the meaning of a life.

In *The Autobiography of W. E. B. Du Bois: A Soliloquy on Viewing My Life from the Last Decade of Its First Century*, Du Bois acknowledges that "autobiographies do not form indisputable authorities." This insight motivates him to reflect upon the difficulties of telling his story "frank and fair":

> [M]emory fails especially in small details, so that it becomes finally but a theory of my life, with much forgotten and misconceived, with valuable testimony but often less than absolutely true, despite my intention.... This book then is the Soliloquy of an old man on what he dreams his life has been as he sees it slowly drifting away; and what he would like others to believe. (12-13)

Refiguring his narrative as a "soliloquy" addressed to "others," Du Bois accepts the impossibility of recording only factual truth and turns to the compensations of an intersubjective truth—partly dream, partly promissory belief—that invites our confirmation of its interpretation.

If we approach self-referential writing as an intersubjective process that occurs within the writer/reader pact, rather than as a true-or-false story, the emphasis of reading shifts from assessing and verifying knowledge to observing processes of communicative exchange and understanding. We could redefine the terms: autobiographical narration is so written that it cannot be read solely as either factual truth or simple facts. As an intersubjective mode, it lies outside a logical or juridical model of truth and falsehood, as models of the paradox of self-reference have suggested, all the way from Epidaurus of Crete to contemporary philosophers of language.[7]

Conclusion

Our working definition of autobiographical or life narrative, rather than specifying its rules as a genre or form, understands it as a historically situated practice of self-representation. In such texts, narrators selectively engage their lived experience through personal storytelling. Located in specific times and places, they are at the same time in dialogue with the personal processes and archives of memory.

With this working definition in mind, let us turn to the components and the features that comprise autobiographical acts.

CHAPTER 2

Autobiographical Subjects

For lack of a natural memory, I make one of paper.

Michel de Montaigne, *Essays*

It is funny this knowing being a genius, everything is funny. And identity is funny being yourself is funny as you are never yourself to yourself except as you remember yourself and then of course you do not believe yourself. That is really the trouble with an autobiography you do not of course you do not really believe yourself why should you, you know so well so very well that it is not yourself, it could not be yourself because you cannot remember right and if you do remember right it does not sound right and of course it does not sound right because it is not right. You are of course never yourself.

Gertrude Stein, *Everybody's Autobiography*

The question of the spontaneity of the *I* belongs in a very different, a (biological?) context.

Walter Benjamin, *Gesammelte Schriften*

Life narratives appear to be transparently simple. Yet they are amazingly complex. To explore this complexity we consider in this chapter what we understand as the constitutive processes of autobiographical subjectivity:

- Memory
- Experience

- Identity
- Embodiment
- Agency

Memory

The writer of autobiography depends on access to memory to tell a retrospective narrative of the past and to situate the present within that experiential history. Memory is thus both source and authenticator of autobiographical acts. But what is memory and how does it work?

Memory as Meaning-making

As memory researchers from fields as diverse as neuroscience, cognitive psychology, and philosophy have argued, remembering involves a reinterpretation of the past in the present. The process is not a passive one of mere retrieval from a memory bank. Rather, the remembering subject actively creates the meaning of the past in the act of remembering (Rose). Thus, narrated memory is an interpretation of a past that can never be fully recovered. As Daniel L. Schacter has suggested, "[M]emories are records of how we have experienced events, not replicas of the events themselves" (6). He goes on to explore how "we construct our autobiographies from fragments of experience that change over time" (9). That is, we inevitably organize or form fragments of memory into complex constructions that become the stories of our lives.

According to researchers in developmental psychology, we learn early in childhood what people around us and, by extension, our culture expect us to remember (Nelson, 12). We learn techniques for remembering. We learn something about who is charged with remembering and what kinds of memories they are charged with keeping. And we learn cultural uses of remembering, how certain ways of remembering are expected, acknowledged, valued. For instance, in the United States public rituals of remembering include such occasions as Memorial Day parades, Veterans' Day marches, and religious holidays. Private rituals include the preservation of objects such as heirlooms and family Bibles, and the continuation of family reunions where people gather to remember, reenact, and reaffirm the family's collective past. Such rituals may be part of the texture of memory evoked in autobiography, but narrators may also struggle with or resist collective forms of cultural remembering, finding other meanings in these moments and activities.

Memory and History

In the early twenty-first century (in the United States at least), memory is organized by such artifacts as the scrapbook and the videotape. But at other historical moments, cultures have used different means or "technologies" of memory.[1] The first Romans carried the *lares*, urns filled with ancestral remains, to their new homes to be honored as household deities and sites of remembering. During the early modern period "memory theaters" became aids to memory. As Frances A. Yates has shown, the memory theater was a mnemonic device for remembering large amounts of material. The material to be remembered was spatially organized as a set of rooms or places in a palace through which the rememberer "walked" in imagination, remembering items "in their place."

James Olney has distinguished two models of memory at work in Augustine's fourth-century *Confessions:* the archaeological and the processual. The archaeological model of memory is spatial, "a site where … [he] can dig down through layer after layer of deposits to recover what he seeks"; memories so recovered will be unchanged, if decaying over time (*Memory and Narrative*, 19). In contrast, the processual model for memory is temporal, "bring[ing] forth ever different memorial configurations and an ever newly shaped self." This kind of remembering is imagined as a process of weaving that makes new forms from strands that are also in process (20–21).

As these examples indicate, techniques and practices of remembering change. How people remember, what they remember, and who does the remembering are historically specific. A particular culture's understanding of memory at a particular moment of its history makes remembering possible for a life narrator. Narrators at a crossroads of competing understandings of memory, such as the contemporary Native

American writer Leslie Marmon Silko, may place these competing practices of memory in creative tension with one another in order to explore and interrogate the cultural stakes in remembering through a dominant modern mode and an alternative indigenous mode. Silko, for instance, in *Storyteller*, interweaves personal narratives with stories not strictly her own, that is, with photographs and the poems and traditional stories of the Laguna Pueblo, in order to remember Pueblo cultural practices and situate herself as a creative and reverential voice bridging multiple cultures. What is valued in memory, then, is never simple.

Memory as Contextual

If remembering is a historically inflected phenomenon, it is also a situated one. Much memory is contextual, as Susan Engel's *Context Is Everything: The Nature of Memory* suggests. Acts of remembering take place at particular sites and in particular circumstances. We remember the history of a relationship in the context of sexual intimacy or as we celebrate anniversaries. We remember our history as national citizens in the context of parades and national holidays. Similarly, the memory invoked in autobiographical narrative is specific to the time of writing and the contexts of telling. It is never isolatable fact, but situated association. In *Family Secrets: Acts of Memory and Imagination*, Annette Kuhn explores her past identity as a working-class child in Britain by rereading her family album and reconstructing the secrets hidden in the camera's official snapshots of familiality. She also rereads public documents of the 1953 coronation of Queen Elizabeth II as forms of remembering that create for the nation a "family drama" generating desire for belonging in that larger "family" of "Britain."

The Politics of Remembering

Contexts are charged politically. What is remembered and what is forgotten, and *why*, change over time. Thus remembering also has a politics. There are struggles over who is authorized to remember and what they are authorized to remember, struggles over what is forgotten, both personally and collectively. For instance, under National Socialism,

Germans in the 1930s were schooled (literally and figuratively) to remember the past of the nation as an Aryan past. After World War II the two Germanys were taught to remember different and competing versions of the war and the Holocaust and highly selective versions of the national past, depending on whether they lived in the socialist East or the liberal-democratic West. German autobiographical writing is still negotiating these different versions of national memory, as the formerly East German writer Christa Wolf suggests in *Patterns of Childhood*.

In the United States in the past two decades, we have seen fierce struggles over how the American past is to be remembered at such crucial junctures as the Civil War, the civil rights movement, and the Vietnam War era. Those who celebrate the nineteenth century as a century of America's Manifest Destiny have strongly differing versions of the meanings of Westward expansion than the descendants of Native Americans displaced across the western plains. Sherman Alexie, a member of the Spokane/Coeur d'Alene tribe, explores the necessity of remembering differently with condensed wit in an autobiographical fragment of diary entries he includes in *First Indian on the Moon* (1993). For the "May" entry Alexie imagines Moses, who "wanted to memorialize every Indian who died in war" by capturing a swallow in his mouth and "breath[ing] out the names" of the men, women, and children killed: "Moses worked for years. After he was finished, Moses released the swallows into the air over the reservation, millions of them. Millions" (12).

These examples suggest how the politics of remembering—what is recollected and what is obscured—is central to the cultural production of knowledge about the past, and thus to the terms of an individual's self-knowledge. Autobiographical narratives, as we will see, signal and invite reading in terms of larger cultural issues and may also be productively read against the ideological grain.

Collective Remembering

If we think about remembering not as an entirely privatized activity but as an activity situated in cultural politics, we can appreciate to what degree remembering is a collective activity. On a daily basis we move in and out of various communities of memory—religious, racial, ethnic, familial. Communities develop their own occasions, rituals, and practices of remembering. They establish specific sites for remembering. Furthermore, particular communities are aided in their acts of remembering by different technologies: the memory theaters of the early modern period, writing, movable type, computers. These become systems of "artificial" memory—not in the sense that the memories are fabricated or false but in the sense that the technologies, as aids to preserving and passing on memories, shape the memories conveyed.

Oftentimes life narrators incorporate multiple ways of accessing memory, multiple systems of remembering, into their narratives. Some of these sources are personal (dreams, family albums, photos, objects, family stories, genealogy). Some are public (documents, historical events, collective rituals). Sometimes one way of accessing memory dominates because it is critical to a narrator's project, his sense of the audience for the narrative, or her purpose for making the story public. For example, in *Maus: A Survivor's Tale*, Art Spiegelman includes many forms of documentary evidence from the death camps to authenticate his father's story of deportation to Auschwitz before the son's birth. And in *Vibration Cooking, or the Travel Notes of a Geechee Girl*, Vertamae Smart-Grosvenor embeds the recipes of African American relatives and friends into stories of communities held together through the senses, rituals, and the "vibrations" of memory.

The collective nature of acts of remembering extends beyond the acknowledgment of social sites of memory, historical documents, and oral traditions. It extends to motives for remembering and the question of those on whose behalf one remembers. Precisely because acts of remembering are implicated in how people understand the past and make claims about their versions of the past, memory is an inescapably intersubjective act, as W. J. T. Mitchell insightfully suggests: "memory is an intersubjective phenomenon, a practice not only of recollection of a past *by* a subject, but of recollection *for* another subject" (193 n. 17). Memory is a means of "passing on," of sharing a social past that may have been obscured, in order to activate its potential for reshaping a future of and for other subjects. Thus, acts of personal remembering are fundamentally social and collective.

Memory and Materiality

Memory, apparently so immaterial and personal and elusive, is always implicated in materiality, whether it be the materiality of sound, stone, text, garment, integrated circuits and circuit boards, or the materiality of our very bodies—the synapses and electrons of our brains and our nervous systems. Memory is evoked by the senses—smell, taste, touch, sound—and encoded in objects or events with particular meaning for the narrator. In the *Confessions*, Augustine's memory of stealing pears from a tree is imbued with the sense-awakening qualities of the pears that momentarily overcome him in writing that moment. In the early twentieth century, the aroma of the madeleine stirs Marcel Proust's narrator as a physiological conduit imaginatively returning him to a scene of his past. And later in the century Vladimir Nabokov exercises a fiercely aestheticized mode of visualizing memory in mnemonic images of the past of his childhood in Russia. In *Speak, Memory: A Memoir*, Nabokov associates his fascination with entomology and butterflies with his art of remembering in pictures and words.

Memory and Trauma

People suffering the agonies of traumatic memory are haunted by memories that obsessively interrupt a present moment and insist on their presence. These memories may come to the surface of consciousness in fits and fragments, again and again, despite the passing of years (see Caruth, and Felman and Laub). This haunting of memory is entangled with profound crises in people's lives. Crises of a personal sort, such as a sexual assault, or of a political sort, such as state-sponsored torture or imprisonment during war, may be speakable only in the halting fragments of traumatic or obsessive memory.

In life narratives of the Holocaust, sexual abuse, torture, AIDS, and disability, among others, narrators struggle to find ways of telling about suffering that defies language and understanding; they struggle to reassemble memories so dreadful they must be repressed for human beings to survive and function in life. In such narratives, the problem of recalling and recreating a past life involves organizing the inescapable but often disabling force of memory and negotiating its fragmentary intrusions with increasing, if partial, understanding.

In her ten-part autobiographical poem *A Poem without a Hero*, for instance, Russian poet Anna Akhmatova narrates her husband and son's arrest during 1935–40 (the four years of Stalin's regime of terror) and links her son's imprisonment to the larger tragedy of state-sponsored murder. The subjective "I" breaks down midway through the cycle as she confesses her struggle between the pain of memory and the forgetting offered by madness. Negotiating this break, the narrator moves toward a transpersonal identification with those who suffered. Its testimony to political trauma in both her family and the state makes *A Poem Without a Hero* an autobiographical poem that is also a call to collective Russian conscience.

For Holocaust survivors such as Charlotte Delbo in *Auschwitz and After*, Elie Wiesel in *Night*, and Primo Levi in *Survival in Auschwitz: The Nazi Assault on Humanity*, the struggle with memories of the Holocaust necessitates the return again and again to those incomprehensible moments in the past. For instance, Levi struggles to exorcise memories of a regime of living whose logic destroyed all the bases of humanities, including the metaphorical and literal dimensions of language itself. And in Spiegelman's doubly autobiographical *Maus*, the distortions and omissions of the father Vladek's memory are a partial amnesia enabling the telling of his son Art's story of the legacies of postmemory, particularly the inaccessible memory of his dead mother.[2]

For those suffering from traumatic or obsessional memories, autobiographical acts can work as therapeutic intervention, what Suzette A. Henke calls "scriptotherapy." Speaking or writing about trauma becomes a process through which the narrator finds words to give voice to what was previously unspeakable. And that process can be, though it is not necessarily, cathartic. Thus narrators of trauma often testify to the therapeutic effects of telling or writing a story, acknowledging how the process of writing has changed the narrator and the life story itself.

In her story of traumatic childhood sexual abuse, *My Father's House: A Memoir of Incest and Healing*, Canadian writer Sylvia Fraser marks the break between the historically situated and the imaginary modes of narrating with different fonts. In this way, the daughter of the father/lover can shuttle between recollection/commentary and fantasy, using writing to engage "the anxiety and rage against a spectral patriarch who is everywhere and nowhere—whose nefarious deeds are hidden in the recesses of the unconscious, and whose authoritarian presence his daughter can never escape" (Henke, 129). The two modes of self-narrating are mutually enabling, as Fraser seeks to capture the multiple modes in which trauma is scripted and exorcised. In her profoundly disturbing and daring account of child sexual abuse entitled *Don't: A Woman's Word*, Canadian writer Elly Danica pieces together, in a mode of diaristic dailiness, the disjointed memories that form the reservoir of the unspeakable. Her Dantesque progress requires translation into "a woman's word" as a narrative of descent into a private hell and ascent toward that moment when she can write: "The sentence has changed. Once I could not remember. Now I cannot forget" (101).

Moreover, narrators of trauma are often attentive to the therapeutic effects the narrative might have on their readers; for they may understand their projects as acts of collective remembering, offering readers a possibility of community in identifying with their stories. Nancy Mairs, in *Waist-High in the World: A Life among the Nondisabled*, insists on the personal and moral value of her commitment to communicate to people with disabilities and to the "nondisabled" the hopeful and empowering life to be lived despite her "rehearsal of losses" (31). And she incorporates into her narrative the stories of others living with disabilities. But the process of scriptotherapy may subvert its own goal. Texts such as *Prozac Nation: Young and Depressed in America* by Elizabeth Wurtzel or *Wasted: A Memoir of Anorexia and Bulimia* by Marya Hornbacher may become, in the end, more self-absorbed than therapeutic, as writing trauma becomes a means of perpetuating its self-involvement.

Reading for Memory

When we read or listen to an autobiographical narrative, then, we listen for and attend to the role of remembering—and conscious forgetting—in the act of making meaning out of the past and the present. We may notice an emphasis on particular acts of remembering or particular moods and voices identified with certain memories. We may glimpse the triggering devices that stimulate certain memories. Then, too, narrators themselves may make the act of remembering a significant theme within the narrative. That is, they may be self-reflexive about the problem of remembering and the value of particular kinds of remembering, as are, for example, St. Augustine in *The Confessions*, Mary McCarthy at the beginning of *Memories of a Catholic Girlhood*, and Richard Rodriguez in *Hunger of Memory: The Education of Richard Rodriguez, an Autobiography*. They may call attention to things forgotten, times irretrievable, and to the personal and communal stakes of that forgetting. Life narratives, depending on the memory they construct, are records of acts of interpretation by subjects inescapably in historical time, and in their relation to their own ever-moving pasts.

Experience and the Autobiographical Subject

Experience. We have it. It is ours. The intimacy and immediacy and palpability of our memories tell us so. But what does it mean to say we have an experience? While the experience represented in an autobiographical narrative seems simply personal, it is anything but merely personal. Mediated through memory and language, "experience" is already an interpretation of the past and of our place in a culturally and historically specific present.

Experience as Constitutive of the Subject

A provocative exploration of the phenomenon we call experience can be found in Joan W. Scott's essay, "Experience." In this essay Scott challenges the foundational status of experience as a ground of analysis and a ground of knowledge about the world and ourselves. Scott cautions that talking about experience as either internal to an individual (expressive of an individual's consciousness—what we have inside us) or external to the individual ("the material upon which consciousness works"—what happens to us from outside) "leads us to take the existence of individuals for granted" (27). This taken-for-grantedness of the relationship between individual experience and the claim to unique individuality is what Scott calls into question. Its effect is a failure to interrogate how our notion of meaningful experience is socially produced. How do we know what we know about ourselves? How do we know who we are?

Taking the analysis of Teresa de Lauretis as a point of departure, Scott defines "experience" as "a process … by which subjectivity is constructed" (27). "Through that process," de Lauretis writes, "one places oneself or is placed in social reality and so perceives and comprehends as subjective (referring to, originating in oneself) those relations—material, economic, and interpersonal—which are in fact social, and, in a larger perspective, historical" (*Alice Doesn't*, 159). Experience, then, is the very process through which a person becomes a certain kind of subject owning certain identities in the social realm, identities constituted through material, cultural, economic, and interpsychic relations. "It is not individuals who have experience," Scott claims, "but subjects who are constituted through experience." Autobiographical subjects do not predate experience. In effect, autobiographical subjects know themselves as subjects of particular kinds of experience attached to their social statuses and identities. They know themselves to be a "woman" or "child" or "heterosexual," a "worker" or "Native American" because these identity categories come to seem natural, to seem "given characteristics of persons" (27).

Experience as Discursive

And subjects know themselves in language, because experience is discursive, embedded in the languages of everyday life and the knowledges produced at everyday sites. For instance, through the "discourse" of medical institutions (the language, images, metaphors, and narratives through which medical institutions produce and circulate knowledge about people), persons learn to understand themselves—"experience" themselves—as "patients" in need of healing or as "diseased" or "insufficient" bodies in need of surgical intervention. This medical discourse also becomes the language through which doctors understand themselves as "scientists" or "healers." Of course, this is only one example of how we understand what has happened or is happening to us, and thus how we know ourselves through what Michel Foucault analyzed as discursive regimes. Every day we know ourselves, or experience ourselves, through multiple domains of discourse, domains that serve as cultural registers for what counts as experience and who counts as an experiencing subject. But since discourses are historically specific, what counts as experience changes over time with broader cultural transformations of collective history.

At the same time that we say that experience is discursive, we recognize that there are human experiences outside discursive narratives— feelings of the body, feelings of spirituality, powerful sensory memories of events and images. Every day, all day long, the material universe affects us, literally as well as discursively. Bodies bleed. They manifest illnesses. They get hurt. They feel hunger, thirst, and desire. These are among the material events in our lives. But in making meaning of these events, we make that meaning, or the "experience" of those events, discursively, in language and as narrative. Thus, we retrospectively make experience and convey a sense of it to others through storytelling; and as we tell our stories discursive patterns guide, or compel, us to tell stories about ourselves in particular ways.

Experience as Interpretation

The discursive nature of experience requires us to be self-reflexive about what we understand as "our experience" or what we think we mean when we say things like "That's just my experience!" or "I'm a man." That is, what seems "ours" or "mine" has been formed and has changed over time, and we can investigate this process of change. This thing called "experience is," as Scott cautions, "at once always already an interpretation *and* is in need of interpretation" (37).

In autobiographical acts, narrators become readers of their experiential histories, bringing discursive schema that are culturally available to them to bear on what has happened. The multiple autobiographical narratives of Giacomo Casanova, Frederick Douglass, Mary McCarthy, Marguerite Duras, Buchi Emecheta, and Maya Angelou, for example, offer fascinating glimpses into an autobiographer's successive interpretations or revisions of the past. These versions, written at different points in their lives and, in Douglass's case, retelling the "same" story divergently in two subsequent narratives, invite readers to question whether different readings of an experience signal stages of, or changes in, the overall pattern of beliefs encoded in the autobiographical story, or whether changes from one text to its "sequel," or "prequel," signal larger cultural transformations affecting how people know themselves through stories tellable (and discourses available) to them at particular historical moments.

Experience as Authoritative

It is important to theorize what we call experience because the narrator's experience is the primary kind of evidence asserted in autobiographical acts, the basis on which readers are invited to consider the narrator a uniquely qualified authority. Thus, a narrator's investment in the "authority" of experience serves a variety of rhetorical purposes. It invites or compels the reader's belief in the story and the veracity of the narrator; it persuades the reader of the narrative's authenticity; it validates certain claims as truthful; and it justifies writing and publicizing the life story.

In their autobiographical acts, narrators claim the "authority of experience" both explicitly and implicitly. Implicit claims can be as unobtrusive as the appearance of the autobiographer's name on the title page. This is the case for people who are public figures and celebrities whose names on the front cover announce credibility: "Dennis Rodman" or "Greg Louganis" or "Mahatma Gandhi" or "Nelson Mandela" or "Jack Abbott" or "Nancy Reagan." The name itself—well known or notorious— is a kind of guarantee. It assures the reader of the authority of the writer to tell his or her story and promises that the public will find the story a credible disclosure.

In the case of persons outside the dominant culture, persons unknown and marginalized by virtue of their lack of public status, appeals to the authority of experience may be explicit. Such appeals may be made on the basis of sexual, or ethnic, or racial, or religious, or national identity claims. In other words, identity confers political and communal credibility. In such cases, a previously "voiceless" narrator from a community not culturally authorized to speak—the slave, the nonliterate, the child, the inmate of a mental hospital, the formerly colonized, for instance—finds in identification the means and the impetus to speak publicly. Richard Wright, for example, in narrating his autobiography *Black Boy (American Hunger): A Record of Childhood and Youth*, explicitly situates himself vis-à-vis racialized communities, both black and white, inviting his reader to accept his narrative as authoritatively representative of the life script of an African American "boy." Similarly, James Baldwin negotiates his identity as a "native son" in *Notes of a Native Son*.

As the cases of Wright and Baldwin suggest, not all "experience" is accorded social and cultural recognition or legitimacy. Whereas the names of the celebrities cited above bestow the "authority" of experience on the narrator (even in cases where the narratives are ghostwritten), in other narratives the authority to narrate is hard-won in a constant engagement with readers posited as skeptical, unbelieving, resistant, and even hostile. Thus the instability of something called the authority of experience suggests how it is that the category of experience itself is socially, culturally, historically, and politically negotiated.

Experience and the Reader

Because issues of authority can be crucial to autobiographical acts, life narrators have much at stake in gaining the reader's belief in the experiences they narrate and thus having the "truth" of the narrative validated. Persuasion to belief is fundamental to the pact between narrator and reader. Appeals to the authority of experience bring to the fore issues of trust in autobiographical narrating, since the autobiographical relationship depends on the narrator's winning and keeping the reader's trust in the plausibility of the narrated experience and the credibility of the narrator. In certain narratives this makes for a complex relationship between narrator and reader.

Consider the case of Susanna Kaysen in *Girl, Interrupted*. Kaysen addresses the reader with the authority of her experience as a young woman who was incarcerated in a mental institution for two years in the 1960s. That experience is "documented" in one sense by her inclusion of twelve documents in her narrative concerning her admission, treatment, and release. Her experiential history as a resident of McLean Hospital (outside Boston) assures the reader that she knows whereof she speaks. But her project is a politically motivated one, not just an occasion to tell a lively and engaging story of "crazy" young women in the '60s. The adult narrator provides a pointed critique of the medical and psychological discourses through which she had been assigned the status of "crazy." The critique involves her challenge to the either/or differentiation of the worlds of the sane and the crazy, a binary mode of thinking that led doctors and nurses to label her "borderline." But in order to convince the reader of the legitimacy of her claim to having been misidentified as a "borderline personality," Kaysen must persuade the reader that although she was unstable and at times self-destructive she is a reliable narrator and thus more authoritative than either those promoting the cultural norm she is judged by or those readers adhering uncritically to everyday norms. This example suggests that securing the authority of some experiences is a tricky process of speaking credibly and ethically about a dehumanizing and self-alienating past.

Or consider the case of a slave narrative such as *Incidents in the Life of a Slave Girl: Written by Herself* by Harriet A. Jacobs, published in 1861. Defenders of slavery were fiercely invested in debunking the authenticity of narratives about life in the slave system. And certain conventions of slave narratives provided grounds for alleging that these stories were fictionalized. Fugitive or former slaves often gave fictional names to the people in their narratives to maintain secrecy about escapes and to protect people left behind. Often the narratives were "edited," and in the process rearranged and changed, by Northern abolitionists, many of whom helped fugitive slaves to write their narratives and get them published. Given such circumstances, Southern proslavery apologists found grounds upon which to challenge the credibility and veracity of the narratives and thus the whole enterprise of abolitionism. Jacobs's *Incidents* was drawn into this maelstrom of debatable authenticity and authorship. Jacobs fictionalized the names of people in her narrative, including her own, and depended upon the editorial help of abolitionist Lydia Maria Child in revising her text. Soon after publication the narrative was dismissed as a fraud and a fiction. Now, more than one hundred years later, scholar Jean Fagan Yellin has documented its historical veracity and *Incidents* has moved from the status of forgotten fiction to that of much-taught slave narrative because its narrative of brutalization, attempted rape, and imprisonment has a truth value beyond the accuracy of particular facts. The example of *Incidents*, therefore, suggests how narratives, and the authority of experience asserted in them, enter a public arena where issues of verifiability and authenticity are fiercely contested by interested groups and where changing norms of the "truth" of experience lead to reevaluation.

Readers also have expectations about who has the cultural authority to tell a particular kind of life story, and they have expectations about what stories derived from direct, personal knowledge should assert. For instance, readers expect the slave narrative to be written by an ex-slave, or the Holocaust narrative to be written by a survivor or survivor-descendant, or the narrative of nationalization or exile to be written by an immigrant. Readers also accept the authority of the near-and-dear to entwine the biography of a loved one with their own autobiographical reflection, which gets filtered through the account of the loved one. For example, in *Brothers and Keepers* John Edgar Wideman enmeshes his own life narrative with that of his brother. And in *The Woman Warrior: Memoirs of a Girlhood among Ghosts* Maxine Hong Kingston braids her stories with the stories of her ancestor No-Name Woman, her mother Brave Orchid, and her aunt Moon Orchid.

The case of Gertrude Stein's *The Autobiography of Alice B. Toklas* offers a more extreme case of the issue of who claims the authority to tell the story of a loved one. In *The Autobiography* Stein writes in the voice of her lifelong lover and friend Alice, but primarily in celebration of the brilliance and accomplishments of Stein and their expatriate circle in Paris of the 1920s and '30s. Some critics have suggested that this might be a fraudulent act, an act of ventriloquism of Alice's voice. Is it parasitic, an act of appropriation of Alice's experience? Or is it an act of dedicated speaking through the other that commingles the boundaries of identity into a shared subject? For Stein, whose response to publishers' requests for her autobiography was "not possibly," writing "that autobiography" in which "I" and "you," "eye" and "other" become indistinguishable, authorizes a subject that is irreducible to either "Gertrude" or "Alice."

But there are autobiographies that seek to misrepresent the identity of the writer and to persuade readers that the experience of fictive protagonists in fact occurred. This undermining of readerly expectations about the authenticity of experience suggests why autobiographical hoaxes are so troubling. The story of Wanda Koolmatrie is a case in point. In 1994 an autobiographical narrative entitled *My Own Sweet Time* was published in Australia as the first work of Wanda Koolmatrie, an indigenous woman. It narrated Wanda's peripatetic journey from her hometown of Adelaide to the urban landscape of Melbourne. A youthful, hip, urbanized narrative, *My Own Sweet Time* was heralded as capturing the spirit of a new generation of indigenous Australian writers, alienated from traditional Aboriginal community but at home in the multicultural maze of the city. A year later, when the publishing house asked to meet Wanda Koolmatrie after giving the book a literary award, a hoax was discovered. The publisher revealed that Wanda Koolmatrie was really a young white man named Leon Carmen who was cashing in on the popular appeal of the personal narratives of indigenous people because, in his view, white men could no longer get published in Australia. Or take the case of Binjamin Wilkomirski's *Fragments: Memories of a Wartime Childhood*, the purported memoir of a Latvian Jew's struggles as an orphan in two concentration camps during World War II. *Fragments* garnered much international publicity as it was first declared a fraud and then withdrawn from circulation by its German publisher, Suhrkamp Verlag, after it had received such honors as the National Jewish Book Award in the United States. Even when confronted with documentary proof of his identity as a Swiss citizen adopted by a middle-class couple named Doessekker, the author declared, "I am Binjamin Wilkomirski."[3]

Charges of autobiographical bad faith and occasional hoaxes reveal how complex questions of the authenticity of experience and the integrity of identity can become, how critical they are to the central notion of the relationship between life narrator and reader.[4] Through the text the life narrator claims that the memories and experiences are those of the "signature" on the cover, the author. Readers ascribe these memories and experiences to a flesh-and-blood person. Ultimately, of course, the relationship comes down to a matter of mutual trust. Certainly we allow memories, and the experience made out of memories, to be inconsistent (as they are in many autobiographical narratives), probably because we understand our own as inconsistent. While we understand that the source text—the memories of the author—is not accessible or verifiable in any literal sense, we are unwilling to accept intentional duping. The situation of fiction is radically different: a hoax is unimaginable, unless one person claims to have written a fictional narrative actually written by another person. But in the case of autobiography, the hoax is a potent and politically charged possibility.

Identity

Autobiographical acts involve narrators in "identifying" themselves to the reader. That is, writers make themselves known by acts of identification and, by implication, differentiation.

Identity as Difference and Commonality

Identities, or subject positionings, materialize within collectivities and out of the culturally marked differences that permeate symbolic interactions within and between collectivities.[5] One is a "woman" in relation to a "man." One is a "disabled" person in relation to someone who is seen as "abled." Identities are marked in terms of many categories: gender, race, ethnicity, sexuality, nationality, class, generation, family genealogy, and religious and political ideologies, to cite the most obvious. These are differences that, at least for now, have meaning in the material and symbolic structures that organize human experience. But identity as difference implies identity also as likeness. As Susan Stanford Friedman notes, "an identity affirms some form of commonality, some shared ground" (*Mappings*, 19). In *The Sweeter the Juice: A Family Memoir in Black and White*, for instance, Shirlee Taylor Haizlip explores how "black" and "white" identities in the United States are far more fluid than many suspect as she traces a family history that includes the "passing" of certain aunts and uncles as "white." Reconstructing family trees, Haizlip reconsiders the basis upon which racial identities are founded and flounder, and exposes the "dark secrets people have in their white souls" (238).

But social organizations and symbolic interactions are always in flux; therefore, identities are provisional. What may be a meaningful identity, on one day or in one context, may not be culturally and personally meaningful at another moment or in another context. Think, for instance, of how many identities you cycle through in the course of a day, identities linked to gender, national citizenship, work status, sexuality, class location, generational location, ethnicity, and family constellation. And notice the potential for conflict between or among these different identities. Because of this constant placement and displacement of "who" we are, we can think of identities as multiple and as "contextual, contested, and contingent" (Scott, 36).

Identities as Discursive

As Scott argued for experience, so for identities. They are constructed. They are in language. They are discursive. They are not essential—born, inherited, or natural—though much in social organization leads us to regard identity as given and fixed. The Russian theorist M. M. Bakhtin argued that consciousness—which also implies identity as a category of consciousness—is dialogical. That is, it is always implicated in "the process of social interaction." Since social groups have their languages, each member of the group becomes conscious in and through that language. Thus autobiographical narrators come to consciousness of who they are, of what identifications and differences they are assigned or what identities they might adopt, through the discourses that surround them. And because of what Bakhtin calls "heteroglossia" in the social realm, the multiplicity of languages, words, and meanings that "mutually supplement one another, contradict one another and [are] interrelated dialogically" (292), the subject comes to consciousness through multiple identities and multiple voices. This is why, as Stuart Hall argues, identity is "a 'production' which is never complete, always in process, and always constituted within, not outside, representation" (392).

Identities as Historically Specific Models

Cultural identities, according to Hall, are "the unstable points of identification or suture, which are made, within the discourses of history and culture" (395). Thus they are marked by time and place. There are models of identity culturally available to life narrators at any particular historical moment that influence what is included and what is excluded from an autobiographical narrative. Some models of identity culturally available in the United States over the last three hundred years have included the sinful Puritan seeking the signs of salvation, the self-made man, the struggling and suffering soul, the innocent quester, the "bad" girl or boy, the adventurer, and the trickster.

Autobiographers incorporate and reproduce models of identity in their narratives as ways to represent themselves to the reader. Consider the single identities announced in the titles of the following life narratives: *Kaffir Boy: The True Story of a Black Youth's Coming of Age in Apartheid South Africa* by Mark Mathabane, *Autobiography of a Face* by Lucy Grealy, *When I Was Puerto Rican* by Esmeralda Santiago, *Teacher* by Sylvia Ashton-Warner, *Bad as I Wanna Be* by Dennis Rodman, *The Lieutenant Nun: Memoir of a Basque Transvestite in the New World* by

Catalina de Erauso, *An American Childhood* by Annie Dillard. The titles announce a limit of identity that the narratives explore, exploit, and explode. In *Rivethead: Tales from the Assembly Line*, for instance, Ben Hamper reimagines himself as "Rivethead," a figure of renegade agency in the monotonous assembly-line life of General Motors. The "Rivethead" speaks Hamper's fears of fading into the emasculated catatonia of alcohol and mechanized routine and his desire to resist the orders of faceless bureaucrats. As the narrator writes of his alter ego, "Rivethead" is the "thoroughbred of all thoroughbreds, the quickest triggerman this side of the River Rouge" (119).

But autobiographers often incorporate several models of identity in succession or in alternation to tell a story of serial development. In *Confessions*, Jean-Jacques Rousseau presents himself as an eager schoolboy, "a man of very strong passions" (33), a wicked sensualist, a thief, a true philosopher, and "an old dotard" (9). In *The Autobiography of Malcolm X* the narrator presents himself in successive chapters as "Mascot," "Homeboy," "Harlemite," "Detroit Red," "Hustler," "Satan," "Minister Malcolm X," "Icarus," and "El-Hajj Malik El-Shabazz." These apprenticeships in different models of identity are put on for particular occasions but, when cast off, leave traces that may conflict with other models.

The stuff of autobiographical storytelling, then, is drawn from muliple, disparate, and discontinuous experiences and the multiple identities constructed from and constituting those experiences. Sometimes these models of identity are conflictual, as in the cases of Rousseau and Malcolm X. Sometimes narrators are aware of the conflicts and contradictions, sometimes not. Sometimes narrators thematize the conflictual nature of identity in the narrative; oftentimes they do not. Sometimes narrators explicitly resist certain identities. Sometimes they obsessively work to conform their self-representation to particular identity frames. We can read for these tensions and contradictions in the gaps, inconsistencies, and boundaries breached within autobiographical narratives. For example, in *Boyhood: Scenes from Provincial Life*, J. M. Coetzee narrates in the third person a memoir of his childhood in the apartheid nation of South Africa in the late 1940s. Refusing his Afrikaner heritage, identifying as English, aligning intellectually with Soviet Russia, and erotically drawn to the "Coloured boys" marginalized by the official identity assigned them by the state, Coetzee explores identity vectors as multiply constructed, in tension, and shifting with political conditions. While boyhood was a fixed time in his life, it was also a time that the narrator reads retrospectively as both facilitating tryouts of possible identities and undermining their realization in the repressive apartheid state.

Identities as Intersectional

The effects of this multiplicity of identities are not additive but intersectional. That is, we cannot just add the effects of one identity to the effects of another to understand the position from which someone speaks. To speak autobiographically as a black woman is not to speak as a "woman" and as a "black." It is to speak as blackwoman. To speak as an Australian indigenous man is not to speak as a "man" plus as an "Australian" plus as an "Aboriginal." There is no universal identity of "man" or "woman" outside specificities of historical and cultural location.

The South Asian Canadian writer Michael Ondaatje captures this amorphous intersectionality when he maps for the reader his return to the familial and now postcolonial geography of the "Ceylon" of his childhood. *Running in the Family* traces the return home of the migrant writer to a realm of family and myth. Shuttling across identities—"Ceylonese," migrant Sri Lankan, Canadian, commonwealth expatriate—Ondaatje mixes time past and time present to conjure up the past he describes as "frozen opera" (22) in order to understand his identity as multiply positioned and continuously mobile.

In her "biomythography," *Zami: A New Spelling of My Name*, Audre Lorde captures this intersectional aspect of identity and difference when she writes of herself and her friends in Greenwich Village in the 1950s:

> Being women together was not enough. We were different. Being gay-girls together was not enough. We were different. Being Black together was not enough. We were different. Being Black women together was not enough. We were different. Being Black dykes together was not enough. We were

> different.... It was awhile before we came to realize our place was the
> very house of difference rather than the security of any one particular
> difference. (226)

Like Lorde in *Zami*, Gloria Anzaldúa in *Borderlands/La Frontera: The
New Mestiza* effectively traces the hybridity of her own identity in a way
that suggests how multiple and intersectional identities can be. The very
title both differentiates English from Spanish and joins them at the border of the slash. The "I"/eye moves back and forth across the border, just
as Anzaldúa writes of navigating the intersections of sexuality, ethnicity,
gender, and nationality at the constructed borderland of Texas and Mexico. Other postcolonial writers have coined different terms to characterize inextricably mixed identities forged from histories of oppression.
Among these terms are *mixed-race, marginal, migratory, diasporic, multicultural, minoritized, mestiza,* and *nomadic.* All of these terms point to the
fluidity of identities in movement through time and across political and
geographical spaces.

Embodiment

It is easy to think that autobiographical subjectivity and autobiographical texts have little to do with the material body. But the body is a site of
autobiographical knowledge, as well as a textual surface upon which a
person's life is inscribed. The body is a site of autobiographical knowledge because memory itself is embodied. And life narrative is a site of
embodied knowledge because autobiographical narrators are embodied
subjects.

Embodied Memory

Life narrative inextricably links memory, subjectivity, and the materiality
of the body. As Paul John Eakin argues in *How Our Lives Become Stories:
Making Selves,* "our lives in and as bodies profoundly shape our sense of
identity" (xi). The ability to recover memories, in fact, depends upon the
material body. There must be a body that perceives and internalizes the
images, sensations, and experiences of the external world. Memories are

created as the subject reconstructs a sense of identity while engaging with the world in symbolic exchange. Subjectivity is impossible unless the subject recognizes her location in the materiality of an ever-present body (Damasio, 239). Moreover, the embodied materiality of memory and consciousness is grounded in neurological, physiological, biochemical, perhaps even quantum systems.

But embodiment is larger than the neurochemistry of the brain and its systems. Embodied subjects are located in their bodies and through their bodies in culturally specific ways—that is, the narrating body is situated at a nexus of language, gender, class, sexuality, ethnicity, and other specificities, and autobiographical narratives mine this embodied locatedness. In her autobiographical poem cycle, *The Father*, for example, Sharon Olds observes her dying father through an ethics of description. The poet seeks to know this remote and silent father through the very materiality of the body that is shutting down before her. Invoking metaphors of pregnancy and mothering, she imagines her own body full with the body of the father. Hers is an embodied mode of remembering, knowing, and mourning the unloving father and expressing her own filial resentment across a generational divide.

Embodiment and Location

Cultural discourses determine which aspects of bodies become meaningful—what parts of the body are "there" for people to see. They determine when the body becomes visible, how it becomes visible, and what that visibility means. And so life narrators are multiply embodied. There is the body as a neurochemical system. There is the anatomical body. There is, as Elizabeth Grosz notes, the "imaginary anatomy" that "reflects social and familial beliefs about the body more than it does the body's organic nature" (39–40). And there is the sociopolitical body, a set of cultural attitudes and discourses encoding the public meanings of bodies that underwrite relationships of power.

In *Loving in the War Years: Lo que nunca pasó sus labios* Chicana writer and activist Cherríe Moraga directs attention to the very materiality of her skin as a source of her political consciousness. In this way she joins skin to the body politic, observing the different significations of "light" and "dark" in different communities. Taking her body as a narrative point of departure, she elaborates, through multiple modes of address, her complex cultural position as lesbian, biracial Chicana, and daughter of working-class parents. A very different kind of body is narrated into shape in Dillard's *An American Childhood*. Invoking again and again the specificities of "skin" to mark the meeting point of the internal and external worlds, Dillard explores the way in which she learned to fit (and sometimes failed to fit) the skin of her white middle-class identity in America's Pittsburgh. If Dillard tells a story of fitting into the skin of middle-class identity, Rodriguez, in *Hunger of Memory*, explores his failure to fit into the skin of Americanized masculinity. Figuring himself as an upwardly mobile "scholarship boy," Rodriguez exposes the cost of the politics of skin color that associates darkness with poverty and silence at the same time that he masks his own homosexual desire. In his embrace of middle-class intellectual masculinity, he writes eloquently of his failure to fit in with the dark-skinned masculinity of the Mexican braceros/manual workers with whom he works one summer. In shifting modes of masculinity, the younger Rodriguez shifts skins of identity. In all these examples, the body—its skin, anatomy, chemistry—resonates as both a locus of identity and a register of the similarities and differences that inflect social identities.

Narratives of the Body

The cultural meanings assigned particular bodies affect the kinds of stories people can tell. For instance, respectable middle-class women up through the nineteenth century could not, and would not, tell sexual stories about their bodies because the cultural meanings assigned those bodies had to do with myths of the corrupt nature of female sexuality. To speak sex was to shame or pollute oneself. Women who did publish confessional narratives about sexual adventures, notably Charlotte Charke and Laetitia Pilkington in the eighteenth century, incited condemnation of both their narratives and their lives as scandalous. Interestingly, within their "scandalous" narratives, as Felicity A. Nussbaum has noted, the female narrators mapped their own topography of sexuality, "relegat-[ing] unlicensed sexuality to the lower classes" (179). Thus, even as they spoke of sexual desire, these narrators reproduced the identification of sexual license and class status. While violating the norms of female self-disclosure, they reproduced those prevailing norms.

Many men, though not all, up through the nineteenth century also remained silent and self-censoring about their bodies and male embodi-ment, reproducing the identification of the male autobiographer with rationality, objectivity, and the mind. The question of how male embod-iment is presented or concealed in life narratives is a rich prospect for future research. Ken Plummer's *Telling Sexual Stories: Power, Change and Social Worlds*, Martin A. Danahay's *A Community of One: Masculine Auto-biography and Autonomy in Nineteenth-Century Britain*, and Trev Lynn Broughton's *Men of Letters, Writing Lives: Masculinity and Literary Auto/Biography in the Late-Victorian Period* have initiated the exploration of texts, tropes, and critical lenses for critiquing models of masculinity. And David Jackson's *Unmasking Masculinity: A Critical Autobiography* per-forms the dual labor of both critiquing forms of masculinity and telling his own story of discovering the social construction of his gendered and sexual identity. Many coming-out life narratives of gay men similarly implicate critiques of enforced social norms of masculinity and might be read more comprehensively within the project of situating male embod-iment at a nexus of categories of identity. The vaunted sexuality of such eighteenth-century autobiographers as Rousseau and Casanova deserves investigation within the terms of embodied subjectivity. Montaigne's *Essays*, which he at one point characterizes as "some excrements of an aged mind, now hard, now loose, and always undigested" (III: 9, "Of Vanity," 721) also deserve a fuller reading for the "consubstantial" em-bodiment of language as materiality.

Now, in the twenty-first century, sexual confessions have become standard fare of daytime television and published narratives in the West. Recently, Kathryn Harrison in *The Kiss: A Secret Life* and Michael Ryan in *Secret Life: An Autobiography* went public with autobiographical stories of sexual abuse, addiction, and primal scenes of violence inflicted on them in childhood. In other parts of the world, writing about sexual experience, especially by women, is still prohibited and punished. Feminists such as Nawal El Saadawi in Egypt have defied public prohibitions by publishing narratives of sexed and gendered bodies. For some this has come at the cost of incarceration, persecution, and exile.

Autobiographical narrating has also become a means for people to confront the destiny of the diseased or differently abled body, whether their own or someone else's. In a succession of essays Nancy Mairs tracks the physical and psychological losses of/in a body becoming increasingly disabled by multiple sclerosis. But she goes further to write candidly about her sexual desires in order to claim for herself and for people with disabilities a full humanity. In memoirs of living and dying with AIDS, David Wojnarowicz, Harold Brodkey, and Paul Monette explore the conjunction of desire, danger, and disease in the male body at a time of moral panic produced about the AIDS pandemic. In *Close to the Knives: A Memoir of Disintegration*, Wojnarowicz refuses the fixed cultural identities of "queer" or "gay man" as he writes "close" to the body and its desires. Immersed in the visuality of memory, Wojnarowicz recreates the specificity of desire and embodiedness as an "I" who has always "lived with the sensations of being an observer of my own life as it occurs" (149). And it is this distance, this imagination of observing himself, that the photographer taps to recreate sensory experience. He does so in order to counter cultural practices that render invisible "any kind of sexual imagery other than straight white male erotic fantasies" (119). These and other narratives of bodily centered crisis and trauma underscore the centrality of embodiment to the telling of lives.

Reading for the Body

In summary, by exploring the body and embodiment as sites of knowledge and knowledge production, life narrators do several things. They negotiate cultural norms determining the proper uses of bodies. They engage, contest, and revise cultural norms determining the relationship of bodies to specific sites, behaviors, and destinies. And they reproduce, mix, or interrogate cultural discourses defining and distinguishing the normative and ab-normative body.

Agency

We like to think of human beings as agents of or actors in their own lives, rather than passive pawns in social games or unconscious transmitters of cultural scripts and models of identity. Consequently, we tend to read autobiographical narratives as proofs of human agency, relating actions in which people exercise free choice over the interpretation of their lives and express their "true" selves. In fact, traditional autobiography has been read as a narrative of agency, evidence that subjects can live freely. But we must recognize that the issue of how subjects claim, exercise, and narrate agency is far more complicated.

We have noted that discursive systems emergent in social structures shape the operations of memory, experience, identity, and embodiment. People tell stories of their lives through the cultural scripts available to them, and they are governed by cultural strictures about self-presentation in public. If individuals are constituted through discursive practices, how, then, can they be said to control the stories they tell about themselves? Some contemporary investigations of agency are helpful in addressing this question.

Theories of Agency

Analysts of agency have found the theorist Louis Althusser helpful in thinking through these issues. Althusser argued that the subject is a subject of ideology—not in the narrow sense of propaganda but in the broad sense of the pervasive cultural formations of the dominant class. Althusser recognized the power of coercive state institutions to conform subjects to particular behaviors, beliefs, and identities—institutions such as the military and the police. He also recognized that there are less overtly coercive institutions—social services, educational institutions, the family, literary and artistic institutions—that "hail" subjects who enter them. By "hailing" Althusser meant the process through which subjects become interpellated, become what institutional discourses and practices make of them. They are "subjected." Most important, individuals understand themselves to be "naturally" self-produced because the power of ideology to hail the subject is hidden, obscured by the very practices of the institution. In this way, people are invested in and mystified by their own production as subjects, by their own "subjection." That is, they have "false consciousness": they collude in their own lack of agency by believing that they have it. It is not enough, then, to say that people exercise free will. The concept of "free will" is itself embedded in a discourse about the Enlightenment individual, a historically specific discourse through which subjects understand themselves as intellectually mature and free to make their own choices. To claim that all humans have something called "free will" in this way is to misunderstand an ideological concept as a "natural" aspect of existence.

Other theorists have taken this challenge to agency as a starting point from which to rethink its possibility. Political theorist Elizabeth Wingrove, in rereading Althusser, argues that "agents change, and change their world, by virtue of the systemic operation of multiple ideologies." The key here is the multiplicity of ideologies through which the subject is hailed. These multiple ideologies "expose both the subject and the system to perpetual reconfiguration" (871). In that reconfiguration new possibilities emerge for knowing oneself as a subject and for understanding a system. (See also Catherine Belsey on subject construction.)

French sociologist and theorist Michel de Certeau locates agency in what he terms "transverse tactics." Individuals and groups deploy such tactics to manipulate the spaces in which they are constrained, such as the workplace or the housing project. For instance, a factory worker may superimpose another system (of language or culture) onto the system imposed on him in the factory. Combining systems, he can create "a space in which he can find ways of using the constraining order of the place or of the language" to establish "a degree of plurality and creativity." Such modes of "re-use," then, are interventions that open a space of agency within constrained systems (29–30). For the French theorist Jean-François Lyotard the flexible and uncontrollable networks of language, through which people construct their worlds, spawn unexpected moves and countermoves. As a result language itself holds strategic potential for the formation of new sociopolitical subjects.

For postcolonial theorist Arjun Appadurai, agency in this particular historical moment of global capitalism resides in imagination mobilized as "an organized field of social practices" (327). Imagination negotiates between "sites of agency," namely, the imagined communities in which we participate, and "globally defined fields of possibility" (327). Situated amid multiple forms of imagined worlds, individuals as sites of agency deploy their imaginations as a social fact and a kind of work to navigate the disjunctures of global flows that create radically different self-understandings.

Feminist philosopher Judith Butler situates agency in what she calls the "performativity" of subjectivity. According to Butler, identity is enacted daily through socially enforced norms that surround us. Thus it is through our reenactment of the norms of, say, masculinity or femininity that we know ourselves to be "a heterosexual man" or "a woman." But this enforcement of norms cannot be totally effective since individuals fail to conform fully to them because of the multiplicity of norms we are called to reenact in our everyday lives. The failure to conform signals the "possibility of a variation" of "the rules that govern intelligible identity." And with failure come reconfigurations or changes of identities (*Gender Trouble*, 145).

Like Butler, feminist theorist Teresa de Lauretis defines the unconscious as a potential source of agency. The unconscious is a psychic domain of disidentification ("Eccentric Subjects," 125–27), a repository of all the experiences and desires that have to be repressed in order for the subject to conform to socially enforced norms. As such, it lies at the intersection of the psychic and the social. A repository of the repressed, the unconscious is also a potential site of agency; its excess is a source of resistance to socially enforced calls to fixed identities. And the anthropologist Sherry B. Ortner situates agency in the ability with which people play the "games" of culture—with their rules and structures—with wit and intelligence. For Ortner, sociocultural structures are always partial rather than total. And thus there is always the possibility of changing the rules—although not of escaping rules altogether.

We have briefly noted several theorizings of agency as multiple: ideologies; transverse tactics and modes of disuse; the flexible network of language; the navigation of imagined communities; performativity; psychic disidentification; the games of culture. These concepts offer critical frameworks for considering how people, in the act of narrating their lives, might change the stories they tell, might gain access to other cultural scripts, might come to understand themselves differently, might, that is, exercise agency.

The Politics of Agency

One of the compelling contexts in which to consider possibilities of agency is the field of postcolonial writing. The question arises: What about formerly colonized peoples who have been educated as subject populations in the colonizers' language, beliefs, and values (interpellated as "colonized"), while their indigenous culture has been repressed, often brutally? Such subjects are inheritors of the legacies of a colonial history that made them less than fully human beings. For them, autobiographical writing has often served as a tactic of intervention in colonial repression.

When people have encountered representations of themselves as the objects of the surveyor's gaze—the "exotic" native Other of anthropology and the racialized laborer or slave of imperialism—how do they begin to assert cultural agency, especially while using the terms and the medium of the colonizer? To think about the uses of life narrative in postcolonial writing is to encounter these conundrums. As, historically, a master narrative of Western hegemony in its celebration of the sovereign individual, traditional autobiography would seem inimical to people whose modes of expression were formerly oral and collective. Yet its reinterpretation in a range of what Caren Kaplan calls "out-law genres"— such as autoethnography, testimonio, and prison memoirs—has been an important means of asserting cultural agency for postcolonial subjects in many parts of Africa, Asia, and the Americas. For Kaplan an out-law genre "mix[es] two conventionally 'unmixible' elements—autobiography criticism and autobiography as thing itself." The result of this mixing is a textual "politics of location," a specific context in which the text is produced and the self-narrator situated ("Resisting Autobiography," 208).

Employing autobiographical discourse and available generic forms to assert their cultural difference and their subjectivity, postcolonial autoethnographers have both engaged and challenged the Western tradition of individualist life narrative. Senegalese writer Ken Bugul, for example, narrates how she came to consciousness of her separate self in Europe in *The Abandoned Baobab: The Autobiography of a Senegalese Woman*. She tells how, as a student in Brussels, she is confronted by the desirous looks of Europeans who exoticize her as an African female Other in the midst of white Europe. The education and the "privilege" held out to the young woman—a "child" of colonial Francophone Africa studying in Europe—to "agentify" her have the opposite effect, making her more keenly aware of her interpellation as a subject of neocolonial practices. But this crisis of individuation is also one in which her memory of African tradition intervenes to enable her reclaiming of African soil and identity, to re-member herself in the possibility of a future—not yet decolonized—African home. As a subject of the French "empire" Bugul adopts an autobiographical discourse of alienated selfhood (as a child of the West and its modes of self-knowing); yet as an autoethnographer writing in an out-law genre, she critiques the very ground of knowing upon which she stands and elects an alternative ground of an Africa in the making. While Ken Bugul could not be called an agentified subject at the end of her narrative, her quest for a "home" that is as yet virtual suggests her status has been reoriented from dispossessed, colonized subject to a critically aware subject in process.

In such instances, writing becomes a means of re-forming (or deforming) the former "empire" and its enforced symbolic interactions. But the deferral of the achievement of agency at the end of Ken Bugul's narrative suggests that gaining agency in such a situation is complex. For, the language of writing, the means of publication—publishing house, editor, distribution markets—and even the tropes and formulas of individualizing an autobiographical "I" are associated with the colonizer's domination.

Consider the case of *I, Rigoberta Menchú: An Indian Woman in Guatemala*. As Mary Louise Pratt notes, Menchú's narrative, as told to Elisabeth Burgos-Debray, interweaves multiple discourses of identity: ethnographic ritual, parody, political manifesto, familial chronicle, and a tragic personal narrative of loss and renunciation ("Me llamo Rigoberta Menchú"). Throughout, Menchú shuttles between cultures (Quiché, Ladino, and Western European), languages (Spanish and Quiché), and positionings (teacher, political activist, daughter, Catholic acolyte, worker, woman) as she communicates an urgent testimony of the suffering of her people and the injustice done to them. In concluding this testimonio, Menchú vows to keep some aspects of her identity secret, thereby resisting the reader's desire to possess the truth about the survival of this indigenous culture. In her insistence on keeping secrets, Menchú positions herself at once as dutiful daughter, political leader, and social critic of a Western middle-class readership. She also subverts the comfortable cultural assumption of readers that we can "know" the life narrator by reading the narrative. In her testimony to the resiliency of disenfranchised indigenous Guatemalan people, Menchú seeks to change consciousness, enabling herself and her readers to resist an oppressive regime and assert human rights. Her testimony, then, attests to a process of exercising agency both in telling and in withholding cultural stories.

Conclusion

Readers often conceive of autobiographical narrators as telling unified stories of their lives, as creating or discovering coherent selves. But both the unified story and the coherent self are myths of identity. For there is no coherent "self" that predates stories about identity, about "who" one is. Nor is there a unified, stable immutable self that can remember everything that has happened in the past. We are always fragmented in time, taking a particular or provisional perspective on the moving target of our pasts, addressing multiple and disparate audiences. Perhaps, then, it is more helpful to approach autobiographical telling as a performative act.

To theorize memory, experience, identity, embodiment, and agency is to begin to understand the complexities of autobiographical subjectivity and its performative nature. In chapter 4 we will frame that subjectivity by exploring the historical interplay of autobiographical texts and changing concepts of personhood. Now we turn to the complexities of specific autobiographical acts in order to think more deeply about what happens locally, at the intersection of text and context.

CHAPTER 3

Autobiographical Acts

Language is not a neutral medium that passes freely and easily into
the private property of the speaker's intentions; it is
populated—overpopulated—with the intentions of others.

M. M. Bakhtin, *Discourse in the Novel*

All these people—producers, coaxers, consumers—are
engaged in assembling life story actions around lives, events and
happenings—although they cannot grasp the actual life. At the
centre of much of this action emerge the story products: the
objects which harbour the meanings that have to be handled
through interaction. These congeal or freeze already
preconstituted moments of a life from the story teller and
the coaxer and await the handling of a reader or consumer.

Ken Plummer, *Telling Sexual Stories*

We recognize that memory, experience, identity, embodiment, and agency are not separable constituents of autobiographical subjectivity. They are all implicated in one another. But disentangling them in chapter 2, however artificially, allowed us to frame the psychic (memory), the temporal (experience), the spatial (identity), the material (embodiment), and the transformative (agency) dimensions of autobiographical subjectivity. Moreover, the concepts of memory, experience, identity, embodiment, and agency enable us to begin probing the complexity of what happens in a particular autobiographical act.

Let's situate the autobiographical act in a story, a story in time and place. This situatedness is especially crucial since life narratives are always symbolic interactions in the world. They are culturally and historically specific. They are rhetorical in the broadest sense of the word. That is, they are addressed to an audience/reader; they are engaged in an argument about identity; and they are inevitably fractured by the play of meaning (see Leith and Myerson). Autobiographical acts, then, are anything but simple or transparent.

In *Telling Sexual Stories*, sociologist Ken Plummer, considering autobiographical stories through the lens of a "pragmatic symbolic inter-actionist ethnography," differentiates three kinds of people who con-tribute to every story action (xi). There is the producer or teller of the story—what we call the autobiographical narrator. There is the coaxer, the person or persons, or the institution, that elicits the story from the speaker. There are the consumers, readers, or audiences who interpret the story (20–21). While we take Plummer's tripartite schema as a start-ing point in the following discussion, we complicate it by introducing other situational and interactional features of autobiographical acts.

The components of autobiographical acts include the following:

- Coaxers/occasions
- Sites
- Producers of the story, autobiographical "I"s
- The Others of autobiographical "I"s
- Addressees
- Structuring modes of self-inquiry
- Patterns of emplotment
- Media
- Consumers/audiences

Coaxers, Coaches, and Coercers

Every day we are called upon to tell pieces of our life stories. Think of autobiographical acts, then, as occasions when people are coaxed or coerced into "getting a life." The coaxer/coercer, in Plummer's terms, is any person or institution or set of cultural imperatives that solicits or provokes people to tell their stories (21). Telling may occur in intimate situations when someone solicits a personal narrative—for example, that intimate exchange between lovers who seek to enhance desire by giving the gift of their memories to one another. Requests for personal narratives may come in letters or e-mail messages from friends and family members—"Tell me what's been happening to you. I haven't heard from you for so long." Compulsions to confess may be coaxed by our internalization of religious values and practices—the voiced confession of the Catholic Church, prayerful confession in silence in Protestant services, the Jewish day of atonement. Compulsions to confession may also be of a commercial kind, commodified in daytime talk shows that package the obsessions of popular culture in neat segments on "loving too much" or "secret eating." Publishers may invite celebrity figures to tell life narratives to a public hungry for vicarious fame. Friends and colleagues of distinguished people may urge them to tell stories exemplary of public and professional life on formal occasions.

Coaxers and coercers are everywhere. Think of these everyday situations in which people's stories about themselves are elicited in the contexts of social institutions.[1]

- In political speeches candidates often tell compelling personal narratives that may project "character" and "values" or situate them in the major wars and movements of the times or attach them to specific religious, ethnic, or vocational communities.
- In the communal confessions of self-help groups participants conform their life stories to the narrative model, for example, the Alcoholics Anonymous format, required of them to make progress in recovery.
- In family gatherings, individuals participate in the shared communal recollection of the family's stories as rituals that reinforce familial history and the very idea of the family itself.
- In hospital waiting rooms, people fill out forms requesting body narratives—stories of their bodies. Often their body narratives rematerialize on film in mammography, ultrasonography, and MRI scans that make their futures readable in signs of disease or bodily abnormality.

- Every day people fill out standardized forms to get food stamps or housing vouchers, driver's licenses or passports. In each of these institutional settings, personal narratives are conformed to particular routines, bureaucratic imperatives, and identities appropriate to the occasion.
- Through the bold-faced headings of personal ads, people advertise their current fantasies, their sexual histories, and their desires.
- The conventions of the employment resumé require presenting packaged credentials to prospective employers, condensing long years of experience into job skills that signify more than they state: the status of the institutions attended or the career path.
- Every day people present themselves to the scrutiny of members of groups they seek to join—neighborhood associations, churches, veterans' organizations, fraternities, or sororities. Through these narratives they announce their qualifications for membership.
- Raising their hands in court to "tell the truth," people before the bar become implicated in "crime and punishment." Legal testimony requires stipulating the facts of a verifiable identity. When competing truth claims are presented, their adjudication may require further personal revelations, sometimes against the will of the witness.
- And now, as personal information is translated into digital codes, millions of web pages carry personalized visual and verbal narratives around the world in microseconds.

This list could go on and on, taking us through cultural institutions, state bureaucracies, nonstate organizations, friendships, cross-cultural encounters, communities, media, virtual reality. Global culture multiplies the possibilities for both coaxing and coercing multiple life stories.

Although the autobiographical narratives of published writers may, in their highly crafted aesthetics, seem far removed from such everyday sites, the coaxing to which they respond shares a number of concerns and features with the kinds of autobiographical presentations we've described, or that people might engage, in telling parts of their own stories.

Some coaxing is explicit. In his *Confessions* Augustine projects a coaxing God needful of his confession. In the section of his autobiography begun in 1788, Benjamin Franklin includes several letters from friends setting out various reasons all Americans would benefit from reading his life story. The "Benjamin Franklin" friends want to coax from him is, of course, a particular version of Franklin, the statesman, social benefactor, and moral guide. In a comparable way, slave narrators were urged to recite their narratives of slavery's degradations in the setting of abolitionist meetings and for the abolitionist press.

But coaxing is also more broadly diffused throughout a culture. Successive generations of immigrants in the United States, for example, have responded to the need to affirm for other Americans their legitimate membership in the nation by telling stories of assimilation. Some autobiographers publish their life stories in order to defend or justify their past choices, to "set the record straight." In writing his apologia, *In Retrospect: The Tragedy and Lessons of Vietnam*, Robert S. McNamara responded to the continuing widespread debate in the United States about the Vietnam War and the role of government officials in waging it.

Coaxing is an integral part of the life-writing process when more than one person is directly involved in producing the story. It can take several forms. In doubled autobiographical narratives, two (or more) people offer their version of shared events or experiences as do Mary Barnes and Joseph Berke in *Mary Barnes: Two Accounts of a Journey through Madness*, in which patient and therapist reconstruct their versions of the journey. In "as-told-to" or "ghostwritten" narratives, multiple levels of coaxing take place, including those of the ghostwriter or cowriter, whose prompting questions, translations of the autobiographer's oral speech, and revisions are often invisible in the final text, as is the case with Alex Haley in *The Autobiography of Malcolm X* or Ida Pruitt in *A Daughter of Han: The Autobiography of a Chinese Working Woman*, based on the narrative of Ning Lao T'ai-t'ai. Yet another case of invisible intervention is the publisher who requires that the celebrity or recovery autobiography be rewritten and shaped for special audiences.

In collaborative life writing, we think of two people as involved in producing the story: one is the ethnographer, who does the interviewing and assembles a narrative from the primary materials given; and the second is the informant, who tells a story through interviews or informal conversations. But with collaborative narratives of Native Americans and indigenous colonized people, the situation is in fact often triangulated among three or more parties. Someone must undertake the translation and transcription from the indigenous language for the person who finally "edits" the narrative into a metropolitan language, such as English, and a culturally familiar story form, such as traditional autobiography or the ethnographic "life." This complex nexus of telling, translating, and editing introduces a set of issues about the process of appropriating and overwriting the original oral narrative. The case of *Black Elk Speaks: Being the Life Story of a Holy Man of the Ogalala Sioux as Told to John G. Neihardt*, G. Thomas Couser argues, is one in which a native informant in a transcultural interview situation may "speak with forked tongue" ("Black Elk Speaks with Forked Tongue"). Couser thus calls attention to the difficulty of translating what was suggested indirectly or *not* said by an informant. Arnold Krupat has considered another complexity, the "invented" English into which such narratives were often cast. But while the transcription-translation process often effaced characteristics of an Indian language, Krupat argues, a text such as *Black Hawk: An Autobiography* might be reconsidered as a collaborative effort to create a "hybrid or creolized language *based on* English" that nonetheless seeks to convey an Indian mode of language through linguistic invention ("Introduction," 7). A third kind of complexity is suggested by the publication history of *I, Rigoberta Menchú*. Menchú has protested that the intervention of the editor, Elisabeth Burgos-Debray, effaced suggested versions of its narrative by its translators, thus controlling the pattern of meaning of the narrative (see Canby).

This politics of coproduction may be mediated differently when life narrators who are deaf or otherwise prevented from directly recording their life stories depend on someone to transcribe their stories into a standard language such as English. Use of American Sign Language, for example, mediates the life writing differently than does signing to an interpreter who then "translates" the text to a recorder-editor, as H-Dirksen L. Bauman has shown (47–62). As all these cases suggest, collaborative life writing, as a multilingual, transcultural process, can be a situation of coercion and editorial control presented in the name of preserving the voice, the experience, and the culture of the life narrator.

Editorial exercise of censorship is a final example of coercion in the name of coproduction at the point of publishing the life narrative. Zora Neale Hurston's *Dust Tracks on a Road: An Autobiography* is a case of an autobiography in which the publisher, concerned about literary propriety with a 1940s white reading public, excised certain phrases and folkloric turns of speech from Hurston's manuscript, and omitted altogether some "sexy" stories she wanted to tell, as Claudine Raynaud has discussed ("Rubbing a Paragraph with a Soft Cloth?" 34–64).

As we see in all these cases, the roles of a coaxer in assembling a life narrative can be more coercive than collaborative. Complicated ethical issues arise when one or more people exercise cultural authority over assembling and organizing a life narrative (Couser, "Making, Taking, and Faking Lives"). In giving thematic shape to the narrative by virtue of decisions about what is included or excluded, a coaxer can subordinate the narrator's modes and choices of storytelling to another idea of how a life story should read and how its subject should speak appropriately. Although this editorial coaxer often effaces his or her role in producing the narrative, a preface "describing" the working relationship between editor/transcriber and narrating subject may try to control the audience's reading, as Peter Canby suggests in his account of the Menchú controversy.

What is a critical reader to do in engaging the complexities of collaborative texts? All of the examples discussed here argue, first, for specifying the roles of various coaxers in making the autobiographical text, and, second, for relinquishing the widespread notion that indigenous texts produce a kind of unmediated authenticity. The stimulating debates of anthropologists about field notes, historians about the authority of primary documents, and cultural studies theorists about autoethnography offer critics of life-writing sites and tools for situating life narrative as a mode of cultural production in which various voices and versions contest, and contend for, authority.

Sites of Storytelling

The examples we have considered suggest the degree to which coaxing/coercing occurs at particular sites of narration. Think of sites as both occasional, that is, specific to an occasion, and locational, that is, emergent in a specific "mise en scène" or context of narration. The site is, first, a literal place, a talk show, perhaps, or a social service agency, an airplane, or, as in the case of Carolina Maria de Jesus in *Child of the Dark: The Diary of Carolina de Jesus*, the desperate *favelas* (slums) of Sao Paulo, Brazil. But the site of narration is also a moment in history, a sociopolitical space in culture. So we might want to think about how particular sites of narration perform cultural work, how they organize the personal storytelling upon which they rely. And we might think about what kinds of narratives seem "credible" and "real" at particular sites of narration.

The appropriateness of personal narratives for particular sites is a crucial consideration. Sites establish expectations about the kinds of stories that will be told and will be intelligible to others. The autobiographical presentation you make on a website, for example, would not be appropriate in a legal setting and might even cause real problems there. So the needs, practices, and purposes of institutions that seek to manage some aspects of our lives might be very different from our own needs and intentions in telling stories to others in intimate settings, or the ideal self-image we would like others to know and believe from our more public self-presentations.

Occasional and locational, sites are multilayered matrices at which coaxing and narrating take place. They may be predominantly personal, institutional, or geographical, though to some extent these three levels often overlap. Let's return to the family reunion. Autobiographical acts in the context of a family reunion might have a lot to do with a specific coaxer—an uncle asking a niece to recall what it was like to spend time with her grandmother. But where the coaxer might be specific—an uncle—the site would have far broader import, for family reunions are occasions at which the ideology of familiality is enacted and reproduced. In order to appreciate the meaning of autobiographical acts in such contexts, then, we would need to consider the role of family reunions in a family's life, the ways in which storytelling within an extended family binds a group of disparate individuals together, the kinds of stories that are appropriate to such occasions and the kinds that would be seen as violating codes of familiality. In an autobiographical narrative primarily concerned with family relations, such as Mary McCarthy's *Memories of a Catholic Girlhood,* family houses and rituals are primary sites of narration.

Another institutional site is the prison cell. Here the locational norm is forced incarceration, and with it the monotonous and deindividuating routine of daily discipline. Within this context of state coercion, autobiographical narrative can become a site of enabling self-reconstruction and self-determination in its insistence on imagining forms of resistance to those deindividuating routines. This was certainly the case with Eldridge Cleaver as he wrote his manifesto *Soul on Ice,* or Jacobo Timerman in *Prisoner without a Name, Cell without a Number.* Earlier it is the case with Albertine Sarrazin in "Journal de prison, 1959." In her journal, this young French vagabond writes against the cultural construction of the female prisoner as defeminized by imagining (and at least momentarily freeing) herself through writing the libidinal economy of heterosexual love and desire.

In many narratives, the geographical location strongly inflects the story being told. Jane Addams's Hull House is both a social institution and a location of impoverished immigrant Chicago in the early twentieth century. Autobiographies as diverse as Edward William Bok's *The Americanization of Edward Bok: The Autobiography of a Dutch Boy Fifty Years After,* Audre Lorde's *Zami: A New Spelling of My Name,* Vivian Gornick's *Fierce Attachments: A Memoir,* and David Sedaris's *Naked,* all situated in New York City, establish richly textured portrayals of its streets, bars, apartments, and urban scene. In the vast and heterogeneous space of the city, stories of lives engage its particular locations as well as the complexity of urban life for various kinds of subjects to produce not "New York City" but diverse stories of the highly charged, dense, sensorily saturated, and often jarring or hostile world of the city. This aspect of life narrative, as yet rarely studied by critics who tend to see the site as a backdrop, shapes the contexts of both autobiographical subjectivity and the kinds of stories that can be told. Conversely, narratives steeped in the specifics of rural place or wilderness—Kathleen Norris's *Dakota: A Spiritual Geography*, Terry Tempest Williams's *Refuge: An Unnatural History of Family and Place*, Michael Ondaatje's *Running in the Family*—are also sociocultural sites in which struggles about environmental, familial, national, and cultural politics intersect as "layers" of narrative location. Site, then, more actively than notions of "place" or "setting," speaks to the situatedness of autobiographical narration.

The Producer of the Autobiographical "I"

Now let's turn to the producer of the story, the autobiographical "I." What do we encounter as readers/listeners when we come to an "I" on a page or hear an "I" in a story told to us? We know from the discussion in chapter 2 that this "I" is not a flesh-and-blood author, whom we cannot know, but a speaker or narrator who refers to herself. But much more is involved in this marker of self-referentiality. While this speaker has one name, the "I" who seems to be speaking—sometimes through a published text or an intimate letter, sometimes in person or on screen—is comprised of multiple "I"s.

Often critics analyzing autobiographical acts distinguish between the "I"-now and the "I"-then, the narrating "I" who speaks and the narrated "I" who is spoken about. This differentiation assumes that the "I"-now inhabits a stable present in reading the "I"-then. It also assumes a normative notion of life narrative as a retrospective narrative about a separable and isolatable past that is fully past. But, as our discussion of processes of autobiographical subjectivity revealed, this is too limited an understanding of life narrative. It cannot account for the complexities of self-narrating or the heterogeneous array of autobiographical modes. Nor does it adequately capture the complexity of the "I" in even the most traditional of autobiographies. We need to think more critically about the producer of the life narrative.

We propose complicating this autobiographical "I" beyond the "I"-then and the "I"-now framework by attending to the multiple "I"-thens, to the ideology spoken through the "I," to the multiple "I"-nows, and to the flesh-and-blood author. Thus we can talk of the following "I"s:

> The "real" or historical "I"
> The narrating "I"
> The narrated "I"
> The ideological "I"

The "Real" or Historical "I"

Obviously an authorial "I" is assumed from the signature on the title page—the person producing the autobiographical "I"—whose life is far more diverse and dispersed than the story that is being told of it. This is the "I" as historical person, a person located in a particular time and place. This "I," as Chantal Mouffe notes, can be understood as "the articulation of an ensemble of subject positions, corresponding to the multiplicity of social relations in which it is inscribed" (376). This "I" lives or lived in the world, going about his or her business in everyday life.

Because there are traces of this historical person in various kinds of records in the archives of government bureaucracies, churches, family albums, and the memories of others, we can verify this "I"'s existence. We can hear her voice, if she is still alive. But this "I" is unknown and unknowable by readers and is not the "I" that we gain access to in an autobiographical narrative.

The Narrating "I"

The "I" available to readers is the "I" who tells the autobiographical narrative. This "I" we will call the narrator or the narrating "I." This is the "I" who wants to tell, or is coerced into telling, a story about himself. While the historical "I" has a broad experiential history extending a lifetime back into the past, the narrating "I" calls forth only that part of the experiential history linked to the story he is telling.

This narrating "I" usually, though not universally, uses the first-person referent. Some life narratives are told in the third person, as are those of Edward William Bok, Henry Adams, and J. M. Coetzee. Some are in the second person, using the "you" of self-reference, as the African American artist Faith Ringgold does in her *The Change Series: Faith Ringgold's 100-Pound Weight-Loss Quilt*, where she writes of herself as the "you" of disorderly eating habits; or as Christa Wolf often does in *Patterns of Childhood*. These narratives suggest that the narrating "I" is neither unified nor stable. It is split, fragmented, provisional, multiple, a subject always in the process of coming together and of dispersing, as we noted at the conclusion of chapter 2.

We can read, or "hear," this fragmentation in the multiple voices through which the narrator speaks in the text. In fact, an "I" speaks in tongues or heteroglossia, to paraphrase Bakhtin. These voices can include the voice of publicly acknowledged authority, the voice of innocence and wonder, the voice of cynicism, the voice of postconversion certainty, the voice of suffering and victimization, and so on. The narrating "I" of *The Autobiography of Malcolm X*, for instance, speaks in several voices: as an angry black man challenging the racism of the United States, a religious devotee of Islam, a husband and father, a person betrayed, a prophet of hope, to suggest only a few of the many voices we hear throughout this narrative. So the narrator and the speaking voices are not entirely synonymous. The narrator is a composite of speaking voices, the "I" a sign of multiple voices.

The Narrated "I"

The narrated "I" is distinguished from the narrating "I." As Françoise Lionnet suggests, the narrated "I" is the subject of history whereas the narrating "I" is the agent of discourse (*Autobiographical Voices*, 193). The narrated "I" is the object "I," the protagonist of the narrative, the version of the self that the narrating "I" chooses to constitute through recollection for the reader.

For example, the narrator may begin her narrative with memories of childhood. She conjures herself up at the age of five or eight or ten. She sets that child-version in the world as she remembers her. She may even give that younger "I" a remembered or reimagined consciousness of the experience of being five or eight or ten. She may give that child a voice through dialogue. That child is the object "I," the memory of a younger version of a self. But the child is not doing the remembering or the narrating of the story. Nor is that narrated "I" directly experiencing that past at the time of the writing of the narrative or its telling. The narrating "I" before the paper or computer screen or the live audience is remembering and creating the story. Even in cases where the narrator tries to reproduce the sense of what that experience might have been like, through recourse to simplistic vocabulary, to truncated phrases, to sensory description, to citations from a past diary, she can only do so as the older narrator with greater knowledge, narrative experience, and linguistic competence. The narrating "I" is the "I" representing the meaning of that narrated child's experience.

Some autobiographical narratives project multiple narrated "I"s. In *How I Grew*, Mary McCarthy writes of posing for a poor artist whom she met in Seattle. "Canvas cost a lot," she writes. "So I, who was not yet 'I,' had been painted over or given a coat of whitewash, maybe two or three times, till I was only a bumpiness, an extra thickness of canvas" (161). Here McCarthy differentiates earlier girl selves from the writer she would become, "I." But those old selves are visible as a palimpsest, a bumpy textual surface that leaves its trace in the layers of covering wash. McCarthy's narrative is a good instance of our larger point: while we use a single "I" as a pronoun referring to autobiographical acts in the text, both the narrating "I" in the temporal present and the narrated "I"s of earlier times are multiple, fragmented, and heterogeneous.

The Ideological "I"

According to Paul Smith in *Discerning the Subject*, the ideological "I" is the concept of personhood culturally available to the narrator when he tells his story (105). Historical and ideological notions of the person

provide cultural ways of understanding the material location of subjectivity; the relationship of the person to particular others and to a collectivity of others; the nature of time and life course; the importance of
social location; the motivations for human actions; the presence of evil,
violent, and self-destructive forces and acts; the metaphysical meaning of
the universe. Because every autobiographical narrator is historically and
culturally situated, each is a product of his or her particular time. We
need, then, to situate the narrator in the historical notion of personhood
and the meaning of lives at the time of writing.

The ideological "I" is at once everywhere and nowhere in autobiographical acts, in the sense that the notion of personhood and the
ideologies of identity constitutive of it are so internalized (personally
and culturally) that they seem "natural" and "universal" characteristics
of persons. Yet changing notions of personhood affect autobiographical
acts and practices, as do the competing ideological notions of personhood coexisting at any historical moment. For the ideological "I" is also
multiple and thus potentially conflictual. At any historical moment,
there are heterogeneous identities culturally available to the narrator
(identities marked through embodiment and through culture: gender,
ethnicity, generation, family, sexuality, religion, among others). Some
narrators emphasize their ideological complexity (Gloria Anzaldúa,
Jean-Jacques Rousseau), while others may bend aspects of the story to
support a prevailing ideology, as in religious narratives. But the ground
of the ideological "I" is only apparently stable and the possibilities for
tension, adjustment, refixing, and unfixing are ever present.

For instance, in "A True History of the Captivity and Restoration
of Mrs. Mary Rowlandson," the seventeenth-century Puritan Mary
Rowlandson remembers her captivity by the Narragansett Indians.
Rowlandson is at a "remove" from her sustaining Puritan belief system
and subjected to unfamiliar practices and values that seem incoherent to
her. But her experience among the Narragansett also subtly shakes the
foundations of that Puritan ideology as she comes to identify with its
unsaved, savage Other. Despite her return to the community, she now
sees its beliefs as one set of values rather than how the world "is," and

hence struggles with reoccupying the ideological "I" from which she was forcibly removed.

In the early twentieth century the Russian revolutionary Alexandra Kollontai negotiates, in her 1926 *Autobiography of a Sexually Emancipated Communist Woman*, the call for a revolutionary "new womanhood" and the cultural force of what she calls "the given model" of normative femininity. Throughout her narrative the residual imprint of the given model persists even as she insists on the transformation to a new ideological model.

The ideological "I" occupies a different and complex location in Gloria Anzaldúa's *Borderlands/La Frontera*. The narrator is critical of a political ideology of American expansionism that has appropriated Mexican lands and oppressed its people. To counter that prevailing ideology, in which she has been schooled and which has judged her as marginal, she counterposes an indigenous mythology of Mexican figures as a foundation for reorienting Chicanas ideologically toward the "new Mestiza." This figure of hybridity also contests ideologies of the gendered subordination of women and of heteronormativity. Anzaldúa wages her critique across multiple borders, including the linguistic frontier of Spanish-English. In so extensively mapping pressure points of resistance to an imposed ideological "I," she defamiliarizes its naturalness. Her posing of Mexican goddess figures, queer identification, and activist woman-of-color feminism gives these countervailing beliefs new ideological force.

Ideological "I"s, then, are possible positions for autobiographical narrators to occupy, contest, revise, and mobilize against one another at specific historical moments. Only apparently a "choice," they are nonetheless multiple, mobile, and mutating.

Reading the "I"

As we read life narratives, we need to attend to these four "I"s or, rather, to the three that are available in the autobiographical act before us—the narrating, the narrated, and the ideological. We can look for places where the narrator addresses readers directly or where he calls attention to the act of narrating itself, to problems of remembering and forgetting, to a sense of the inadequacy of any narrative to get at the truth of his life as he is defining it. We can watch how the narrator organizes the times of past, present, and future in the telling of the story as a way of teasing out narrated versions of the "I" presented and the ideological stakes of those representations in the present of narration.

Sometimes the narrating "I" produces an apparently continuous chronology from birth to adolescence to adulthood. Sometimes she produces an explicitly discontinuous narrative, beginning "in the middle" and using flashbacks or flash-forwards. Sometimes the exactness of chronology is of little importance to the narrator. Always there are moments in the text when that impression of narrative coherence breaks down, in digressions, omissions, gaps, and silences about certain things, in contradiction. While we may read the narrator's recitation to us as one long, continuous narrative, the text signals discontinuities that will not bear out our own fiction of coherence.

As one example, consider how, in *The Education of Henry Adams*, Henry Adams omits the story of his wife Clover's suicide in his narrative. Just at the chronological moment of her suicide, the narrative breaks into two parts. Reading for this gap, we can explore how our knowledge of the silence and the split structure resonates, undermining the illusion of narrative coherence Adams's narrator seems to project. We construct a coherent "Henry Adams," or other ideologically coherent "I"s, only by underreading the ways in which the narrative calls attention to its own fissures.

Relationality and the Others of Autobiographical "I"s

The self-inquiry and self-knowing of many autobiographical acts is relational, routed through others, as Nancy K. Miller ("Representing Others"), Paul John Eakin (*How Our Lives Become Stories*, 43–98), and G. Thomas Couser (*Recovering Bodies*) in different ways have argued. This concept of relationality, implying that one's story is bound up with that of another, suggests that the boundaries of an "I" are often shifting and flexible. Relationality invites us to think about the different kinds of

textual others through which an "I" narrates the formation or mod-
ification of self-consciousness. These include historical others, the iden-
tifiable figures of a collective past such as political leaders. In some
autobiographies a narrator reads his or her "I" as having engaged such
figures as models or ideals. For example, the idea of American presidents,
as well as his contact with actual former presidents, drives Bok's narrative of self-formation as an ambitious assimilated American. Such historical others often serve as generic models of identity culturally available
to the narrator that we have already discussed in chapter 2.

There are also contingent others who populate the text as actors in
the narrator's script of meaning but are not deeply reflected upon. And
there are what we might call significant others, those whose stories are
deeply implicated in the narrator's and through whom the narrator understands her or his own self-formation, as in the case in Edmund Gosse's
Father and Son: A Study of Two Temperaments and Abraham Verghese's *My
Own Country: A Doctor's Story of a Town and Its People in the Age of AIDS*.
Significant others appear in narratives of several kinds. Relational narratives incorporate extensive stories of related others that are embedded within the context of an autobiographical narrative. For example, in
Brothers and Keepers, John Edgar Wideman seems to focus on the story
of his brother Robby, who became a street criminal while Wideman
became a writer and college professor. In his effort to understand their
different lives and to memorialize his brother, Wideman interweaves his
own story, not just of growing up together but of deeply felt emotions
about African American manhood. In *In My Mother's House: A Daughter's
Story*, Kim Chernin weaves the narrative of her mother, and her mother's
voice, into her story of a complex filiality among several generations of
mothers and daughters. Traditional stories of empowered women as well
as communal proverbs and family histories of valueless women transmit-
ted through generations and in contexts of immigration and cultural
change also form the core of Maxine Hong Kingston's autobiographical
narrative, *The Woman Warrior: Memoirs of a Girlhood among Ghosts*.

A relational narrative of a different sort is at the center of
Paul Monette's life narrative, *On Borrowed Time: An AIDS Memoir*. The

partner of Roger Horwitz, a gay man who died of AIDS, Monette remembers a partner and a relationship in a text that, as Couser notes, blurs the line between auto- and biography. Monette struggles to narrate several stories simultaneously—a chronological journal of illness and death, a romantic love story that contests popular representations of gay men, an AIDS story of cultural crisis in the gay community, a narrative of rereading and revising a crisis in the gay community, and a narrative of rereading and revising a journal's gaps and emotions (Couser, *Recovering Bodies*, 155–60). Monette's second memoir, *Becoming a Man: Half a Life Story* is a prequel of his life that ends with meeting Horwitz and realizing that his previous life, alone and in the closet, was one of being "bodiless" (38) and "frozen" (173), without a life. While family members, spouses, or lovers are not always the focus of narratives of significant others, they are understandably prominent forms of deeply felt relationship (Couser, *Recovering Bodies*, 160–63).

Another form of significant other to whom a narrative may be addressed and in whom it may invest special meaning is the idealized absent other, whether secular or divine. Such narratives cannot "tell" the Other because of the profundity and inextricability of the relationship, but allusions to it as central to self-understanding resonate throughout the narrator's telling of a narrated "I." In his *Confessions*, for example, Augustine rereads his experience before conversion through a language transformed by conversion and his implicit dialogue with God. For Montaigne, his friend La Boétie, who died young, is the significant other whose absence underwrites the *Essays*. While Montaigne praises La Boetie as a "brother" and has La Boétie's essay "Of Voluntary Servitude" published posthumously, he does not embed this "brother's" biography in his own narrative. Rather, in "Of Friendship" Montaigne asserts the impossibility of differentiating his friend from himself: "Our souls mingle and blend with each other so completely that they efface the seam that joined them" (1:28, 139). Similarly, in his collaborative narrative *Black Elk Speaks* (1932), the Lakota shaman incorporates the voices of multiple others as he tells his story through the dreams, visions, and voices of other spiritual leaders. Doing so, Black Elk secures the authority of his own visions by situating himself in a genealogy of visionaries.

Yet another textual model of the significant other organizing autobiographical discourse is the subject other, the other internal to every autobiographical subject. As Jacques Lacan has argued in *The Language of the Self: The Function of Language in Psychoanalysis*, the illusion of a whole self acquired in the "mirror stage" is an identification taking place in "the imaginary." The infant is both captivated and trapped in an image of self, an alienation upon which the ego constituted at this stage maintains a false appearance of coherence and integrity. Life narrators by definition cannot address the subject Other that in a sense speaks them. But critics can perform Lacanian readings of the fissures and gaps of texts, as, for example, Shari Benstock does with Virginia Woolf's *Moments of Being* (10–33). Or the gap can be read in the tensions of narrative strategies. In *The Lover*, for instance, Marguerite Duras's narrator shifts between the confessional mode of first person narrative and the novelistic mode of third-person narrative. Duras, according to Suzanne Chester, "undermines the objectification to which she was subjected ... [and] appropriates the masculine position of the observer" (445). Here the narrator exploits the otherness of her identity as a young white woman in colonial Indochina to undermine the stability of a colonizer and a colonized "I."

These multiple others—historical, contingent, significant, idealized but absent, and subject Others—suggest the range of relational others evoked and mobilized within a life narrative for the purposes of self-narrating and self-knowing. The routing of a self known through its relational others undermines the understanding of life narrative as a bounded story of the unique, individuated narrating subject. What these examples suggest is that no "I" speaks except as and through its others.

But we need to look more closely at the explicit textual other addressed within the text, the other to whom the narrator tells his story. For, as narrative theory suggests, a text's narrator constructs an implied reader to whom the narrative is addressed, even if never named.

The Addressee

The narrator of necessity tells his story to someone. That someone might be in the same room, if the narrator's story is told orally. But even in the case of a written or published narrative, the narrator is addressing someone. Sometimes, as in a diary, that someone might even be another version of himself. We call this someone "the addressee," although we note here that scholars of narratology (the study of narrative structures) differentiate the "narratee" from the "implied reader." "The narratee," notes Shlomith Rimmon-Kenan, "is the agent which is at the very least implicitly addressed by the narrator. A narratee of this kind is always implied, even when the narrator becomes his own narratee" (89). Although narratologists differ in their understanding of the relationship of narratee to implied reader, they concur on the importance of the ways in which narratives depend upon addressees in the process of storytelling.

The implied reader is a particularly interesting addressee. The self-narrator whose story is published cannot know who in fact her readers (or, in Plummer's schema, consumers) will be. But she cannot tell her story without imagining a reader.

The implied readers to which self-referential modes are addressed vary across time, cultures, and purposes. Some speakers imagine an addressee as an intimate, as Glückel of Hameln does as she addresses her children in her 1690–91 "Memoirs in Seven Little Books" (5), or as the Englishwoman Frances Anne Kemble does when she addresses her journal entries describing her sojourn in the Georgia Sea Islands in the late 1830s as letters to her friend "Elizabeth." Others imagine an addressee at some distance. Spiritual life narrators may identify "God" as the implied reader. Still others idealize an addressee, as Anne Frank does in constructing the implied reader of her diary as a sympathetic friend whom she names "Kitty." And, of course, letter writers who employ the opportunities the form offers to engage in self-reflection, social or political critique, and philosophical speculation in condensed form address their letters to particular persons who are at once specific and universalized, as is the case with the letters of the Indonesian writer and activist Raden Adjeng Kartini (whose *Letters of a Javanese Princess* includes letters written from 1899 to 1904). Sometimes the narrator addresses a universalized implied reader directly, as Susanna Kaysen does in *Girl, Interrupted.* "Do you believe him or me?" (71–72), she challenges her addressee as she contests the power of the doctor who labeled her personality disordered and sent her to McLean Hospital as a teenager in the late 1960s. Or this implied reader can be a category of people—the white Northerners whom Frederick Douglass addresses in the first of his three autobiographies, or the white Northern "sisters" whom Harriet Jacobs addresses explicitly in her *Incidents in the Life of a Slave Girl.*

Addressees can be imagined, and addressed directly in the text or indirectly through the text. And often there are multiple addressees in the narrative, narratees and implied readers addressed simultaneously or in sequence. For instance, when the medieval mystic Margery Kempe dictated her narrative to an amanuensis, she addressed a multiplicity of interlocutors: the God to whom she would manifest her purity of soul; the amanuensis upon whom she depended for the preservation of her story; the Church fathers who threatened her with excommunication, perhaps even death; the community of Christians before whom she would claim her rightful membership as a true believer and thereby secure her social status.

Narrator and addressee(s), then, are engaged in a communicative action that is fundamental to autobiographical acts and the kinds of intersubjective truth they construct. Attending to the addressee or implied reader of a life narrative allows us to observe subtle shifts in narrative intent. That attention also allows us to consider the kind of reader the text asks us to be as we respond to such rhetorics of intent.

Structuring Modes of Self-inquiry

Autobiographical acts are investigations into and processes of self-knowing. But both the modes of inquiry and the self-knowledge gained or produced change over time and with cultural locations. Thus there is a history to presentations of self-knowledge. How one knows oneself today is very different from how one would have known oneself in a Socratic dialogue or in the *Imitatio Christi* of Thomas à Kempis in the early modern period. Or in the ritual Dreaming through which contemporary indigenous Australians in traditional communities understand their place within a system of totem and kinship and through which they enact their systems of values, beliefs, and relationships.

Some life narrators formalize schemes of self-investigation through a method. And these have varied dramatically. In *The Autobiography of Benjamin Franklin*, Benjamin Franklin produces self-knowledge through his "Project of arriving at Moral Perfection." John Donne produces his through relentlessly self-questioning sermons; Montaigne through the self-tryouts of his *Essays;* William Butler Yeats through the mythical system of *A Vision;* St. Teresa through the topography of "interior landscape"; Robert Burton through the anatomy as a physiological and systemic metaphor. Each narrator developed and improvised upon a particular structure of self-knowing.

Some well-known patterns for presenting processes of self-knowing are linked to other genres of literature, such as the novel, and provide templates for autobiographical storytelling. Among them are the Bildungsroman or narrative of social development, the Künstlerroman or narrative of artistic growth, the confession, memoir, conversion narrative, testimonio, and quest for lost identity or a lost homeland or family. The Bildungsroman, for instance, unfolds as a narrative of education through encounters with mentors, apprenticeship, renunciation of youthful folly, and eventual integration into society. The conversion narrative develops through a linear pattern—descent into darkness, struggle, moment of crisis, conversion to new beliefs and worldview, and consolidation of a new communal identity. In the quest or adventure narrative, a hero/heroine alienated from family or home or birthright sets forth on a mission to achieve elsewhere an integration of self that is impossible within the constraints (political, sexual, emotional, economic) imposed in a repressive world and to return triumphant. The testimonio unfolds through the fashioning of an exemplary protagonist whose narrative bears witness to collective suffering, politicized struggle, and communal survival.

Conventions that are culturally and historically specific govern storytelling options, narrative plotting, and the uses of remembering. And those conventions have histories: that is, at certain historical moments and in specific milieux, certain stories become intelligible and normative. Yet such stories stretch and change, gain cultural prominence or lose their hold over time. Think, for instance, of the genre of feel-good narratives that have recently emerged as part of contemporary America cultural life. Conventions can also be displaced by newly emergent ones. For instance, autobiographical narratives published in the late twentieth century—at least those by women and people of color—have radically altered the inherited conventions of life narrative by their reworking of the Bildungsroman to account for the lives of formerly subordinated subjects.

And so, when we read or listen to autobiographical narratives, we need to attend to methods of self-examination, introspection, and remembering encoded in them through generic conventions. Sometimes the narrator turns his method upon particular kinds of experiences—such as dreams—and particular kinds of knowledge—such as intuitive, irrational, supernatural, mystical, or symbolic knowledge. Sometimes the narrator interrogates cultural forms of knowledge valued at the historical moment of writing. Sometimes he establishes complex linkages between knowledge of the world/others and self-knowledge. Sometimes he imagines alternative knowledges. And sometimes he refuses the very possibility of self-knowing, as is the case with the avant-garde narrators of works by Michel Leiris and Roland Barthes.

Patterns of Emplotment

The expanded concept of autobiographical acts that this study proposes leads us to review narrative plots or patterns from the perspective of a theory centered in narrative modalities. We might broadly frame these as of two kinds, although in practice these kinds are always mixed:

temporally based patterns, which concern the organization of narrative times; and spatially based patterns, what might be termed, in the phrase of Susan Stanford Friedman, the "geographics" of narrative subjectivity (*Mappings*).

There are temporal patterns both *of* the narrator's telling and *in* the telling. Some narrators tell their stories from a relatively fixed moment of their lives, as does, for instance, Isak Dinesen in *Out of Africa*. In this haunting memorial return, Dinesen reflects, after returning to Europe, on her years in Kenya as irretrievably lost. But many narratives seem to have been written at different times. Franklin's *Autobiography*, for example, identifies the narrator at different ages and in various professions rereading his past. His autobiographical "I"s are serial, multiple, and heterogeneous, in part because of the long life span over which he narrated his life.

Autobiographical narratives can be plotted strictly by chronology, with the narrator looking back upon the life course and organizing the segments of telling according to the movement of historical time. But a strict linear organization of narrative can be and often is displaced by achronological modes of emplotment. A narrator may employ a scheme of associational, or digressive, or fragmented remembering told through multiple flashbacks and flash-forwards, as does, for example, Janet Campbell Hale in *Bloodlines: Odyssey of a Native Daughter*. Such a pattern is multidirectional rather than linear-progressive.

Friedman, in her invocation of a "geographics" of subjectivity, foregrounds the spatial mapping of identities and differences as distinct from the chronological tracking of identity.[2] "[T]he new geographics," she suggests, "figures identity as a historically embedded site, a positionality, a location, a standpoint, a terrain, an intersection, a network, a crossroads of multiply situated knowledges" (*Mappings*, 19). As narratives of identity, autobiographical stories offer particularly potent sites for this geographics. Such geographic "mappings" emerge through allegorical, imagistic, and rhetorical modes negotiated by the narrating "I" as she moves into and out of various subject positions within the narrative. Moreover, since autobiographical narratives also enact the relationality of identity, a geographics of self-narrating involves the multiple modes of emplotment through which the narrating "I" entwines a personal story with the stories of others, both individuals and collectivities.

In *The Words to Say It: An Autobiographical Model*, Marie Cardinal locates the struggle with her female body in the context of the Algerian struggle for liberation from colonialism. Mapping the intersections of political oppression and psychological repression of colonialism and sexism, the agony of Algeria and the agony of her mother, Cardinal enacts the revolutionary potential of a psychoanalysis that links the psy chological to the sociopolitical. Similarly, in contemporary Australia, narratives such as Labumore: Elsie Roughsey's *An Aboriginal Mother Tells of the Old and the New* and Ruby Langford Ginibi's *Don't Take Your Love to Town* map the diverse geographies of individual struggles within collective histories of physical displacement, cultural dislocation, and state forms of oppression affecting the lives of indigenous peoples.

A pastiche of memories may layer the narrative by incorporating multiple forms of self-inquiry, perhaps borrowed from such genres as the lyric sequence, fable, essay, diary, meditation, or public testimony. A narrative may also incorporate multiple media—graphic images, photographs, tables, or charts—that juxtapose other geographies to that of the verbal narrative. Such narratives composed of heterogeneous modes and media of self-inquiry, achronologically organized, often enable us to see more clearly how narrated "I"s are indeed multiple.

The conscious diffraction of times of telling and the fragmentation of chronological sequence are narrative means of emphasizing that a subject is not unified or coherent. That is, different modes of emplotment and different media of self-presentation offer possibilities for and constraints upon the kind of "I" that can be narrated. Let us briefly consider some narrative genres that have provided occasions for autobiographical acts. The fable presents the narrated "I" as an allegorical type enacting human aspiration, as in, for example, John Bunyan's *Grace Abounding to the Chief of Sinners*. The meditation presents the stages of a narrated "I"'s reflections, with increasing understanding or momentary glimpses of the meaning of her spiritual history, as occurs in the *Shew-ings of Julian of Norwich*, Teresa of Avila's *Interior Castle*, and Thomas Merton's *The Seven-Storey Mountain*. A secular narrative, such as Robert Burton's *Anatomy of Melancholy* or Loren C. Eiseley's *The Star Thrower*, also performs a meditative exploration occasioned by situating a life within the context of a system of thought. The lyric sequence may present the narrating "I" as a subject charting its own moments of intense emotion and rereading the narrated "I"s of previous poems as an increasingly complex structure of self-reflection, as do, for example, the sonnet sequences of French Renaissance poet Louise Labé and, in quite different ways, American poets Robert Lowell in *Notebook 1967–68* and *Life Studies* and James McMichael in *Four Good Things*. The sketch (or way of life) presents the narrated "I" as a subject enmeshed in a way of life that may be recalled precisely because it is a time now past, as is the case in Mark Twain's *Life on the Mississippi*.

The emplotment of autobiographical narratives, then, can be described as a dense and multilayered intersection of the temporal and the geographic. By teasing out the complex ways in which life narratives are organized, readers may discover the cultural, or historic, or generic specificities of these emplotments. As life narratives increasingly innovate on modalities of self-representation, critics are called upon to inventively contextualize the host of strategies that autobiographical texts employ.

The Medium

While we normally think about autobiography as an extended narrative in written form, it is possible to enact self-presentation in many media. The kinds of media that can be used to tell an autobiographical story include short feature and documentary films; theater pieces; installations; performance art in music, dance, and monologue; the painted or sculpted self-portrait; quilts, collages, and mosaics; body art; murals; comics; and cyber art. As Plummer suggests, "[Storytellers] even and more complexly can perform their stories—not just in words and scripts but as emotionally charged bodies in action" (21).

Examples of the uses of mixed media for projects of autobiographical telling abound in the twenty-first century. In such story quilts as "The French Collection" series, Faith Ringgold chronicles, as a Künstlerroman, the life of a black woman artist in Paris and in America. Quilt, painting, text on cloth, the story quilts present, through a fictionalized narrative of African American woman artist Willia Marie, Ringgold's struggle to find her place "in the picture" of Western art history and to make a place in that history for the aesthetics of her African American quilting heritage. The performance pieces of such artists as Laurie Anderson, Carmelita Tropicana, Rachel Rosenthal, Guillermo Gómez-Peña, and Bob Flanagan become occasions for staging ethnically, racially, and sexually marked bodies and for remembering and dismembering the psychic costs of identity, cultural visibility, and the social construction of difference. Since the Renaissance, artists' self-portraits have powerfully imaged the social milieu, virtuosity, and cultural myths of mastery through which the artist has claimed the authority of his or her professional status.

In these visual media artists of the autobiographical can achieve effects that verbal narrators cannot. They can place the material body in the picture to make embodiment visible. They can palpably push the autobiographical to the very interior of the body, as Mona Hatoum does in her photographic renderings of the insides of her body. They can visualize the psychic interior of such drives as hunger and sexual desire, as Janine Antoni does. In her installation entitled "Gnaw," Antoni presents the viewer with two 300-pound cubes, one made of chocolate, the other of lard, that the artist has eaten during off-hours in the gallery; out of the regurgitated gnawings she has fashioned new consumer products—lipsticks and chocolate hearts—identified with the social construction of heterosexual femininity. Here the autobiographical body, while absent, remains present in its traces: the teeth marks left on massive cubes of chocolate and lard, the chewings that reform into lipstick and hearts. Through these traces of the body, Antoni puts autobiographical drives in the picture.

Of course, the medium that comes most readily to mind in

self-representation is photography. Because photos individually or in family albums seem literally to memorialize identity, they often accompany written life narratives. Photographs can be found in the autobiographical works of Mark Twain and August Strindberg, and more and more commonly in contemporary narratives, among them Roland Barthes's *Camera Lucida*, Norma Elia Cantú's *Canícula: Snapshots of a Girlhood en la Frontera*, Donna Williams's *Nobody Nowhere: The Extraordinary Autobiography of an Autistic*, and Sheila Ortiz Taylor and Sandra Ortiz Taylor's *Imaginary Parents: A Family Autobiography*. But there are separate conventions in visual and verbal media. Photographs never simply illustrate a written narrative. Each photo tells a separate story and, taken together, they form a separate system of meaning. And the stories in photographs may support, or be in tension with, or contradict the claims of the verbal text. To read these multimedia texts we need to develop familiarity with the narrative and generic conventions of visual compositions, a field beyond the purview of this study.

Photograph(s) may accompany an autobiographical narrative, be alluded to but absent, or stand in the place of an absent but suggested narrative. The latter is the case with photographic series, multiple self-portraits that expose an autobiographical subject to view as they engage the illusory and unstable nature of the subject so exposed. For the photograph presents the "I" in the photograph as at once a flesh-and-blood subject and a dematerialized phantom of an invisible photographer. The uncanny self-portraits of such self-photographers as Claude Cahun, Francesca Woodman, and Cindy Sherman interrogate self-identity, doubling "I"s, unfixing gender, and unmasking conventions of self-portraiture by the impersonation of popular or artistic images. This power of the photograph to "tell a story" of subjectivity has become a fascinating focus of theorizing about life narratives, as recent studies by Marianne Hirsch (*Family Frames*), Linda Haverty Rugg, and Timothy Dow Adams (*Light Writing and Life Writing*) suggest.

Finally, media may be assembled into what might be described as an ensemble text of life narrative. This is the case with Kate Bornstein's *Gender Outlaw: On Men, Women, and the Rest of Us*. Bornstein takes her experience as a male-to-female transsexual as a starting point for critiquing the binary social construction of gender and gendered desire. Her strategy of engaging the reader in actively interpreting gendered experience produces a hybrid text, composed of photographs, a play, interviews, the analyses of social critics and scholars, and a dispersed, nonchronological personal narrative. No one medium or generic mode is sufficient to this ensemble narration, and her "cut-and-pasted" text suggests both the suturing of body parts and social networks, and the subversion of the system of gender identity that its collage method achieves.

As the example of Bornstein's narrative suggests, the media for self-narrating are and have always been multiple—although critics until recently have not often emphasized the autobiographical dimension of genres other than published texts.[3]

The Consumer

We noted above that a life narrative is addressed to one or more narratees and the implied reader within the text. Both addressees are implicit in autobiographical acts. But there are also actual readers of, and listeners to, personal stories. Plummer calls these readers and listeners the "consumers" in the tripartite symbolic interaction that is personal storytelling. Most literary critics call them audiences (or flesh-and-blood readers).

When someone tells his life story before a "live" audience, that audience is palpably there, soliciting, assessing, even judging the story being told. Thus the audience directly influences the presentation of identity. It influences the inclusion of certain identity contents and the exclusion of others; the incorporation of certain narrative itineraries or intentionalities and the silencing of others; the adoption of certain autobiographical voices and the muting of others. In a sense, then, the performativity of such an autobiographical act minimizes the distances between the narrator and narratee, the implied audience, and the consumer. The story is being addressed to a live audience that, to a greater or lesser extent, immediately and audibly responds.

But reading audiences are not comparably homogeneous communities. They are heterogeneous collectives for whom certain discourses of identity, certain stories, certain truths make sense at various moments. They come to their readings of an autobiographical text with expectations about the kinds of narrative that conform relatively comfortably to criteria of intelligibility. But they come from different experiential histories and geopolitical spaces. There is, then, no way to predict what kind of "reading" they will take away from, or give to, an autobiographical act.

Think of the further complications involved in understanding the responses of audiences to written texts, given distances of both space and time. Scholars of the history of the book try to discover, through research into the material conditions of publication, who constituted "reading publics," the historical consumers of narratives at various times. They analyze what meanings reading publics assigned to the narratives they read in order to understand the cultural meanings the narrative acquired when, and since, it was first published. And they assess the investments that religious, juridical, political, and/or cultural institutions may have had in the reproduction—or suppression—of genres of personal narrative or in a particular personal narrative.

Published narratives circulate among reading publics. But how they are produced, how they circulate, what routes they take, how they get into people's hands, what institutions they circulate in and through are issues that affect the ways in which narratives achieve their ongoing effects in social interactions. Moreover, personal narratives come to communities of readers along with many other kinds of cultural productions (from elite, as well as popular, culture). Readers "consume" narratives along with other cultural stories. So their interpretations of and their responses to narratives are influenced by other kinds of stories in general circulation—in families, communities, regions, nations, diasporas.

Take two examples of popular American life narratives that circulated among reading publics throughout, and even beyond, the nineteenth century: Barbary Coast narratives and Mary Jemison's captivity narrative. A fascinating subgenre of captivity narrative, the Barbary captive narratives (both English and American, white and black) were usually narrated by mariners captured by pirates and held in North Africa. During the sixteenth through the nineteenth centuries, these tales were widely read as popular exploration and adventure stories. But in the United States they were also read in the nineteenth century as cautionary tales, warning of the vulnerability of the new nation to its European trading partners, all of whom sought wealth in Africa (Baepler, 25). These tales also mobilized divisions in American discourses of race at a key moment, the first half of the nineteenth century, when the slave trade had greatly intensified and slave narratives were circulating. A captive such as African American Robert Adams, who told his narrative to a white editor in 1816 in London, Boston, and elsewhere, was variously read as "white," "Arab," or "negro" by readers whose interpretations of his narrative varied wildly according to their location and politics (21). A female Barbary captive, Eliza Bradley, wrote "an authentic narrative," published in 1820 as the true and harrowing tale of a white English woman who, in captivity, was sheltered and never the victim of sexual advances (247). This narrative, borrowing large parts of its story from a best-selling adventure narrative of its time, captivated readers with its contradictory notions of fragile and independent white womanhood. Barbary Coast narratives traded on the exoticizing of Africa as a land of extremes in bizarre stories of grotesque spectacles: they rationalized and critiqued slavery in the United States, and they inaugurated a public taste for Barbary captive narratives in print and, much later, on the stage and screen (50–51).

A different aspect of reading publics is evident in the changing responses to the narrative of Mary Jemison, popularly known as "the white woman of the Genesee," told to James E. Seaver. Jemison was captured in 1755 by the Seneca in what is now upstate New York and stayed voluntarily for life with her captors, raising a large family. Her narrative, first published in 1824, was so popular it went through twenty-seven printings and twenty-three editions that ranged in size from 32 to 483 pages. In these editions the story was reshaped as, at various moments, an ethnographic record of life among the Seneca and Iroquois; a "true history" of captive experience; a document attesting to settler stamina; a nostalgic mourning for the decline of Indian life; a site for displaying photos of the new sites and monuments of western New York; and a popular children's book (Namias, 4–6). In examining its successive editions, we can trace shifts in reading tastes by observing the modifications of content and presentation of the edition over time. To date, the study of audiences for autobiographical narratives is not a developed field. More scholarly work needs to be done on the reception of popular narratives, the international transmission of such narratives, and the shifts in content and emphasis that occur from edition to edition in response to changing public tastes.

In sum, changes in reading publics are signaled by the most subtle of changes in the material production of the book (from print size to the use of illustrations, from introductions to appendixes) and in the framing of the narrative for readers whose interpretative schema have shifted dramatically from those of an earlier time. And since narratives are riddled with the play of meaning beyond any fixed referentiality, reading publics, or consumers, become cocreators of the text by remaking the story through the social codes and psychic needs of their times.

"The meanings of stories are never fixed," concludes Plummer, "but emerge out of a ceaselessly changing stream of interaction between producers and readers in shifting contexts. They may, of course, become habitualised and stable; but always and everywhere the meanings of stories shift and sway in the contexts to which they are linked" (21–22). This instability and periodic renewal of meaning accounts for the ever-shifting effects of the autobiographical, and for the joint action of life narrator, coaxer, and reader in constructing the narrative. Umberto Eco aptly captures this dynamism of publics for narrative by titling a section of his 1979 book, *The Role of the Reader: Explorations in the Semiotics of Texts*, "How to produce texts by reading them" (3).

Conclusion

Getting a life means getting a narrative, and vice versa. In his influential essay, "Life as Narrative," Jerome Bruner powerfully articulates the complex interconnections between lives lived and the narratives of lives:

Eventually the culturally shaped cognitive and linguistic processes that guide the self-telling of life narratives achieve the power to structure perceptual experience, to organize memory, to segment and purpose-build the very "events" of a life. In the end, we become the autobiographical narratives by which we "tell about" our lives. And given the cultural shaping to which I referred, we also become variants of the culture's canonical forms. (15)

It is in our autobiographical acts, contextual, provisional, performative, that we give shape to, and remake ourselves through, memory, experience, identity, embodiment, and agency. Understanding the profound complexities of these acts enables us to better understand what is at stake in our narratives, in the narrator-reader relationship, and in the culture of the autobiographical so prevalent at the beginning of the twenty-first century.

CHAPTER 4

Life Narrative in Historical Perspective

> I'm losing myself! An explosion of identity. Searching for oneself
> in death to get to know birth! Beginning with the origins in order
> to understand the end. Inventing a detail, patching it up and
> adjusting it to suit one's destiny.
>
> Calixthe Beyala, *Your Name Shall Be Tanga*

Our goal in this chapter is to trace the production of autobiographical subjects over time. This history does not claim to trace a simple chronology of successive notions of personhood. Competing versions of personhood overlap and intersect at a given historical moment. Our focus is double, on demarcating autobiographical subjects in their historical context and on noting the emergence of various autobiographical genres through which those subjects fashion themselves. Our aims in constructing this history are both to identify exemplary autobiographical texts and to explore the kinds of subjects those narratives inscribe.

Thus, we look beyond individual texts to the formation of the subject in relation to larger collectivities of social classes, nation, religious community, ethnic group, and other defining identities. Understanding how individual representations of subjectivity are "disciplined" or formed enables readers to explore how the personal story of a remembered past is always in dialogue with emergent cultural formations. This brief anatomy, then, examines autobiographical genres that are both formed by and formative of specific kinds of autobiographical subjects.

We noted in chapter 1 the relatively recent coinage of the term *autobiography* in the West. The practice of writing autobiographically, however, has a history extending back to, and perhaps before, the Greeks and Romans in antiquity and extending beyond Western culture. The oral performance of self-narrative has existed in many indigenous cultures prior to literacy—in, for example, the naming songs of Native American cultures, the oral narratives of genealogy and descent among Africans, the communal self-locating of the "song lines" of indigenous Australians, and others. In addition to the long-standing practices of oral tradition throughout the world, there are modes of written self-inscription in China as early as two thousand years ago, in Japan as early as a thousand years ago, in Islamic-Arabic literature as early as the twelfth century,[1] in India during the medieval period (the *bhakti* poetry of devotional engagement with the sacred), and in North Africa in the fourteenth century (Ibn Khaldûn's *At-Ta'rîf*). This widespread use of self-representation in both preliterate and literate non-Western cultures contradicts the allegation of an earlier generation of literary critics that "autobiography" is a uniquely Western form and a specific achievement of Western culture at a moment of individuation in the wake of the Enlightenment.[2]

Given the current interest in the study of life narratives, we fully expect that scholars in the next decade will continue research into autobiographical traditions and their transcultural influence; and we anticipate that autobiography studies will become increasingly comparative and multicultural. For the purposes of this study, however, we have limited our focus to written life narrative as it has developed in the West.

Autobiographical Subjects in Antiquity and the Middle Ages

When we think of self-knowledge in classical antiquity, we are likely to think first of the figure of Socrates and his self-interrogatory understanding of the Delphic oracle's injunction, "Know thyself": Socrates knows that he knows nothing. But although Socrates engaged others on the limits of their knowledge and revealed their blindness about themselves, even the "Apology" and the "Symposium" are, at best, obliquely self-referential. While the Platonic dialogues show the paradox of self-knowledge in the wise man's knowing admission of ignorance, they do not resemble autobiographical texts as we now understand them. Georg Misch, an eminent early-twentieth-century German scholar of autobiography, however, identified hundreds of texts and inscriptions in his multivolume history translated in part as *A History of Autobiography in Antiquity*.[3] Misch found evidence of an "I" commemorated in funerary inscriptions about feats of battle and in early texts such as funeral orations, familiar letters, and travel narratives that have both the autobiographical content and the structure of self-reference. Certainly the lyric poems of Sappho of Lesbos (c. 600 B.C.E.) present the voices of a woman candidly exploring her emotions and the somatic designs of love and physical desire, often with self-mocking wit, as feminist scholars have recently argued.

The "first" book-length autobiographical narrative in the West is generally acknowledged to be the *Confessions* of St. Augustine, written around 397 C.E. Augustine's "I" retrospectively views his early life from the perspective of his conversion to Christianity. Saved, he looks back to assess the workings of grace in his wayward life and the steps to his spiritual salvation. The postconversion Augustine construes the first half of his life as a chronological narrative of errors and self-indulgence from his youth through his pursuit of education and erotic love. He narrates, in Book 8, the turning point of his life, the moment of conversion when he was called by a spiritual voice to seek dialogue with an unapproachable god, and to reflect on the centrality of memory to spiritual salvation.

Unlike Plutarch and other biographers of the Roman emperors who focus on the public careers of their subjects, Augustine writes extensively of his childhood, with its intimate desires; he writes as well about the psychology of virtue and vice that marked his troubled journey toward conversion and confesses a Christian sense of sin and shame. The identity that is the subject of Augustine's text is a paradoxical one. In this process of conversion, loss of self as it is commonly understood defines identity, and self-effacement becomes a means to a higher state, being subsumed in God. The mode of this autobiography as postconversion "confession" is directed simultaneously to Man and to God, in a narrative at once exemplary and highly personal.

In the next thousand years, most autobiographical writing was done by religious men and women as a form of devotion in the service of spiritual examination. Their narratives sought the signs of God's grace in the life of Christ and Christian saints and tried to erase the traces of sin by effacing the stubborn self. Medieval spiritual testimonies include such works as the *Shewings* of Dame Julian of Norwich and the meditations of mystics such as Hildegard of Bingen and Hadewijch in Germany, and Angela of Foligno in Italy. In the narrated visions through which they attempted to represent their relationship to the unrepresentable, female mystics, according to Laurie Finke, "claimed the power to shape the meaning and form of their experiences" even though they "did not claim to speak in [their] own voice[s]" (44).

In the fifteenth century in England Margery Kempe, a medieval mystic, told to a scribe a most remarkable story of one woman's life. Her *Book* sought to convince readers and Church authorities that she was a mystic, perhaps even a saint, who belonged in the genealogy of Christian saints. As a married mother, Kempe had to remake herself as a public religious through a narrative of God's manifestations in her life and in her very body, a body whose testimony included weeping and wailing. Like other religious mystics, Kempe co-constructed the story of a subject in dialogue with a god who commanded her attention to the signs of his wonders. This version of life narrative offered a destiny and an itinerary for self-location and promised salvation through self-overcoming.

In fourteenth-century Italy, Francis Petrarch and Dante Alighieri introduced self-referentiality into traditional poetic genres to present the spiritual quests of their narrators and to define their relationship to a classical tradition. Petrarch's letter, "The Ascent of Mt. Ventoux," addressed to St. Augustine, applies the terms of self-understanding in Augustine to his own arduous journey up the "mountain" of life. In his *Vita Nuova (The New Life)* Dante's young poet-narrator recasts his entire life in light of that transformative moment when he glimpsed Beatrice, a figure for, and a foreshadowing of, the encounter with the divine. And Dante the pilgrim, at the beginning of the *Divine Comedy*, represents himself as a straying wanderer who "woke to find myself in a dark wood" (*Inferno*, 1:67), both a writer on a personal quest to resolve the dilemma of his identity *and* a figure of the struggling Christian soul.

Medieval Christian writers deployed a rhetoric of self-reference in their quests for salvation. It is important to note, however, that the challenges and complexities of self-reference and self-study in medieval mystics do not yet present the self-fashioning private individual of much early modern narrative. But as forays into autobiographical writing, these narratives, with their applications of sacred discourse to the profane private self, anticipate the terms of a dialogue about the private and public loci of self-conception that later humanist self-narrators will explore.

We know far less of everyday medieval uses of the autobiographical. The letters, journals, and chronicles of the secular world take place at the margins of records of official tasks, private communications, and household management. Chronicles recorded and celebrated the public actions of aristocrats and merchants. Letters and ledgers recorded the everyday workings of families, notably families whose members achieved prominence due to their social status and inherited identity. There is no one category of personhood to which we may assign these many modes of encoded self-presentation in medieval texts. In fact, much exploration of the forms of subjectivity in medieval texts remains to be done by scholars.

The Humanist Subject, Secular and Spiritual

As part of the transformations wrought in the early modern period of the fifteenth and sixteenth centuries, the problem of writing and imaging a secular and public self became increasingly pressing as people struggled with landscapes of interiority other than that of Christian spirituality and an exteriority other than that defined through the material signs of God's grace. In the poetic traditions of Italy, France, England, Germany, Spain, and the Netherlands, the sonnet sequence offered lyrical occasions for a narrator's extended introspective exploration of the range of emotions evoked by the beloved and the conflicting effects of love produced in the lover. Although highly conventionalized in form, meter, and rhyme, the sonnet sequences of writers such as William Shakespeare and Louise Labé conduct explorations of heightened states of feeling and evolve a vocabulary of interiority to delineate a nuanced subjectivity.

In his *Autobiography* Benvenuto Cellini, a sixteenth-century Florentine sculptor, narrated the story of his life, fulfilling what he considered the duty of all men "who have done anything of excellence" (7). Cellini mixes discussion of his everyday work as an artist with accounts of the manners and customs of his time, stressing his own importance as someone at the center of power and accomplishment. His text combines chronicle with a kind of early ethnography to construct a humanist subject who centers himself in the public world as both evaluator and actor. This humanist subject is epistemologically oriented in writers such as Desiderius Erasmus and Michel de Montaigne, engaging with a material world that it can significantly act upon and enter into dialogue with. As Stephen Greenblatt suggests, such "Renaissance self-fashioning" reoriented poets and thinkers toward a human measure and mode of the self.

Contemporaneous with Cellini, the mathematician Girolamo Cardano composed *The Book of My Life*, considered by some to be the first psychological life narrative. Cardano minutely inventories aspects of his life in chapters with such titles as "A Meditation on the Perpetuation of My Name," "Those Things in Which I Take Pleasure," "My Manner of Walking and Thinking," and "Things in Which I Feel I Have Failed." His emphasis on self-evaluation remains open-ended, never coming to rest in the completed composition of his self-portrait. In *St. Ignatius' Own Story, As Told to Luis Gonzáles de Cámara* in three short sessions in 1555, Ignatius represents his history of inward growth and interior transformation differently. He presents himself as a contemplative in action by alluding to particulars of the world in which he studied, taught, and traveled. In such narratives the autobiographical subject objectifies himself as an actor in the world and records the externalization of his character, showing how the subject becomes a subject of history. Here the presentation of subjectivity is, as with the medieval mystics, in the service of an external source; that source is now not timeless and transcendent, but embedded in the material conditions of history.

Teresa of Avila, working within a tradition of spiritual autobiography, engages the form to explore her visions and present herself to her confessors. In this process, she introduces a metaphorics drawn from everyday domestic experience that works against a discourse of transcendent spirituality, thereby creating a kind of personal, material subject and giving embodiment to interiority. In authorizing herself as a subject, Teresa challenges her confessors' suppression of women religious and articulates a mode of self-interrogation congenial to women mystics who also inhabit earthly realms of power. Similarly, Madame Guyon, trapped in a ruthless marriage, embraces in her narrative a mysticism that promises empowerment in its exaggeration of model femininity. By exploring their own private experience, then, some women writers find alternative access to self-knowledge in a church that forbade them formal learning. Here, autobiographical practice becomes an alternative form of education.

The first specific, sustained self-exploration in Renaissance prose occurs in the *Essays* of Montaigne, who for nearly thirty years used colloquial prose to test or "try" his reading of the writers of antiquity against the perspectives of his own times and his personal idiosyncrasies. In his extended self-portrait, Montaigne dramatizes his situation as both the subject and object of his own discourse. Asking himself "Que sçay-je?" ("What do I know?"), he pursues an inquiry into how self-knowledge shapes the terms of subjectivity.

Montaigne's *Essays* are not a retrospective chronicle of his lived life; rather, they comprise a sustained investigation into the conditions of knowledge that enable his enunciation of an "I" in the terms of the self-portrait formed of ever-shifting perspectives. Montaigne's interlinear habit of writing commentary on his previous layers of text, however, adds reflexivity as his narrating "I" enters into ongoing dialogue with past narrating "I"s. Montaigne's "I" studies itself in a succession of moments refracted through the lenses of topics as exalted as "Of Experience" and as humble as "Of Thumbs." This mix of everyday topics, details of personal life, and classical learning makes a textual body that, in an act of secular incorporation, is recursively referential.

This practice of taking oneself as a subject of inquiry in time is engaged discursively by such dramatic figures as Hamlet and explored in the prose of John Donne's sermons, Robert Burton's *Anatomy of*

Melancholy, and Thomas Browne's "Religio Medici," among others. Each of these writers, working within a received prose genre of the meditation, reshapes it as a forum for self-investigation by posing systems of knowledge against one another and locating his investigatory "I" at their nexus. With the philosophers Francis Bacon, John Locke, and David Hume, however, that inquiring "I" becomes embedded in new ontologies, the "I" a subject of a new system, as the interrogatory, experientially based stance of Montaigne is transformed in emergent systems of metaphysics.

The Migratory Subject of Early Modern Travel Narratives

The self-exploration of the early modern period both motivated and paralleled geographical exploration of the globe as travelers began to record the findings of their journeys in narratives that comprise another kind of autobiographical practice. These travel narratives posed an "I" in migration, encounter, conquest, and transformation.

The genre emerges in the West with *The Travels of Marco Polo* in 1271, which inaugurated, over the next four centuries, a plethora of narratives of voyages to exotic destinations. European adventurers and explorers returned home with tales of hardships and survival, of dangerous transit and wondrous encounters (Pratt, *Imperial Eyes*, 20). Presenting themselves as heroic survivalists and their project as one of mapping new worlds, these writers used their self-referential narratives to articulate the subjectivity identified by Mary Louise Pratt as "a European global or planetary subject" (9). This global subject was "male, secular, and lettered," and viewed the world through the lens of a "planetary consciousness" (29–30).

Journeys to the New World provide a focus for these narratives of exploration, conquest, and empire, from the Portuguese through the French, Spanish, Dutch, German, and American explorers. Perhaps the best known of these is Columbus's log, a personal set of informational entries for the years of the Hispaniola visits, and the journals of Cortés, registering both the hardships of travel and the wonders of encounter. In letters such as those of Dominican friar Bartolomé de Las Casas to King Philip of Spain concerning the cruelties of Spanish conquest in the West

Indies beginning in 1542 (translated into English in 1583), the critique of the predatory mentality and abusive practices of a "global or planetary subject" is fully achieved. Another kind of travel narrative was developed by Jean de Léry in the *History of a Voyage to the Land of Brazil, Otherwise Called America* written in 1578. Speaking alternately as "I" and "we," Léry provides an eyewitness account that mixes encounters with "exotic" natives, tales of hardships at sea, religious controversy among the Huguenots, and personal reflections on contact with other worlds, a narrative project that gradually forms his own subjectivity. As in Montaigne's "Of Cannibals," which indicts colonizing Europeans as more barbaric than the "barbarians" of the New World, for Léry contact with indigenous people calls "civilizing" practices into question and suggests that an "indigenous" collectivized subjectivity may be superior to that of the Western "new man."

Narratives of colonization, captivity, and contested hegemony continued to abound into the seventeenth century, wracked as it was by political conflict. While Captain John Smith's brash fabulations signaled one possibility of storytelling, captivity narratives in the New World reworked certain tropes of conversion narratives in the context of the radical dislocations created by contact in the New World. In the American colony Mary Rowlandson's narrative of captivity, with all its ambivalences, became well known. As we noted in chapter 3, Rowlandson charts her shift from victim to flexible survivor among the Narragansetts, from the assumed superiority of an inerrant Puritanism to the less certain subjectivity and more complex worldview of transcultural encounter.

The Enlightenment Subject

Contemporaneously, in seventeenth-century Europe, Descartes situated the contemplative, epistemological self in a new house of philosophy. The solitary "I" of his *Discourse on the Method* subordinates body to mind, nature to intellect, and others to a sovereign philosophical self, the *cogito*. In isolating and individuating an identity, he transforms experience into metaphysical principles, stripped of everyday particulars. In the reflection of the cogito on its own mental processes, the enlightenment subject is born and, with it, a new world of Cartesian dualism created from its desires and certainties.

In the wake of the cogito, forms of rational and scientific knowledge gained preeminence. Privileging sight and visual clarity, philosophers identified Enlightenment rationality with the intellectual standpoint of objectivity and understood the goal of man's intellectual labor as comprehending the totality of a problem. This claim to objectivity and universal knowledge enabled the postulation of a rational or objective subject able to transcend the perspectival sight of humanist writers and define his knowledge as outside that which he surveys. And the notion of an ideal knowledge, linking sight, knowing, rationality, and power, reordered conceptions of self-understanding, as the autobiographical investigations of such philosophers as Blaise Pascal and Thomas Hobbes suggest.

Motivated by this cultural belief in the thinker's objectivity, enlightened men set off on sustained journeys into interiors of continents, as scientific journeys superseded journeys of conquest. Enlightened men of science traversed the globe, collecting samples and information about flora and fauna, peoples and geographies. Bringing the entirety of the globe within sight and rationalizing it through the systematic classification of Linnean taxonomy, these scientists exercised their enlightened subjectivity by naming the profligate chaos of the world and writing narratives of scientific inquiry through which they presented themselves as benign agents of reason and order (see Pratt, *Imperial Eyes*, 14–37).

But the limitations of an overreaching rationalism and the social orthodoxies of emergent nation states also provoked resistance and gave rise to the articulation of alternative subjectivities among dissenting marginal groups, including Protestant sects as well as some wives of the gentry.

The Dissenting Subject

After the sixteenth-century rise of dissenting sects in the Protestant Reformation, spiritual autobiography was increasingly employed to defend a community of believers. The Puritan revolution in England engendered John Bunyan's *Grace Abounding to the Chief of Sinners* and George Fox's "Journal." In his "Journal" Fox attempts to acquaint readers with his character and religious views. In Bunyan's project of self-biography, an ideal dissenting self assesses itself in terms of Puritan religious prescriptions. Eager to establish a place for both the dissenting self and the dissenting community in the body politic, Bunyan's narrator constantly attunes his salvation to what Felicity Nussbaum describes as "the promise and the threat of the loss of identity" (69). Often, she notes, his writing plays out a dialectics of subjection and agency for subjects of self-regulation: "The autobiographical subject may describe subjection to an authority's control while being bound to a belief that one is a free agent with an independent conscience and self-understanding" (77). The dissenting subject is an ethical subject located in the space of paradox. He or she is at once subservient and free: subservient to the extent of being free to choose the path to salvation; and free in the sense of choosing the path of subservience.

Men and women writing secular life narratives in the seventeenth century had few models clearly available to them, in part because many of the narratives written during the period remained unpublished for several hundred years. There were, however, two generalized conventions—the narrative of religious conversion, as we have seen, and the secular *res gestae* (the story of deeds done), tracing its roots back to classical antiquity. Some educated aristocratic women, finding means to write within the general constraints on women's writing, chronicled the deeds and achievements of their husbands, as did Lucy Hutchinson and Ann Lady Fanshawe. But others hesitantly asserted their own voices. For example, Anne Lady Halkett appended a narrative of her life to the biography she wrote of her husband. Margaret Cavendish wrote a personal account, one of the earliest secular life narratives written by a woman, but only after she had dutifully written a biography of her husband. In *The True Relation of My Birth, Breeding, and Life* she negotiated her ambivalent desires for public recognition and for proper femininity. In this struggle for meaningful autobiographical identity, Cavendish sustains two competing self-representations, the story of feminine self-effacement and that of masculine self-assertion.

The Bourgeois Subject

Perhaps the best-known life narrative of the English seventeenth century is Samuel Pepys's *Diary*, although it was not published until the early nineteenth century. In six large volumes, written over forty years (1660–1703), Pepys recounts in minute detail London life, the great fire and the plague, as well as everyday life, trips to the country, and his weakness for women. Written as regular weekly entries throughout his life, the diary composes a secular world in which Pepys takes account of his daily life. His might be thought of as the accumulative subject, along the lines of Defoe's pseudo-autobiographers Robinson Crusoe and Moll Flanders, all of whom are nascent bourgeois subjects accumulating the capital of experience. In some ways, too, this accounting resembles the self-survey of spiritual autobiographers. In both genres, the diurnal record and the narrative of spiritual progress, the life narrator becomes an eyewitness to events, both great and daily, a kind of interested social historian.

Bourgeois subjects, like aristocrats before them, also set off on the road, traveling through Europe on what became known as the "grand tour" and writing about their travels as a *peregrinatio academica* (Leed, 184–85; Chard, 1–39). In their travel journals James Boswell, Charles Burney, and Thomas Nugent recorded their observations as educational journeys through successive cultures. Typically, grand tourists followed a prescribed curriculum and set of exercises codified in guidebooks written by their tutors, such as *The Compleat Gentleman, or, Directions for the Education of Youth as to Their Breeding at Home and Travelling Abroad*, written by Jean Gailhard. The bourgeois subject of both tour and journal imagined himself as the newly enlightened man of broad learning and experience preparing to assume "the responsibilities of the well-born male to family, class, and nation" (Porter, *Haunted Journeys*, 35).

At least one grand tourist discovered that the education she received through the grand tour made the return to family responsibilities impossible. Lady Mary Wortley Montagu, traveling with her husband, who was British ambassador to the Sultanate of Turkey, carefully composed and copied her letters to friends and family in England. In these "embassy letters," published after her death, Montagu turns an observant autobiographical eye/"I" into a detailed and revisionary ethnographic account of women's lives in the Turkish seraglio, refiguring the woman of the seraglio as a sign "of liberty and freedom" (Lowe, *Critical Terrains*, 45) in comparison to the women of England.

In France the rise of the epistolary form enables other kinds of autobiographical presentation. Madame de Sévigné's renowned letters, many of which are addressed to a daughter unwilling to engage her in speech, reform for private disclosure the genre that Abelard and Héloïse had used centuries earlier for self-presentation as devout lovers. In a remarkable epistolary conversation with her daughter, de Sévigné creates herself as a woman writing and, like Montaigne with the essay form before her, comments upon the act of letter-writing. The occasion of writing to her daughter provides de Sévigné an occasion for dialogue in her absence; to herself, at least, she sustains her identity as "mother" to her daughter. Along with some novels of the century, such as Madame de Lafayette's *The Princess of Clèves*, her writing signals a nascent bourgeois maternal subject characterized by nurturance and the appeal to filiality.

The Exceptional Subject of Modern Life Narrative

The eighteenth century comprises a vast and complex network of autobiographical discourses among the French encyclopedists, German Pietists, British diarists, American adventurers, and others. The figure of Augustine in the *Confessions* is revived for varied uses by philosophical autobiographers investigating issues in cognition and epistemology, how we know and how we know we know. In the *Autobiography of Giambattista Vico*, written between 1725 and 1731, Vico narrates his intellectual development as a philosophical historian and figure of all humanity. Vico's "true art of autobiography," in distinction to what he views as Descartes's false autobiography, is modeled on Augustine's mode of self-searching. In a fable written in the third person he presents himself as an autodidact engaged with the ancient problem of self-knowledge (Verene, 71, 58, 48).

Another mode of autobiographical self-presentation occurs in *History of My Life*, the twelve-volume memoirs of Giacomo Casanova, who prided himself on being gifted as both a seducer and a memoirist. In contrast, Edward Gibbon, in the six versions of *Memoirs of My Life* written between 1788 and 1793, wavers between confidence and doubt about his mastery of the world and ability to shape his experience, as Roger Porter suggests.[4]

Jean-Jacques Rousseau employs another autobiographical strategy, reviving the genre of the confession before the French Revolution for very different ends. In his *Confessions* he turns the lens of his analysis upon himself in all his licentious frailty, "confessing" not to some god in pursuit of conversion, but to a diverse "public" that rejects him and evokes his hostility. Rousseau's assertions about his project of self-representation are both well known and notorious: "I am commencing an undertaking, hitherto without precedent, and which will never find an imitator. . . . I am not made like any of those I have seen; I venture to believe that I am not made like any of those who are in existence. If I am not better, at least I am different" (3). His claim to being the exceptional subject, characteristic of much Romantic autobiography, is linked to his self-portrayal as natural man, in solitary quest of lost innocence in a corrupted society. Here confession becomes a method of self-justification and social indictment, as well as a medium for posing radical individuality.

If the *Confessions* celebrates a discourse of selfishness and egotism in pursuit of an ideal world, it also mirrors a self-reflexive imagination untiringly engaged in recording its own sensations, impressions, and motives. For some, Rousseau inaugurates modern autobiography, with his focus on childhood, his retrospective chronology, his radical individualism, and his antagonistic relationship with both his readers and the reader. For others, Rousseau's legacy in the *Confessions* is a radical individualism that privileges the white male citizen. For them, Rousseau inaugurates traditional autobiography, which, as we suggested in chapter 1, has become a suspect site of exclusionary practices. Rousseau's massive project of self-absorbed individualism continues to be an influential and controversial model of life narrative.[5]

New Subjects of Life Narrative in the Eighteenth Century

The eighteenth century saw an explosion in both the kinds and the sheer numbers of life narratives. New reading publics emerged with the rise in literacy, the expansion of print media, and the increased circulation of texts, goods, and people between Europe and the American colonies, and within both Europe and the colonies. In effect, there was a democratization of the institution of life writing. More and more people—merchants, criminals, middle-class women, ex-slaves—turned to life narratives as a means to know themselves and position themselves within the social world. We will consider two sites of such activity, in the American colonies and in England.

In retrospect, it has become clear that life narrative was one cultural location for negotiating the terms of the "new world" subject in the American colonies. In the context of settling the continent, life narrative took on added importance as people had to invent both their landscape and themselves. Outward exploration and inward exploration became coextensive, as Daniel Shea observes. This dual mapping of new terrains signaled "the flourishing of the Renaissance idea of the self as a microcosm in a period when the discovery and exploration of the macrocosm seemed to offer transformative possibilities directly to the person of the explorer" (Shea, "Prehistory of American Autobiography," 27).

Among the Puritans, Quakers, and other dissident religious communities in the New World, writers of spiritual autobiography found themselves in a dilemma: how could they validate narratives of conversion and salvation as authentic and irreversible when the self was "fallen"? Their autobiographical narratives indicate at once profound self-preoccupation and abject self-effacement. In these religious communities, too, the spiritual seeker was a profoundly public subject, commemorating the relationship of the introspective individual to the community of God's people. In different ways the mid-eighteenth-century spiritual narratives of Elizabeth Ashbridge, Jonathan Edwards, and John Woolman read community and self through each other, in dialogue and dissent. The community's history and the individual's spiritual life narrative are interdependent, inextricable.

In the secular community self-writing became self-making, as can be seen in Franklin's foundational text of American republicanism. Franklin's self-examination, written in part in the same decades as Rousseau's, diverges sharply from that of the French philosopher in the social and prescriptive character of its self-examination. Aimed at molding the individual to the community, Franklin's autobiography represents the Rousseauian individualist as corrupt and unproductive in the new republic. It presents a flexible, pragmatic subject, adaptive to the needs and possibilities of the new republic and critical of the old world privileges of inherited status and legacy. Franklin secularizes the heritage of Puritan life narrative and emphasizes self-invention as an ethical, rather than a spiritual, project.

In Franklin's rhetorical drama, as Daniel Shea suggests, the "pose of casual self-invention" disarms readers with its provincial tone, its lack of interiority, and its notion of an endlessly revisable self, which enable "the cunning of its didactic design" to re-arm them (*Spiritual Autobiography in Early America*, 38–39). Written over several decades and only published in the mid-nineteenth century, well after his death, Franklin's autobiography becomes a prototypical narrative for America's myth of the self-made man and the entrepreneurial republican subject, specifically marked as male, white, propertied, and socially and politically enfranchised.

In England, middle-class women who were sufficiently educated wrote letters (Mary Delany, Elizabeth Carter) and kept diaries (Hester Thrale, Fanny Burney), seemingly the marginal forms of marginal subjects that since have been revalued as precise records of everyday life. Even as they wrote about themselves in what appeared to be a "free space of interiority beyond the boundaries of a gendered hierarchy in the unwomanly, the unspoken, and the undervalued," their writing of daily selves reproduced gendered ideologies which they both trouble and reproduce. Other women, such as Charlotte Charke and Laetitia Pilkington, led more public lives and wrote "scandalous memoirs," encoding the sexual desire of an out-of-control female sensuality that escaped the control of the bourgeois family, at the cost of their own social status (Nussbaum, 203, 179).

Other marginalized subjects struggled to find their own spaces of inscription. Take the case of slave narratives, which began to be recorded around 1750, in tandem with the intensification of the transatlantic slave trade. Many of the earliest slave narratives were by illiterate men, "as-told-to" recorders. A remarkable exception is *The Life of Olaudah Equiano, or Gustavus Vassa the African*, purported to be the life narrative of an Igbo West African captured as a child and enslaved on various merchant ships. Equiano told a tale of escaping the repressive American colonies for the relative liberty of England, buying his freedom, and becoming a legislator active in repealing Britain's slave laws in 1806. Although this narrative traces a stirring journey to freedom, literacy, and masterful self-representation, its authenticity has recently been called into question as suspect (Carretta, 221).[6] If this eventuality proves to be the case, it will only suggest how important the discourse of the autobiographical had become as a means to imagine another life and identity for oneself and how salable autobiographical narratives had become in the marketplace of print culture.

The Romantic Subject of Lost Illusions

The struggle of marginal subjects for spaces of inscription becomes more prominent in the nineteenth century as, with the post-Revolutionary decline of aristocratic patronage, artists and writers move increasingly to the social margin. More dependent on selling their works in this less secure social position, writers began to rework the Romantic quest narrative to explore their own subjectivity outside the mainstream of national life.

In the Romantic quest narrative, the autobiographical becomes an allegorical pursuit of an ideal or transcendent self desiring to merge with some "absolute" of nature, love, or intellect that is beyond the ego, that is sublime. The legacy of Rousseauian radical individualism was reshaped by Goethe in *The Sorrows of Young Werther*, an epistolary fictionalized life narrative of self-preoccupation to the point of suicide. *Werther* powerfully influenced the artistic self-portrayal of passionate obsession. Such Romantic writers as Novalis, Byron (in the pseudo-autobiographical *Don*

Juan), and Mary Robinson in Europe all in different ways engage this model of a self on a solitary quest. And Walt Whitman in *Specimen Days* and "Song of Myself," and Henry David Thoreau in *Walden* adapt the quest of the introspective seeker to the landscapes, both rural and urban, of the American Republic in crisis and transformation.

The most elaborate reflection on the growth of the poet's mind, cast as a retrospective autobiography of childhood, education, and external and internal voyaging, is William Wordsworth's extended poem, *The Prelude*. The life of the artist is represented as that of a creative spirit, outside of and at odds with society, seeking to mirror his longing in the isolated grandeur of nature. (The legacy of this lyric autobiographical writing is seen in the early-twentieth-century works by such poets as T. S. Eliot, Ezra Pound, and Robert Frost.) Even life narrative treating the quest for the absolute ironically, as in Stendhal's diaries and *Life of Henry Brulard*, Thomas Carlyle's *Sartor Resartus*, or Thomas DeQuincey's *Confessions of an English Opium Eater*, construct what we might call a subject of lost illusions whose legacy can be discerned well into the twentieth century. Not all life narratives, of course, were as caught up in this dynamic of ideal, loss, and self-surrender, whether philosophical, political, or erotic. The narrator of Goethe's late and lengthy autobiography, *Truth and Poetry: From My Own Life* looks back on Romantic idealism as a disease he overcame by immersion in the European classical tradition and relentless self-critique.

As the "modern" world exerted its conforming pressures on the Romantic subject, travel to "exotic" locales offered another avenue of escape. In narratives of exotic travel and erotic encounters, the traveler reimagined himself through exoticist tropes that had their genealogical roots in earlier travel narratives of biracial love, such as John Stedman's sentimental *Narrative of a Five Years' Expedition Against the Revolted Negroes of Surinam*. But their most elaborate iterations emerged in the late nineteenth and early twentieth centuries. Through these tropes the traveler/narrator enacted his desire for the return of the repressed body, forced into routine conformity by the radical changes wrought by industrialization and urbanization (Bongie, 12). In chronicling his experience of "going native," he enacted his surrender to the Other, and to the other in himself.

The subject of lost illusions is, however, conspicuously white and masculine in both its privilege to wander and its freedom from labor. Dorothy Wordsworth's *Journals* sketch a different set of daily preoccupations, as do the spiritual narratives of such African American "sisters of the spirit" as Jarena Lee, Zilpha Elaw, and Julia Foote, or the letters and autobiographical fragments of such German writers as Rachel Varnhagen and Karoline von Günderrode. By mid-century George Sand (Aurore Dudevant Dupin) serializes a life narrative, *Story of My Life*, in a Parisian newspaper (1854–55) to raise money. Introducing the melodramatic structure of a popular novel into the telling of her life, and parodying the call to writing in Augustine's conversion in the *Confessions*, Sand's chatty text interpolates biographies of her parents, letters, sermons, stories of lovers and friends into the story of her early life and discovery of an inner voice. And throughout the last half of the century European and American women such as Harriet Martineau, Frances Trollope, Margaret Fuller, Nancy Prince, and Isabella Bird took to the roads and seas, bringing back home stories of adventures survived, accounts of knowledge gained, and/or tales of "civilizing" colonized subjects. Often these narratives represented acts of female agency in the midst of continuing bourgeois constraints that coded travel as a male activity.

The Bildungsroman and the Bourgeois Subject

Perhaps the most influential genre of the nineteenth century was the Bildungsroman or novel of development. Writ large in such narratives as Goethe's *Wilhelm Meister's Apprenticeship*, Dickens's *David Copperfield*, Mme. De Staël's *Corinne, or Italy*, and Charlotte Brontë's *Jane Eyre*, its structure of social formation unfolds through a narrative of apprenticeship, education in "life," renunciation, and civic integration into bourgeois society. The mode of the Bildungsroman, as the pseudo-autobiography of a fictional character distinct from the text's narrator, had some influence on forms of nineteenth-century life narrative and would be of growing significance in the twentieth. Its developmental model is evident, for example, in the autobiographies of John Stuart Mill, John Henry Newman, and Harriet Martineau, which, in different ways, use its paradigm of a self developed through education, self-directed "intellectual cultivation" through reading, and encounters with social institutions (Mill, 45).

The Bildungsroman narrates the formation of a young life as gendered, classed, and raced within a social network larger than the family or the religious community. But, as feminist scholars note, gendered norms differ for women, who historically have not chosen, but been chosen (or not); who are not initiated into social life, but retreat from participation; who awaken more to limitations than possibility (Fuderer, 4–5). For women life narrators, then, the Bildungsroman's model was inverted. This inverted structure of expectations disappointed by barriers of gender is implicit in such late-nineteenth-century works as the diaries of Alice James, for instance.

The structure of the Bildungsroman is also implicit in many nineteenth-century slave narratives. Ex-slaves found a powerful rhetorical means of intervening in the repressive institution of slavery by telling or writing their narratives of enslavement, self-education, and quest for entry into the free society of American citizens. They at once testified to the circumstances of their degradation and the achievement of status as full human beings. The slave narrative became one of the most popular forms in the United States and Europe. In the nineteenth century hundreds of slave narratives began to be published, often by abolitionist societies of the Northern United States. Unquestionably the most widely read of these now are *Narrative of the Life of Frederick Douglass* and *Incidents in the Life of a Slave Girl* by Harriet Jacobs.[7]

Douglass's *Narrative*, the first of three quite different and even contradictory accounts of his enslavement, fugitive days, and liberation, tells a story of conversion from an imposed mental enslavement to liberation as much through literacy and the creation of a community as through the struggle against and rejection of his slave status. Douglass writes as the subject of freedom, "a free man on free land," willing to indict the hypocrisy of Christian slavers. His narrative, important in the abolitionist cause before the Civil War, has been celebrated and taught in school curricula. Jacobs's narrative, by contrast, was long assumed to be the work of white abolitionist Lydia Maria Child, recording the story of pseudonymous Linda Brent. Only in the last two decades, with Jean Fagan Yellin's restoration and defense of Jacobs's text, has it gained recognition as a compelling narrative of the binds and brutality of the slave system for a young woman lacking a community of abolitionist sisters. But Jacobs's quest for liberation is at best ambivalently realized, and troubled by the impossibility of either avoiding sexual encounters or achieving real economic and personal freedom. Douglass's subject of development and liberation is not realizable for Jacobs.

American Subjects in the Nineteenth Century

Scholars in the last decade have begun to integrate nineteenth-century life narratives into the literary canon of the United States. For Lawrence Buell, rethinking American literary culture through the lens of autobiography studies involves paying serious attention to Douglass's *Narrative of the Life*, Emerson's *Journals*, Thoreau's *Walden*, and Whitman's *Specimen Days*. It means, as well, looking at generic inventions such as the carnivalesque of Franklinian entrepreneurship in *The Autobiography of P. T. Barnum: Clerk, Merchant, Editor, and Showman, with His Rules for Business and Making a Fortune*, Lydia Sigourney's *Letters of Life*, the "first full-dress autobiography written by an American author of either sex whose primary vocation was creative writing" (Buell, "Autobiography in the American Renaissance," 60), and at travel narratives such as John Neal's *Wandering Recollections of a Somewhat Busy Life: An Autobiography* (1869) and Francis Parkman's *The California and Oregon Trail: Being Sketches of Prairie and Rocky Mountain Life*. For Buell most of these autobiographers, particularly Whitman, are ambivalent about conventional, chronological narrative and adapt an "improvisational" and spontaneous style to resist its norm of linear plotting. While *Walden* pursues the symbolic "quest-into-nature-and-return story" of narratives of exploration and discovery, it also, Buell argues, portrays its "I" as untypical, its experience as mysterious, and its intricate autobiographical representation as inadequate to the complexity of the author (Buell, "Autobiography in the American Renaissance," 62, 64–65).

In the mid-nineteenth century American authors, then, employed multiple models of life narrative that introduce a tension between an "I"-centered model of the exceptional individual and a narrative model centered in events that either objectify or subordinate the "I" to communal discourses of identity, such as the narrative of conversion and the slave narrative (Buell, "Autobiography in the American Renaissance," 64–65). If American myths of self-realization emerge powerfully in the life narratives of this century, most are also conflicted and unresolved.

After the Civil War autobiographical writing in the United States becomes more "self"-conscious, Susanna Egan argues, posing life writing not as memoir, but as "history in the making," with the life narrator as a participant in that dialectical process ("'Self'-Conscious History"). In different ways Henry James, Henry Adams, Mark Twain, Booker T. Washington, and W. E. B. Du Bois locate themselves as subjects of American progress, if oftentimes with ambivalence.

The importance of affirming an American identity drives many life writings as, with westward expansion, people become increasingly mobile and migratory. Lucy Larcom nostalgically recalls her childhood in the mills of New England from the "west" of an Illinois college in *A New England Girlhood*. Jane Addams in *Twenty Years at Hull-House* charts the significance of professional work to both her life and the immigrant community of Chicago as a means of making Americans and American history of its many immigrants at the century's turn.

The life narratives of Native Americans tell stories of mobility and migration from perspectives of loss and expropriation, often intermingled with other discourses of American subjectivity. Crucial to reading these narratives is the distinction Arnold Krupat makes about the production of life writings in these cultures that had not emphasized either the "auto" of the isolate individual or the "graph" or alphabetic writing of lives prior to contact. One kind, Krupat argues, is Indian autobiographies, which are "not actually self-written, but ... of original, bicultural composite composition" and often composed by a white editor-amanuensis, a Native "subject" who orally presents a life, and a mixed-blood interpreter/translator in a process of unequal collaboration. The other kind is autobiographies by Indians, "individually composed texts ... written by those whose lives they chronicle" (Krupat, "Introduction," 3). For example, in 1831 William Apess, in what is considered the "first" Native American life narrative in his own words, *A Son of the Forest*, mixes a narrative of exile from both his birth and adoptive families and a travel/adventure story with an account of his conversion to evangelical Christianity, all the while negotiating his indigenous identity in a Euro-American discourse that lacks a language for it. Zitkala-Ša in *Impressions of an Indian Childhood*, however, contrasts her experience of growing up in an indigenous culture on the Sioux reservation and at a missionary school to show the brutal repressions of the latter conducted in the name of its civilizing and Christianizing missions. Her "sketches" at the turn of the twentieth century reflect on how an education intended to form her as a docile citizen in fact motivated her to reclaim the Indian culture being erased by assimilation and to narrate a personal history as a collective story of loss and a quest for dignity.

In the last half of the nineteenth century, too, in both the United States and England, the industrial revolution and the rise of the union movement led to the emergence of narratives by working-class people, as well as increased literacy among working classes and women. In the United States, narratives of immigrants begin to appear at the end of the century. Jacob Riis, in *The Making of an American*, writes and photographs his growing up as a Danish immigrant in the streets of New York from the perspective of an assimilated American, as does Dutch immigrant Edward William Bok in his Franklinesque *The Americanization of Edward Bok* and Mary Antin in *The Promised Land*. Making oneself an American, as both a personal and an exemplary figure, involved learning the value of the individual in a land of opportunity and promise, a lesson that was largely successful for most European immigrants (Egan, "'Self'-Conscious History," 82), but much more ambiguous for indigenous peoples, immigrants from Asia and Africa, and Latinos and Latinas at the borders.

Recent scholarship has begun to focus increasingly on these other stories of Americanization among populations dominated and spoken for by the myth of the American melting pot. As Anne E. Goldman suggests, many early-twentieth-century Chicana women encoded the communal values of their heritage in everyday forms such as folkloric tales, cookbooks, and family narratives that can be read autobiographically as resistant to dominant cultural myths. Sau-Ling Cynthia Wong argues that immigration narratives among Chinese- and Japanese Americans are by no means assimilationist, given the histories of racism both groups experienced in the United States, and points out that generational factors also reshape the story of Americanization ("Immigrant Autobiography").

For more politically radical autobiographers, such as Emma Goldman in *Living My Life* and Alexander Berkman in *Prison Memoirs of an Anarchist*, America is a corrupt land of greed and unequal privilege to be resuscitated by the international socialism propounded in the essays and manifestos of Rosa Luxemburg, Vladimir Lenin, and Leon Trotsky. Although in the United States, Mother Jones in her *Autobiography*, Charlotte Perkins Gilman in *The Living of Charlotte Perkins Gilman: An Autobiography*, Elizabeth Gurley Flynn in *I Speak My Own Piece: Autobiography of "The Rebel Girl,"* and Dorothy Day in *The Long Loneliness: The Autobiography of Dorothy Day* link their autobiographical writing to social critique and a call for greater equity between the sexes and among classes, this representation of the autobiographical subject as interventionary social radical is, among Euro-American writers, male and female alike, less influential than is the presentation of immigrant Americans assimilated in the project of retrospectively writing their histories as new American subjects.

New Subject Formations

In the twentieth century life narrative became a dominant form in the West, and thus impossible to review here in any systematic way. The forms of life writing have multiplied, and the field of autobiography studies has begun to fracture as scholars address issues specific to particular modes of self-narrating. To give the reader some sense of the diversity of these modes, we provide in our appendix A, "Genres of Life Narrative," brief descriptions of fifty-two modes of life writing, modes both historical and contemporary.

Here we can only telescope, through bullets, a sampling of the kinds of narratives through which people have produced autobiographical meaning as they have negotiated their cultural locations.

- Immigrant narratives and narratives of exile become sites through which formerly marginal or displaced subjects explore the terms of their cultural identities and their diasporic allegiances.
- Narratives of ethnic identity and community become a call, sometimes to revolution, other times to reforming ethnic subjects through autobiographical acts.
- Ethnographies and as-told-to narratives, the foundational texts of anthropology and folklore studies, considered "authentic" throughout the first half of the century, have given way to auto-ethnographic texts in which formerly colonized subjects narrate their own stories, both individual and collective, of coming to consciousness of their histories of oppression.
- Testimonios inscribe a collective "I" that voices stories of repression and calls for resistance in ways that have influenced political struggle around the globe.[8]
- Prison narratives, a contemporary form of captivity narrative, record the struggles of incarcerated subjects with dehumanizing systems and the forging of identity in resistance.
- Narratives of childhood, in the wake of the popularization of the Bildungsroman, mine the psychic landscapes of a lost past (see Coe and Rooke studies) and the repressed past of traumatic childhood abuse.
- The Bildungsroman continues to be a decisive model for the presentation of twentieth-century lives, for postcolonial writers who cast their narratives in terms of encounters with powerful mentors at cultural crossroads of metropole and colony and of conflicting concepts of education and social value.

- Postmodern narratives undermine the foundations upon which identity is posited by shifting the ground of reference and explode the relationship of individual memory to any certain chronology of experience.
- Autopathographies, such as narratives of illness and disability, offer stories of loss and recovery at the same time that they function as a call for increased funding for research, new modes of treatment, and more visibility for those who have been assigned the cultural status of the unwhole, the grotesque, the uncanny.
- AIDS narratives entwine memoirs of caring and loving with arguments for the destigmatization of the disease, thereby intervening in national and international debates about how to signify and respond to the pandemic.
- Coming-out narratives make visible formerly invisible subjects, as gay, bisexual, lesbian, and transgendered subjects inscribe stories of the costs of passing as heteronormative subjects and the liberatory possibilities of legitimation.
- Narratives of sport figures, movie stars, military heroes, and other public figures, a growth industry in self-advertisement, reproduce the culture of celebrity and project possible role models for young people.
- Narratives of the life cycle and of aging, particularly in women's life narratives, foreground the social construction of some elements of age and the shift in family position from child to elder, as well as the relationship to aging and dying.[9]
- And in cyberspace, self-producing websites introduce digitized subjects to anonymous others in the virtual world where time and space are reconfigured.

As this chapter's brief survey indicates, the history of autobiography in the West cannot be read solely as a literary history. Life narrative and its multiple genres have been foundational to the formation of Western subjects, Western cultures, and Western concepts of nation, as well as to the ongoing project of exploration, colonization, imperialism, and, now, globalization.

As this survey also indicates, autobiographical acts have always taken place at conflicted cultural sites where discourses intersect, contradict, and displace one another, where narrators are pulled and tugged into complex and contradictory self-positionings through a performative dialogism. The terms of the narrator-reader relationship are continually being renegotiated as writers and practitioners develop new rhetorics of identity and strategies of self-representation for being heard in new ways, as different subjects and subjects in difference. Contemporary investigations into the subject-in-process of, say, Michel Leiris, Gloria Anzaldúa, Art Spiegelman, or Bessie Head, read those texts as characterized by discontinuities, openness, mobility, transcultural hybridity. These innovative life narratives can now serve as productive sites for rethinking and retheorizing the practices, politics, and possibilities of "authoring" one's life.

In the Americas, at least, the autobiographical gesture has become endemic. Increasingly we incorporate autobiographical genres, modes of address, and consciousness into our everyday lives. This contemporary fascination with life narratives derives in part from the power of an ideology of individualism and its cultural hold on us—and Americans in particular are attracted to Horatio Alger-esque fantasies of the self-made individual. We are also witnessing, in an outpouring of memoirs, the desire of autobiographical subjects to splinter monolithic categories that have culturally identified them, such as "woman" or "gay" or "black" or "disabled," and to reassemble various pieces of memory, experience, identity, embodiment, and agency into new, often hybrid, modes of subjectivity. In this pursuit, life narrative has proved remarkably flexible in adapting to new voices and assuming new shapes across media, ideologies, and the differences of subjects.

As Jeff Bridges's character, Max Kline, says in the film *Fearless:* "Hell, this is America in the nineties. Nobody apologizes anymore. They write a memoir."

CHAPTER 5

A History of Autobiography Criticism
Part 1: Defining the Genre

As autobiography has been the dominant mode in literature of the
twentieth century, so critical attention to the questions posed by
the autobiographical act has become the principal preoccupation
of theorists across the entire critical spectrum.

James Olney, "Autobiography and the Cultural Moment"

No autobiography can take place except within the boundaries of a
writing where concepts of subject, self, and author collapse into
the act of producing a text.

Michael Sprinker, "Fictions of the Self: The End of Autobiography"

In the last chapter we offered a historical overview of self-narrating in
the West. In this chapter and the next we consider how critics have
responded to life narratives in the past half-century. What questions
motivate their readings? And what are the implications of the readings
they promote? In effect, these chapters offer a brief overview of theorizing about autobiographical narratives.

Books and articles about autobiographical narrative have appeared
at an increasing rate in the last half-century, and particularly the last two
decades. The year 1980 saw the publication of two bibliographical essays
that interpreted the history and shifting preoccupations of criticism up
to that time: the essay appended to William C. Spengemann's *Forms of
Autobiography: Episodes in the History of a Literary Genre*, and "Autobiography and the Critical Moment," the introductory essay to *Autobiography:
Essays Theoretical and Critical*, edited by James Olney. Spengemann situated the first surge of critical interest in the practice of life narrative in

the late nineteenth and early twentieth centuries, citing three contributing phenomena: the increasing number of life narratives reaching an interested public; the increasing number of critical essays focused on such narrative; and the influence of German historian Wilhelm Dilthey, who defined the genre of "autobiography" as "the highest and most instructive form in which the understanding of life comes before us" (85–86) and called for its use in the writing of history.

But earlier cultural influences forming notions of personhood, unacknowledged by Spengemann, also contributed to a surge of interest among critics and readers. These include:

- the eighteenth-century privileging of an Enlightenment or liberal-humanist subject understood as universal man and transcendent mind;
- the revolutionary movements of the late eighteenth century, with their pressures for greater democratization of society and the enfranchisement of women and some classes;
- the radical individualism celebrated by Romantic movements throughout Europe and the Americas in the early nineteenth century;
- Victorian Darwinism, most particularly social Darwinism, with its emphasis on the survival of the fittest and the primacy of evolutionary progress;
- the Industrial Revolution and its informing myth of the self-made man;
- the writing of history through the paradigm of the "great man";
- Freud's theory of the unconscious and the analytical methods used in psychoanalysis to organize self-reflection;
- the rise of literacy and the great outburst of literary activity that accompanied increasing democratization.

In sum, social and philosophical transformations from the seventeenth through the early twentieth centuries contributed in new ways to the formation of the Western subject as an accomplished and exceptional individual; the consolidation of that subject was a key means of legitimating the spread of imperialism around the globe. As we have suggested elsewhere (introduction to *De/Colonizing*), an important historical use—although by no means the only use—of "autobiography" has been as a master narrative of Western rationality, progress, and superiority. And the readings of generations of critics of life narrative shaped and authorized this understanding.

The First Modern Generation:
Misch and the Representative Autobiographer

Dilthey's student and son-in-law, German philologist Georg Misch, inaugurated the first wave of modern criticism of the field. Misch argued in his vast, multivolume *History of Autobiography in Antiquity* that the progressive unfolding of Western history can be read in the representative lives of the leaders who participated in this achievement of civilization; and he discovered particular types of Western man in the self-representational strategies of each generation of autobiographers.

As Misch's theory has had a profound impact on subsequent studies of the genre, his concept of life narrative is worth noting. Misch defines it as autobiography, "the description (*graphia*) of an individual human life (*bios*) by the individual himself (*autos*)" (5). Two introductory passages from Misch's *History of Autobiography in Antiquity*, taken together, suggest his critical orientation:

> Among the special relationships in life it is chiefly the self assertion of the political will and the relation of the author to his work and to the public that show themselves to be normative in the history of autobiography. (14)

> Though essentially representations of individual personalities, autobiographies are bound always to be representative of their period, within a range that will vary with the intensity of the authors' participation in contemporary life and with the sphere in which they moved. (12)

For Misch, the normative generic characteristics of autobiography and the criteria for the success of any particular life narrator rest in the writer's relationship to the arena of public life and discourse. People who have lived their lives in the public sphere, people who have been actors in important historical events or moments, people who have achieved fame or notoriety in public, are the "representative" and appropriate subjects of what he designates as autobiography. Misch's emphasis on the autobiographer's role as a public presence is part of his scheme of a division between the "high culture" of achieved and elite civilizations and the "low culture" of popular and everyday forms. High cultural forms, such as classical music, painting and sculpture, the literary epic, and, for Misch, the autobiography of the great man, summarize the achievement of culture, entwined with the making of the nation-state, which reached its apogee in Western Europe in the nineteenth century.

Misch's criteria, drawn from the German tradition of *Geistesgeschichte* (the spirit of the historical moment), are both restrictive and prescriptive in arguing for what is "great." Consequently, while they have been influential in shaping a canon of the great books of autobiography, they have exacted a cost: the exclusion of other kinds of life narrative practiced for much of human history—letters, diaries, journals, memoirs, and other autobiographical modes of everyday and private life. Misch's criteria informed the kinds of critical reading practiced for much of the twentieth century.

To take a case in point, consider Misch's theorizing of who and what is the proper autobiographical subject. Factoring in issues of gender, race, class, and political status, how might a concept of autobiography such as Misch's inflect our reading of the life narratives of a woman, a slave, or a "postcolonial" writer? Before the late twentieth century, patriarchal notions of white women's inherently irrational nature and their primary social role of reproduction severely restricted their access to public space and education. Male distrust and repression of female speech condemned most women to public silence, which in turn qualified their relationship to writing as a means of exploring and asserting an identity publicly. Women who presumed to claim fully human identity by seeking places in the public arena were seen as transgressing patriarchal definitions of their nature, or "acting like men." To challenge cultural conceptions of the nature of woman was to invite public censure. If women bowed to pressures to remain anonymous, however, they denied a human desire to articulate a voice and claim an identity.

For slaves and, in different ways, for colonized peoples, the assertion of human status and the exercise of the rights of social subjects were even more severely and brutally repressed. Slaves were legally understood as "chattel" to be bought and sold; indigenous colonized peoples were treated as children suitable only for labor and entertainment. While the formerly enslaved or colonized were denied any human identification, they also struggled with the tensions and double binds of representation. As W. E. B. Du Bois noted early in this century, a "double consciousness" was imposed on African Americans by their historical situation. For women of color, that double consciousness was redoubled. Of course, many other groups were also seen as marginal to the public sphere of great men: the lower classes, religious minorities, persons disabled, and the sexually "deviant." The bind of becoming nominally enfranchised while remaining culturally invisible "others" has been a central tension of the past century for groups with no access to textual histories of their subjectivity.

If we turn to Misch's other prescriptive definition, the "representative" nature of autobiography, additional problems become evident. His definition of the "supreme example" of human accomplishment is "the contemporary intellectual outlook revealed in the style of an eminent person who has himself played a part in the forming of the spirit of his time" (12–13). Consider the trouble the term *representative* makes for women or the formerly enslaved or colonized. In what ways could they compose a "representative" narrative of a period? Prior to the twentieth century, few women, former slaves, or colonized people achieved the status of "eminent person," and those who did were usually labeled "exceptional" rather than "representative." Perhaps the life narratives of such people, had they been written, would more accurately have been "unrepresentative" of their times.

Framing the question to foreground gender, we could ask: How might women narrating their lives have negotiated the tension between idealized codes of femininity and idealized codes of masculinity? Since women who wrote necessarily identified with codes of both sorts, how did they write themselves into cultural narratives and how were they read by readers "representing" the patriarchal order? Framing the question to foreground race and ethnicity, that is, to consider the formerly enslaved, colonized, or subordinated, we could ask: How could subalterns have negotiated the tension between idealized codes of humanity as white and Western and the less than fully human status assigned them?

Just as historians have dismantled the notion of *Geistesgeschichte*, "the spirit of [the] time," recent literary critics have dismantled this notion of the "representative life" that haunted earlier critical definitions of autobiography, asking such questions as the following: What is at stake when a life is described as "representative"? Whose lives can be considered representative of a culture or a historical moment? Who determines which lives are representative? Where life narratives of the past are concerned, should Misch's notion be definitive? As cultural critics have argued for well over a decade, such labeling of what is—or is not—representative is part of the cultural project of "naming, controlling, remembering, understanding" (Jardine, 118–19) that sustains the patriarchal, and imperial, power to produce "knowledge" about the world. If only those people authorized as agents of existing institutions determine the economic value of lives, what are the consequences for our sense of which people can "get a life" and become cultural subjects?

We want to be clear here. We are not arguing that only "great" public men could and did write autobiographies in the past, or that others were always excluded from cultural production. Though their access was certainly constrained, many people, from diverse cultural locations, produced, wrote, and told their stories to confessors, amanuenses, and editors before the twentieth century. Our point is that the texts produced, some quite popular and influential in their own times, did not acquire the status of "representative autobiographies"; these life narratives were not seen as formative of "civilization" and thus not celebrated as the appropriate subject of study.

In effect, then, Misch's notion of autobiography as the record of a representative life of the great man has long served as a norm, a "master narrative" about the meaning and role of a particular model of life narrative in western civilization.

Let's return these considerations to our history of autobiography criticism. Misch's study, produced over forty years and translated in part into English only in 1951, did not play a major role in the criticism of life narrative until mid-century. But its assumptions appear, less fully formulated, elsewhere in early scholarship, as in Anna Robeson Burr's 1909 *The Autobiography: A Critical and Comparative Study*, because the notion of a representative life dominated concepts of textual personhood. Once interest in autobiography, which the New Critics had eschewed as an inferior literary mode, began to reawaken in a few corners of the academy in the late 1950s, Misch's work began to be invoked in scholarly definitions of "autobiography." Historians and literary critics seeking to write the long history of life narrative turned for guidance to Misch's erudite and exhaustive—but, we have suggested, inescapably selective and normative—study.

In Anglo-American literary scholarship generally, the New Critics crafted a concept of the literary text as aesthetic object and work of value, most fully achieved when irresolvably ambiguous. William K. Wimsatt Jr. and Cleanth Brooks trace a critical tradition since Plato in which the genre of autobiography and the practice of life narrative go unmentioned. Remarkably, the highly influential 1966 study, *The Nature of Narrative* by Robert Scholes and Robert Kellogg, also situates narrative only in the history of the novel, the epic, and the film, and nowhere alludes to life narrative. This striking omission is perhaps best understood as an enactment of Wimsatt's condemnation of "the intentional fallacy" as anathema to the work of verbal art, a romantic and positivist construing of verbal indeterminacy that privileges the author's psychology and reduces poetry to literary biography, "whether written by the author or a critic" ("Intentional Fallacy," 10). Wimsatt's concept of the autobiographical is implicit in his argument that self-referential narrative would be "external, ... private or idiosyncratic; not a part of the work as a linguistic fact; it consists of revelations (in journal, for example, or letters or reported conversations) about how or why the poet wrote the poem" (10). In effect, Wimsatt reads the self-referential reductively as "evidence of what the author intended" in his literary works; at best, he implies, the autobiographical is a form of marginalia about great works, not a kind of artful text in itself (11). For the dominant Anglo-American critical tradition, then, autobiographical writing was a suspect mode of "trivia" or "personal" writing, the site of writers' flawed notions about their artistic works, and therefore was to be bracketed out of the canon of poetic and narrative texts and critical theory that the implementation of New Criticism enabled in the academy.

Thus the master narrative set in motion by Misch's landmark study has influenced subsequent studies of the genre—with significant effects in terms of the texts discussed and critical assessments of their cultural importance. Critics whose readings of texts are informed by Misch's criteria, for instance, might engage a life narrative by a woman, such as the *Life* of St. Teresa of Avila but would read her text as the record of an exceptional life. The life narratives of vocationless women might be locally interesting, even delightful to read, as is Anne Lady Halkett's seventeenth-century narrative appended to her biography of her husband. But such texts will be considered culturally insignificant because the *bios* (or life) is not of public historical significance and the mode of self-representation not of aesthetic significance in literary history, according to Misch's criteria. Given these standards of theme, structure, and public prominence, critics could not help but misread and, for example, label women's narratives inferior or trivial. Moreover, the dominance of Misch's criteria precluded inquiry into how women's narratives intersected with or informed the "master narrative" of autobiography, which assumed that the appropriate subject was white and male.

Similarly, critics reading through these assumptions rarely turned to forms of self-representation outside the West in the great biographical traditions of China, Japan, India, and Persia; and they omitted the North African ancestry of an immigrant such as Augustine. Nor did they recognize the significance of oral, nonalphabetic traditions of collective self-inscription in indigenous cultures throughout the world. If, by definition, Western Europe signified "civilization," then life narrative from elsewhere and nonwritten self-representation would be understood as properly the focus of disciplines outside literary studies, that is, of anthropology and folklore.

In sum, Dilthey and Misch were significant in inaugurating this century's critical fascination with "autobiography." They offered a working definition of the genre and its controlling trope—the life of the "great man." They situated that man and his actions in specific historical and cultural contexts and assessed how he and his deeds were "representative" of the times. Scholars following Dilthey and Misch assumed the notion of the great man as normative subject and the representative life as its narrative trajectory. But, as we've noted, while these normative standards and judgments elevated some life narratives to a literary mode, and no longer a form of biographical marginalia, they constricted the field of study, excluding the heterogeneous narratives and texts of many kinds of people. While such writings might be mined by historians as documentary evidence about the past, they were thought to lack the coherence and cultural status that made a "life" worth reading.

The Canon of Autobiographical Texts

To this point, we have discussed the history of autobiography criticism in terms of texts and perspectives excluded from consideration. But of course scholars contributing to the norms of autobiography criticism as a field of study did focus their interpretations and build their theories around several key life narratives of "great men." Their readings of this core of texts constituted and promoted what could be understood as a canon of autobiography. In chapter 4 we set forth in some detail a historical overview of both canonical and noncanonical autobiographical texts. Now it is important to comment on how the canon of life narrative was generated by, and to an extent, informed by, the criticism of autobiography.

A "canon" is a culturally valued set of texts that are agreed to represent the "best" that the culture has produced—the "best" novels or plays or poems, for instance. Or the "best" life narratives, deemed auto-biography. As Griselda Pollock argues, in considering the notion of the canon in art history,

> Canons may be understood … as the retrospectively legitimating back-bone of a culture and political identity, a consolidated narrative of origin, conferring authority on the texts selected to naturalise this function. Canonicity refers to both the assumed quality of an included text and to the status a text acquires because it belongs within an authoritative collec-tion. Religions confer sanctity upon their canonised texts, often implying, if not divine authorship, at least divine authority. (3)

Canons are determined by widely recognized sources of cultural author-ity, a person or group of persons charged with establishing criteria of inclusion and exclusion and with making determinations about what fits, and by implication what doesn't fit, the criteria. Their decisions affect which texts get read (or viewed), which texts get taught, indeed which texts are read, or even published, in the first place.

Canonical texts are held to be the "most important" or "most authoritative" ones available to the culture. But what criteria determine inclusion in the canon? Clearly, the criteria used vary with culture, the national language, and the historical period. Particular titles included in a canon will change over time. But the idea of a core of "the best" remains. Critically, items included in the core of "the best," as Pollock notes, are assigned "transhistorical aesthetic value." They are read as "timeless." And that "timelessness," paradoxically, assures their value at a particular moment in time. For this reason, what is included in the canon "must be studied as a model by those aspiring to the practice" (Pollock, 3). The canon both establishes and reproduces codes of value; it enforces an obligatory curriculum.

In the case of autobiography in the West, a set of texts achieved canonical status by the 1960s and influenced what scholars wrote, profes-sors taught, and students read. The establishment of this canon served to legitimate the field of autobiography studies by affirming that the field could boast a set of weighty, substantive texts that students should study. Obviously, articulating a canon of sacrosanct texts also served to organize and "police" the subject of inquiry by limiting the kinds of questions that were addressed in reading canonical texts.

Some of the life narratives that emerged as "landmarks" in the critical study of self-exploration, confession, and self-discovery will be familiar, for example, St. Augustine's *Confessions*, Cellini's *Life*, Rousseau's *Confessions*, Fox's "Journal," Franklin's *Autobiography*, Goethe's *Truth and Poetry*, Mill's *Autobiography*, Cardinal Newman's *Apologia Pro Vita Sua*, and Thoreau's *Walden*. To mid-century, shifts in this canon meant moving beyond a Eurocentric focus and acknowledging significant life narrative in the Americas, especially by Franklin, Thoreau, Whitman, and Adams. These core texts, seen as the highest achievements of life narrative, were the focus of interpretation in articles and book-length studies of autobiography; the accumulation of interpretations contributed to their maintaining canonical status.

It is illuminating to consider the assumptions that scholars brought to their readings of these texts. They assumed the autobiographer to be an autonomous and enlightened "individual" who understood his relationship to others and the world as one of separateness in which he exercised the agency of free will. They focused on a teleological pattern of development in narratives usually written late in life as retrospections on public and/or writing careers. They assumed a concluding point at which some kind of self-understanding through reflection upon past achievement takes place. And, after Dilthey and Misch, they assumed the representative status of the narrator; that is, they assumed that even though the narrator speaks of his individual life, the patterns of behavior, achievements, intellectual preoccupations, and relationships with others he rehearses are the norm or—in the case of rebels such as Augustine, Rousseau, or Thoreau—become an inspired choice of the culture. That all of these texts can be (and are being) read very differently now suggests that these categories of freedom, individuality, coherent life design, and comprehensible, connected events of past life were norms at a particular historical moment that informed acts of critical reading.

The canon of texts became a common reference point for scholarly discussion and debate as autobiography studies emerged as a field in the 1960s. As a reference point, the canon encoded a "tradition" of representative lives identified with texts privileged by scholars in the academic establishment. These were "traditional autobiographies," often different from the life narratives of celebrities, military leaders, religious figures, and politicians that ordinary people sought out with pleasure during the century. Later we will consider how new "countercanons" have formed during the last twenty years, as many forgotten life narratives were republished, as modes of autobiographical narrating proliferated, and as theoretical approaches to many hybrid genres collected under the umbrella term "life writing" have been formulated. With this countering of the canon (and the loosening of the hold of a concept of "representative lives"), scholars have brought a diversity of reading strategies to canonical autobiographies, offering innovative readings of, say, the "gay" Goethe or the "maternal" Augustine.

Second-Wave Approaches: Gusdorf, Hart, and Creative Self-Representation

James Olney ascribes the second surge of autobiography criticism to 1956 and the publication (in French) of Belgian critic Georges Gusdorf's article "Conditions and Limits of Autobiography." William Spengemann traces a new critical moment back to 1970 and the publication of Francis R. Hart's essay, "Notes for an Anatomy of Modern Autobiography," arguing that much of the work done before 1970, including Gusdorf's seminal article, remained unknown in the English-speaking world. For both Olney and Spengemann, the significance of the critic named is in his application of a systematic literary analysis to canonical autobiography that parallels in intent and seriousness that addressed to the novel, poetry, and drama.

The shift identified as occurring at different moments by Olney and Spengemann has a common denominator: namely, the critic's focus on self-narrating as the distinctive hallmark of autobiography. To better understand this shift, we will contrast how first- and second-wave critics frame the questions of the truth of autobiographical narratives and their mode of self-representation.

First-wave critics were preoccupied with the "bios" of the autobiographer because they understood autobiography as a subcategory of the biography of great lives and excluded other modes of life narrative. Truthfulness in autobiography meant consistency with the biographical facts of the life. The historical record could easily confirm or refute textual inconsistencies, since the assumption, as James Olney astutely notes, was that "there was nothing problematical about the *autos*, no agonizing questions of identity, self-definition, self-existence, or self-deception—at least none the reader need attend to—and therefore the fact that the individual was himself narrating the story of himself had no troubling philosophical, psychological, literary, or historical implications" ("Autobiography and the Cultural Moment," 20). In other words, formerly the narrator was thought to speak self-evident truths of his life, and the autobiography critic acted as a kind of moralist, evaluating the quality of the life lived and the narrator's ability to tell that truth.

But new understandings of the autobiographical subject involved new understandings of these key concepts of self and truth. While the Enlightenment or liberal-humanist notion of selfhood understood the "I" as the universal, transcendent marker of "man," radical challenges to the notion of a unified selfhood in the early decades of the twentieth century eroded certainty in both a coherent "self" and the "truth" of self-narrating.

- The Marxist analysis of class-consciousness, linking individual consciousness determinatively to larger economic forces, defined the individual as subjected to economic structures and relationships, rather than as autonomous agent. In this framing, humans lose agency; they are defined as perversely manipulated subjects who, in Louis Althusser's terms, will exhibit false consciousness and be "interpellated" by ideologies (see chapter 2).

- Freudian psychoanalysis destabilized the notion that the human being is a rational actor by reconfiguring "self" as a struggle of forces occurring outside conscious control. A subversive unconscious continuously threatens the individual's precarious illusion of conscious control over identity and experience.

- Freud also redefined the function of language in knowing oneself. Never neutral, language is always "interested." It speaks through the subject and is mysterious to its speaker because it encodes his desire. Indeed, in Lacan's reinterpretation of Freud, the unconscious is a language through which the subject spoken is always other to his own desire.

- Linguists such as Saussure and the Russian Formalists further problematized language by questioning the transparency of what was formerly conceptualized as a medium of self-expression. According to Saussure, language cannot and does not imitate reality or merely designate things through words. Language is a system of meaning produced through the relationship of signifier ("parole" or "word") and signified ("langue" or "referent"). As a system, language operates outside the individual subject; and so, entering into language, the individual becomes more "spoken by" language than an agentic speaker of it. The individual is more a product of discursive regimes (culturally dominant knowledges) than the self-creator and explorer of any essence of self outside culturally coded systems of meaning. And the individual cannot know herself through language.

What had been assumed by earlier generations of critics to be a universal "self"—achieving self-discovery, self-creation, and self-knowledge—became, in the wake of multiple theoretical challenges of the first half of the century, a "subject" riven by self-estrangement and self-fragmentation. Moreover, the relationship of language to what it claims to represent becomes problematic. Any simplistic notion that writers could "intend" what they say is undermined. As a result, the project of self-representation could no longer be read as direct access to the truth of the self. The truth of autobiographical acts had to be understood differently as an always inaccessible knowledge.

As a consequence of this new understanding of subjectivity as constructed by language, the second wave of autobiography critics began to attend to what Olney labeled the "agonizing questions" of self-representation. For these critics, truthfulness becomes a more complex and problematic phenomenon. Life narrative is seen as a process through which a narrator struggles to shape an "identity" out of an amorphous experience of subjectivity. And the critic becomes a psychoanalyst of sorts, interpreting an encoded truth in the welter of details of the narrative as a psychological design rather than a factual or moral profile.

Why did Olney and Spengemann accord the Gusdorf and Hart essays the status of groundbreaking reconceptualization of the "literariness" of some life narratives? Let us turn to these essays in more detail.

In "Conditions and Limits," Gusdorf argues that autobiography is a uniquely Western genre of life narrative, and more particularly a Christian form of self-writing, one that requires a historical rather than a cyclic notion of time and a concept of the individual as separate from the collectivity and as the highest achievement of civilization. Autobiography is, he says, an act of "reconstructing the unity of a life across time" (37). As such it functions for the writer as "a second reading of experience, and it is truer than the first because it adds to experience itself consciousness of it" (38). Thus, Gusdorf emphasizes the creative aspect of autobiographical writing. It is for him "art" rather than "history." As art the autobiographical act always fixes that which is in process, making it a cultural artifact. By definition, then, autobiography must fail to create the life of the writer, but it enshrines consciousness, the ability to reflect upon oneself through the autobiographical process.

Olney himself extends this exploration of the "creative" nature of autobiographical acts by developing a theory that all writing, but most pointedly, life narrative creates "metaphors of self." For Olney, the autobiographical is a unique mode of writing because it has the potential to postulate self-reflection as a process rather than an essence, through the "doubling" of self-observation. But only certain writers, for instance,

Montaigne and T. S. Eliot, realize this potential of autobiographical writing to create a structure of self-reflection in which the narrated "I" and the narrating "I" are interlocked.

Hart, by contrast, "maps" the anatomy of life narrative by taking up issues of form and intentionality. Conceding that "'unreliability' is an inescapable condition" (488–89), that is, that narrators cannot tell the truth disinterestedly, Hart redefines life narrative as a drama of intentions that "interact and shift" (491). Thinking about the comprehensive, or restricted, or created "I" that is selected for narrating, Hart establishes three categories of autobiographical intention: the confession, the apology, and the memoir; each has its own principles of memory selection and narrative perspective. But these intentions and forms are not categorically distinguished as genres; rather, they are modalities of relationship to the addressee and reader. Hart acknowledges "the continuous refocusing of expectation and intention as each autobiographer discovers his own fluctuating mixture of confession, apology, and memoir" (508). Subsequent critics of life narrative, such as Spengemann in *Forms of Autobiography*, followed Hart's example by examining in more detail formal conventions and intentions.

These explorations of generic conventions fostered more nuanced readings of autobiographical texts by situating them within the parameters of literary production rather than the realm of history writing. But even as the Gusdorf and Hart essays directed readers to the creative complexities of life narratives, they continued to encode certain cultural models of selfhood. Gusdorf explicitly defines "autobiography" as "Western," only possible in a culture with a historical notion of time and a concept of the isolate individual. While a notion of individual, progressive time—as opposed to cyclical temporality—may underwrite certain narratives in the West, overemphasis on progressive time ignores the subjective time of memory and constrains recognition of autobiographical acts to a narrowly defined scope and limited possibilities.

Similarly, while Hart's anatomy seems applicable to all life narrative, definitions of the autobiographical situation become problematic for the self-representational practices of many people, among them men and women in diverse situations and narrators from cultures outside the West. For Hart, the "truth" of the narrative emerges from "the relation between the autobiographer and his personal, historical subject." The reader must attend to the selected "I," which "is made and remade according to such criteria as naturalness, originality, essentiality, continuousness, integrity, and significance" (492). Hart appropriately exposes the constructed nature of the autobiographical project that remakes the "I." Yet for him, the specific criteria for shaping the "I" privilege individuality and separateness over relationality.

The staying power of Misch's and Dilthey's identification of autobiography with individuality and greatness, even in this second wave of critics, can thus be traced in these pivotal essays by Gusdorf and Hart, and in historian Karl Joachim Weintraub's *The Value of the Individual: Self and Circumstance in Autobiography*, another key work in this transitional phase of autobiography studies. In this exploration of Western individuality, Weintraub traces the comparative value given to "individuality" and to the "pursuit of the typical and the model" by various self-narrators. Weintraub comments in his introduction:

> This heuristic device posits, on the one hand, the adherence of men to great personality ideals in which their culture tends to embody its values and objectives—and on the other hand, a commitment to a self for which there is no model.... There existed, and continue to exist, many ... model conceptions of the personality in our tradition: the ideal of the Homeric Hero, the Germanic hero, the truly "polis-minded" man, the Roman paterfamilias, of Aristotle's "great-minded man," of the unshakable Stoic, the ideal monk, the ideal knight, the ideal gentleman, the ideal teacher, and so on. (xv)

Again we see how his critical discourse defines male and Western norms as human and universal norms and enshrines the sovereign self. And we see how such a typology does not mark alternative racial origins or gendered identities. In this second-wave critic, expressions of personhood have been reduced to a narrow range of the "ideal."

To sum up, the second wave of autobiography critics opened up the discussion of autobiographical narrating by insisting on its status as an act of creation rather than mere transcription of the past. Reconceiving self-referential narratives not as sites of the truth of a life but as creative self-engagements allowed them to elevate autobiography to the status of a literary genre. This critical move enabled critics to turn their attention to the history, forms, themes, and tropes of self-narrating, but it also required that they bracket out other kinds of life narratives, assigning them subliterary status. Wayne Shumaker, Margaret Bottrall, Paul Delany, Daniel B. Shea (*Spiritual Autobiography*), and other scholars of autobiography, for example, charted their versions of the genre's historical development. Roy Pascal and Jean Starobinski, like Hart, formulated concepts of generic conventions and poetics. William Spengemann and William L. Howarth defined its paradigmatic patterns. And others, from a variety of critical perspectives, attempted to categorize life narrative's manifold expressions in a more expansive hierarchy of types, including memoir, confession, diary, journal, amd chronicle.

But, as we have noted in the discussion of Gusdorf, Hart, and Weintraub, an ideology of the autonomous selfhood of autobiography underlies much of the theorizing in this second wave and informs the texts privileged and the practices of self-creation valued. The focus on self-referential narratives as narratives of autonomous individuality and representative lives narrowed the range of vision to the West. Little was written on life-narrative traditions globally. That focus also privileged "high" cultural forms, a focus that obscured the vast production of life narratives by ex-slaves, apprentices and tradespeople, adventurers, criminals and tricksters, saints and mystics, immigrants, and the representation of lives in such documents as wills and treaties. The gendering of the representative life as universal and therefore masculine meant that narratives by women were rarely examined; and on those rare occasions when their narratives were taken up, they were accorded a place in an afterword, a paragraph, a note—in marginal comments for what were seen as marginal lives. Or their achievements were defined through normatively feminine terms.

But if we recall the diverse modes of life narrating by marginalized, minoritized, diasporic, nomadic, and postcolonial subjects throughout the history of life writing, the concept of individuality is insufficient as a determining force. And it may not be the only motivation of canonical writers, many of whose autobiographies deserve fuller rereadings through the theoretical lenses we discuss below.

Avant-Garde, Postcolonial, and Postmodern Interventions

Olney's 1972 *Metaphors of Self: The Meaning of Autobiography* is a transitional work, at once a culmination of the second wave's opening of the field to complex issues of self-knowing and self-writing and an invitation to a more theoretically nuanced reading of the autobiographical ("Autobiography and the Cultural Moment," 9–11). Since the publication of *Metaphors* in the early 1970s, numerous approaches to reading self-referential narratives have emerged in the field of autobiography studies that gradually shifted the terms of debate from a concept of "self" to one of "subjectivity." Such interventions are responding to the explosion of activity in both the writing of life narratives and theorizing about subjectivity. As a conclusion to this chapter, we briefly consider avant-garde, postcolonial, and postmodern interventions that have amplified the possible modes of self-narrating and undermined canonical norms of autobiographical inscription.

Avant-garde autobiographical writing at mid-twentieth century registered the cultural break of modernism (or what Thomas Kuhn described as a "paradigm shift") from a polis-centered to a decentered metropolitan habitat of identity. William Boelhower, in his structural analysis of the avant-garde autobiographical model, suggests that in attempting "to create a coherent grammar of the self out of the spatial vocabulary of the metropolis" the avant-garde autobiographer "ends up with a loosely bound inventory of fragmented forms" ("Avant-Garde Autobiography," 275). On narrating their successive displacements in the new metropolitan centers, such artists as Ernest Hemingway, Frank Lloyd Wright, Louis H. Sullivan, Malcolm Cowley, and Le Corbusier register the mobility of identity in transit in the fragmented, centerless spaces of the city and the resulting nostalgia for "a proper dwelling" (276). In such narratives, spatial dynamics displace the temporal emphasis of much earlier canonical autobiography, and the bricolage of description displaces narrative teleology (279). In Boelhower's view, the self of avant-garde autobiography becomes less an agent of inhabitable space and a synthesizing point of view and more a subject of urban architecture, fragmented and decentered. While Boelhower does not engage the narratives of women or autobiographical representations of the post-colonial urban center, all of which contest and reverse the terms of avant-gardism, his mapping of decentered identities and spaces suggests a provocative new direction of study.

The avant-garde experiments of subsequent architects and writers have continued this decentering of any stable "I" or narrative point of reference. French writer Michel Leiris, in his sustained four-volume autobiography, *Rules of the Game*, of which two volumes, *Scratches* and *Scraps*, have been translated into English, parallels self-study to the study of others. A student of ethnography and an ethnologist, Leiris states that the logic of his self-study is to discover the masks and rules that govern human games. Confounding "I" and "other," "inside" and "outside," language and idea, Leiris makes the autobiographical a moving point of exchanges that transmit the writer's "corrections" to others in an ongoing communicative circuit. He writes that memory, for example, "even though it has come to me from outside, even though it is the result of an absolutely fortuitous conjunction of circumstances, … is nonetheless an integral part of me." In this exchange an image from outside becomes a mirror, "the only solid thing I look at and that throws my reflection back at me" (*Scratches*, 14). The exchange of memory and image becomes an interplay momentarily creating traces of an "I," what Leiris calls "a set of needle points" that scratch upon, and inscribe, an impalpable "me" (17). Leiris's "I," elusive and ubiquitous, idiosyncratic and insubstantial, explodes the boundaries of particularized lives as sites of the autobiographical.

Similarly, Roland Barthes, in *Roland Barthes*, explores the conundrum of being both the subject and the object of an always impossible autobiographical discourse. More recently, French expatriate Luc Santé in *The Factory of Facts* enunciates the "I" as an effect of the constellation of objects in particular moments of everyday life. And at an extreme of the depersonalization of the autobiographical, the "novels" of Kathy Acker challenge the very ground upon which any utterance can be labeled "autobiographical." Acker herself noted that, in her provocative meditations on identity titled "The Childlike Life of the Black Tarantula by the Black Tarantula,"she placed "autobiographical material next to material that couldn't be autobiographical" (Friedman, "Conversation," 15). Throughout her experimental writing Acker contests the signature upon which the narrator-reader relationship rests, as she appropriates, cannibalizes, even plagiarizes work from male writers in order to explore how the woman quester can constitute an identity in the contexts and terms established for her by men and the phallic economy (Friedman, "'Now Eat Your Mind,'" 43). In such experimental writing Acker exposes the malleability of identity through outrageous acts of appropriation and impersonation, becoming others so as not to become too securely the kind of self reproduced in postmodern consumer patriarchal capitalism. "I'm trying to become other people," she declares in "Black Tarantula," "I'm trying to get away from self-expression" (86). In her plagiaristic impersonations of others, she exposes at once the very instability and overdetermination of something once understood as "the true self" and its autobiographical acts.

These experimental writers, then, purposefully mine the problematics of language and representation to interrogate old meanings of "selves." Through complex plays of signification in which the present is ever-escaping and the "I" an impersonation, they both call the autobiographical into question and relentlessly employ it to demonstrate its impossibility.

A second site of intervention has been the production by postcolonial and multicultural writers of texts that propose, constitute, and reframe alternatives to an individual self. Calling Western norms of identity and experience into question, these writers, at diverse global locations, produce self-narrations through which they both call attention to their status as the West's former "Others" and seek to be heard in different terms, to be accountable, to count. For such autoethnographers the emancipatory dimension of contemporary autobiographical practices and cultural work is primary, as they creatively inquire into the histories of their own cultural erasure in the name of civilizing missions and employ modes of oral storytelling.

Fueled, on the one hand, by the critiques of Frantz Fanon and Aimé Césaire and, on the other, by a need to construct subject positions through which to negotiate neocolonial regimes of truth in the name of liberation, writers around the globe are proposing new concepts of subjectivity, as transcultural, diasporic, hybrid, and nomadic. Such autobiographical acts move the "I" toward the collective and shift the focus of narration toward an as-yet virtual space of community, across and beyond the old boundaries of identification. The uses of such life narratives in witnessing torture, disappearance, and imprisonment have been transformative, from Gandhi's *The Story of My Experiments with Truth* through the narratives of Malcolm X, Rigoberta Menchú, Nawal El Saadawi, Jacobo Timerman, Aung San Suu Kyi, and others. Yet international dissemination requires translation into Western languages and distribution by transnational publishers, conditions that have been unavailable to many writers of resistance texts. Despite these constraints, however, increasing numbers of life narratives contribute to a resistance literature that has begun to reorganize global knowledge.

The third site of intervention is poststructural and postmodern theorizing about the subject. At the same time that the practices of postcolonial life narrative proliferated around the globe, larger debates within critical theory of the 1970s through the 1990s led to the reconceptualization of subjectivity and, therefore, of autobiographical acts. Derridean deconstruction, Barthesian semiotics, and Foucaultian analysis of the discursive regimes of power energized the dismantling of metaphysical conceptions of self-presence, authority, authenticity, and truth. As for Lacan, for Derrida the self is a fiction, an illusion constituted in discourse, a hypothetical place or space of storytelling. A true self can never be discovered, unmasked, or revealed because its core is a *mise en abîme*, an infinite regress. The origin and history of the self, then, are fictions, although the history of utterances of that fiction can be traced. Because the self is split and fragmented, it can no longer be conceptualized as unitary. At a given moment what calls itself the self is different from itself at any other given moment. As Virginia Woolf remarked, "'I' is only a convenient term for somebody who has no real being" (*A Room of One's Own*, 4).

In telescoped fashion we might summarize the theoretical interventions of the last quarter century, also discussed in chapters 2 and 3, as follows:

- The Lacanian revision of Freudian psychoanalysis challenged the notion of an autonomous self and proposed a split subject always constituted in language.
- The Derridean notion of "différance" captured the way in which "language, whose meanings are produced by differences ... tries to set up distinctions necessary for there to be meaning." Meanings, always emergent in the system "as a whole," are never fixed, but rely on other signifiers, that "lie in waiting, negatively supporting the signifier that has been uttered or written" (Pollock, 30). Consequently, meaning is always in process, continuously put off, or deferred.
- Derridean and Lyotardian critiques of universalized or "master" narratives contributed to the deconstruction of "Truth" with a capital 'T' and challenged the firmness of generic boundaries between fact and fiction.
- Althusser's critique of ideology argued that ideology constitutes not only socioeconomic relations but subjectivity itself. Social subjects are subjects of ideology, "interpellated" or "hailed" as a particular kind of subject by the very institutions through which those ideologies are reproduced.
- Foucault's emphasis on discourses of identity and his critique of power analyzed the multiple, dispersed, local technologies of selfhood through which subjects come to self-knowledge in historically specific regimes of truth.

- Bakhtin's concept of the dialogism of the word and the consequent heteroglossia of utterances replaced the unitary "I" with multiple dialogic voices spoken as the autobiographical "I" speaks in language that has "a multitude of concrete worlds, a multitude of bounded verbal-ideological and social belief-systems" (288).
- Anthropological research exposed critics and theorists to ideologies of selfhood outside the West that challenge the universality and homogeneity of Western models. It also exposed the ways in which the framing of human thought and language is determined by the culture in which that framing takes place, as mediated by investigators themselves.
- Feminist theories of representation problematized "experience" as a transparent category of meaning, examined the political dynamics of the "personal," focused on the body as a site of cultural inscription and practices of embodiment, and critiqued the notion of a universalized "woman" by exploring the differences among women.
- Fanon's critique of the specularity of the colonial gaze reconceptualized relations of domination and subordination in formerly colonized regions and linked the subjection of colonial peoples to international racism at a moment when national liberation movements were disrupting the interdependencies of identity in colonial relationships between the West and its Others.
- Postcolonial, ethnic, and feminist studies analyzed the effects of discourses of identity and cultural practices on minoritized and/or de/colonized subjects and proposed enabling models of margins and centers.
- Gay and, more recently, queer studies resituated subjectivity as performative and criticized binary models of the organization of gender and sexuality.
- Cultural studies, long-standing in Great Britain and taking hold in the United States, turned to popular, public, and everyday forms of textuality, including everyday practices of self-narrating in verbal, visual, and mixed modes.

- Alternative concepts of time challenged the primacy of notions of chronological and progressive time, relativizing external and internal temporalities of history and of memory.
- Interdisciplinary studies of memory and its encoding in the materiality of the brain offered new ways of understanding the processes of remembering and forgetting, and the effects of traumatic memories.

Taken together, these theoretical reframings suggest a paradigm shift in understandings of the subject.

Such challenges to the concept of a unified, sovereign subject and to belief in language's transparency have shattered the cultural authority of what Lyotard calls the "master narratives" of the West, including the institution of canonical autobiography. Although at this time the unitary self of liberal humanism remains a prevailing notion governing Western configurations and disciplines of selfhood, that universal self and the narratives through which it has claimed its authority are increasingly open to challenge. Around the globe, contesting versions of selfhood are posed, above all, in diverse kinds of life narratives that introduce collective, provisional, and mobile subjects. And they are explored in a third wave's engagement with the poetics and politics of the autobiographical, to which we now turn.

CHAPTER 6

A History of Autobiography Criticism
Part 2: Contemporary Theorizing

> We are never really the cause of our life, but we can have the
> illusion of becoming its author by writing it, providing that we
> forget that we are no more the cause of the writing
> than of our life.
>
> Philippe Lejeune, "The Autobiography of Those Who
> Do Not Write"

The Third Wave of Autobiography Criticism

With the practical and theoretical interventions described in chapter 5, what we loosely call a third wave of autobiography critics, writing in the last twenty years, responded to the diversity of practices of subjectivity and modes of analyzing that we have traced. As notions of an authoritative speaker, intentionality, truth, meaning, and generic integrity have been challenged, the former preoccupations of autobiography critics with the nature of its truth, its formal structures, the struggle with identity, even the assumption of a motivating self, have been displaced. A new emphasis on *graphia*, "the careful teasing out of warring forces of signification within the text itself" (Johnson, *Critical Difference*, 5), has assumed central importance. Readers now ask whether there are practices of graphing the *autos* and framing its *bios* that are particular to texts that perform self-reference, be they written, imaged, spoken, and/or figured. Emergent theorizing of the autobiographical at interdisciplinary boundaries suggests new ways to engage the canon of autobiography and the larger field of life narrative, including other media of self-presentation.

Many critics have contributed to the ferment of theorizing the institution of autobiography and practices of life narrative since the 1970s. Our bibliography of secondary sources lists many of those critics and historians. We want now to mention critics within autobiography studies whose work enabled the transition to a third wave of theorizing life narrative.

Elizabeth Bruss's 1976 *Autobiographical Acts: The Changing Situation of a Literary Genre* and her related essay generated from that book argue for understanding autobiography neither mimetically, as a chronology of the representative life, nor expressively, as the writer's baring of experience, but as a performative act: "Autobiography is a personal performance, an action that exemplifies the character of the agent responsible for that action and how it is performed" (Bruss, "Eye for I," 300). While "act-value" is only one of three defining features of her theory—the others are truth-value and identity-value—and her orientation is toward the unitary makers of speech acts, her promising emphasis on autobiographical acts and her turn to filmic life narrative anticipate a dominant trend of the 1990s toward theorizing autobiographical performativity.

Some theorists considered the vexed relationship of the autobiographer to his or her own past, his or her own status as an "I." Louis A. Renza's important 1977 essay, "The Veto of the Imagination: A Theory of Autobiography," theorized autobiographical temporality and the relationship of the autobiographical subject to the only apparent "pastness" of the past. Renza argues that, in the act of writing, the life narrator "presentifies" that past; never simply recollected, it informs the present moment of writing. Furthermore, Renza argues, autobiography only appears to be an activity of imaginative cognition manifesting the writer's "screen [set up] between the truth of the narrated past and the present of the narrative situation" (3). The writer engages imaginatively in what Renza terms the "'impersonating' effect of discourse" as a "diacritical retention of the 'I,'" a split intentionality (9). Renza's insistence on the self-referentiality of an "I" that both "presentifies" and privatizes its public presentation anticipates theories of the split subject of life narrative.

Michel Beaujour's 1980 theoretical work on self-representation was translated into English as *Poetics of the Literary Self-Portrait* only in 1991 and has been less influential in the United States than in Europe. Beaujour distinguishes the literary self-portrait from the autobiography as a "polymorphous formation, a much more heterogeneous and complex literary type than is autobiographical narration" (25). Self-portraiture is not self-description but "the mirror whose reflecting function is mimicked in the symmetrical statement: me by me" (31). He claims for self-portraiture many of the texts Olney would view as sites of "doubled" metaphors of self: the self-representations of Augustine and Montaigne, Nietzsche and Malraux, Leiris and Barthes.

And finally, Paul de Man's influential essay of 1979, "Autobiography as De-Facement," challenged autobiography as an inevitably self-deluded practice unable to represent the life or *bios* it took as its subject. De Man asserts:

> We assume the life produces the autobiography as an act produces its consequences, but can we not suggest, with equal justice, that the autobiographical project may itself produce and determine the life and that whatever the writer does is in fact governed by the technical demands of self-portraiture and thus determined, in all its aspects, by the resources of its medium? (920)

For de Man autobiography as a genre is the exemplary case of prosopopeia, or the representation of an imaginary or absent person as speaking and acting. While this strong challenge to the genre's legitimacy may be qualified by de Man's own troubled lapses about his past collusion with occupying Nazi forces, his reading of prosopopeia framed a question of autobiographical representation as an act of impersonation that remains a key issue. The impact of de Man's poststructuralist interrogation of self and author (as well as that of other poststructural theorists) is insightfully assessed in Candace Lang's 1982 "Autobiography in the Aftermath of Romanticism," in which she also historicizes the concept of individualism and frames new terms for conceptualizing autobiographical practices.

Since the 1980s critics in the United States have been more concerned with issues of the referentiality and relationality of life narrative. If Bruss had earlier insisted on the autobiographical occasion as an act,

Philippe Lejeune insists on its function as a pact. In his theory of the autobiographical pact, Lejeune integrates a concept of both implied and actual (flesh-and-blood) readers into the meaning-making of autobiographical writing. As he refines distinctions between autobiography and biography, on the one hand, and autobiography and fiction on the other, by considering linguistic modes of the "I," Lejeune takes the position of the reader as his starting point. According to Lejeune, the autobiographical text establishes a "pact" between narrator and reader that "supposes that there is *identity of name* between the author (such as he figures, by his name, on the cover), the narrator of the story, and the character who is being talked about" ("Pact," 12). For Lejeune the "deep signature" of autobiography is the proper name: "What defines autobiography for the one who is reading is above all a contract of identity that is sealed by the proper name. And this is true also for the one who is writing the text" (19–20). Lejeune subsequently modified his schema in "The Autobiographical Pact (bis)" by acknowledging that "the real reader can adopt modes of reading different from the one that is suggested to him," and he acknowledged "especially that many published texts in no way include an explicit contract" ("bis," 126). While modifying the concept of the pact to account for the fictionality of the proper name, however, Lejeune reconfirms the necessity of an author-reader pact as a starting point for both the writer and reader.

In another version of the autobiographer-reader contract, Janet Varner Gunn in the 1980s situated a theory of autobiography in two moments of reading—the reading "by the autobiographer who, in effect, is 'reading' his or her life; and by the reader of the autobiographical text," who is also, in the encounter with the text, rereading his or her own life by association (8). For Gunn, the reader, like the narrator, is engaged in an autobiographical act.

In his 1985 *Fictions of Autobiography: Studies in the Art of Self-Invention*, Paul John Eakin argued that autobiographical writing is a form of self-invention that constitutes the self. In this sense, the self is the origin of "the reflexive center of human subjectivity" (198), although self as a concept is both historically demarcated and culturally specific. For

Eakin the autobiographical act both reenacts and extends earlier phases of the entry into identity through language (226). While Eakin modifies this view of the textuality of the self in *Touching the World* by insisting on autobiography's referentiality to a historical and material world, his emphasis has remained on the processes by which lives are made into stories and on self-experience as "a kind of awareness in process" (*How Our Lives Become Stories*, x). In his most recent study, *How Our Lives Become Stories*, Eakin probes interdisciplinary approaches to life narrative based on recent work in neurology, cognitive science, memory research, and developmental psychology, and he inquires into the implications of those approaches for contextualizing "the registers of self and self-experience" captured in autobiographical stories (xi).

Like Eakin, Nancy K. Miller has investigated the intersectionality of the autobiographer, the critic, and the world. While Eakin argues persuasively for the difference of life narrative in its proximity to historical materiality, Miller insists on the inextricability of genre and gender ("Representing Others"). Both have pointed out that the notion of autobiographical relationality, taken to characterize the difference of women's autobiography in early feminist scholarship by such critics as Estelle Jelinek and Susan Stanford Friedman, in fact characterizes modes of relationship in much autobiographical writing by both men and women. As she has explored autobiographical subjectivity since *Getting Personal*, Miller has developed an innovative style that interweaves the practice and critique of autobiographical writing into a mode of "getting personal" that reads significant life experiences and moments through both memory and the terms of critical discourse.

Theorist Sidonie Smith, in her 1987 *Poetics of Women's Autobiography: Marginality and the Fictions of Self-Representation*, also takes up the linkage of gender and genre in exploring how women engage autobiographical discourse to renegotiate their cultural marginality and enter into literary history. As Smith's 1993 *Subjectivity, Identity, and the Body: Women's Autobiographical Practices in the Twentieth Century* makes clear, autobiographical subjectivity is enacted in cultural spaces between the personal "I" and the body politic. A life narrator's inscription of embodied textuality is thus an effect of discourses of embodiment. Smith has since gone on to examine the range of both geographic sites and generic modes of life narrative in several subsequent studies.

In *Telling Lies in Modern American Autobiography*, Timothy Dow Adams examines limit cases in which autobiographers deliberately propounded lies to exploit or, in other cases, to expand the boundaries of autobiographical discourse. Moving to another limit, the interface of photography and life writing as modes of representing subjectivity for Americans over two centuries, Adams, in *Light Writing and Life Writing: Photography in Autobiography*, explores the "vexed history of referentiality" encountered in theorizing the ways in which photography and autobiography "represent" the world. Thinking about the two modes of referentiality together enables Adams to understand that "since reference is not secure in either, neither can compensate for lack of stability in the other" (xxi). In both studies Adams is preoccupied with the ways in which acts that expose and refer are also acts that conceal and blur.

The work of these critics over three decades signals that a third wave of theorizing life narrative has coalesced. It engages the challenges posed by postmodernism's deconstruction of any solid ground of selfhood and truth outside of discourse. These challenges are confronted directly, and through a productive variety of theoretical lenses, in the collection of essays entitled *Autobiography and Postmodernism*, edited by Kathleen Ashley, Leigh Gilmore, and Gerald Peters. Its essays investigate how subjectivity both resists and produces identity by reading subjectivity dialogically. Attentive to the instability of texts, contributors such as Betty Bergland raise questions about the possibilities of human agency in ethnic autobiographies and emphasize the dynamic and fundamentally discursive character of self-representation. For these critics self-narration occupies multiple and contradictory discursive spaces in voicing the discontinuities of remembered pasts.

At this moment in the history of autobiography criticism, then, critical/theoretical approaches to life narrative do several things. They draw upon and adapt aspects of postmodern and postcolonial theory, which are themselves heterogeneous rather than unified fields. They consider generic instability, regimes of truth-telling, referentiality, relationality, and embodiment as issues that contest the assumptions of the earlier critical wave's understanding of canonical autobiography. And they expand the range of life narratives and the kinds of stories criticism should attend to in constructing a field of study. To suggest some modalities in which contemporary criticism of life narratives is couched, we foreground the following set of terms: performativity, positionality, and heteroglossic dialogism. We will go on to suggest how new forms of critical inquiry are being organized through the rhetorics of identity, location, and address.

A *performative* view of life narrative theorizes autobiographical occasions as dynamic sites for the performance of identities constitutive of subjectivity. In this view, identities are not fixed or essentialized attributes of autobiographical subjects; rather they are produced and reiterated through cultural norms, and thus remain provisional and unstable. Much contemporary discussion of life narrative as performative is informed by Judith Butler's deconstruction of a binary gender system and her assertion that gender is performative. For Butler, performativity "must be understood not as a singular or deliberate 'act,' but, rather, as the reiterative and citational practice by which discourse produces the effects that it names" (*Bodies That Matter,* 20).

Critics of life narrative have found in theories of performativity a vocabulary for describing the complexities of the relationship of regulatory discourses of identity and material bodies, as well as autobiographical agency. Sidonie Smith, for instance, reads autobiographical telling as performative because it enacts the "self" it claims has given rise to the "I." Responding to Butler's assertion that "the 'I' neither precedes nor follows the process of . . . gendering, but emerges only within and as the matrix of gender relations themselves," Smith explores how "the interiority or self that is said to be prior to the autobiographical expression or reflection is an *effect* of autobiographical storytelling" ("Performativity, Autobiographical Practice, Resistance," 18).

There are also other ways of understanding the performativity of life narrative. Paul John Eakin has noted what he terms a "shift from a documentary view of autobiography as a record of referential fact to a performative view of autobiography centered on the act of composition" (*Touching the World*, 143). Eakin is concerned, however, to argue for life narrative as a process of "narratively constituted identity" rather than to theorize the autobiographical subject, in Barthes' terms, as "merely . . . an effect of language" (*How Our Lives Become Stories*, 139). Current discussions on the significance of memory to autobiographical storytelling suggest that new understandings of memory will inflect theorizing of autobiographical performativity, and that the terms and modes of autobiographical subjectivity will remain open to debate.

Another critical turn prescient of the third wave is the exploration by Philippe Lejeune. In "The Autobiography of Those Who Do Not Write," he elaborates the many dimensions of everyday modes of narrative. Lejeune begins by questioning, in the as-told-to narrative, whether the life "belongs" to the one who lives it or the one who writes it. Profoundly problematizing the notion of authorship, Lejeune notes how "a person's life can appear through someone else's narrative" in collaborations such as interview situations where questions are erased and the oral stories of those who do not write recorded (190). A life, Lejeune states, "is always the product of a transaction between different postures" (197). This is particularly clear in working-class autobiography, where the narrative records a struggle between the class consciousness of the worker and the form and patterns of the life story, which ideologically belong to the ruling class. While typically the lives of workers have been "studied from above," with the effect that the workers did not speak (199), the publication of everyday lives—by autodidacts, or as manifestos, or orally, as in talk-show accounts—begins to redress a situation in which those living everyday lives could not write but only be written. Lejeune's extensive studies of the life narratives collected as ethnographies by social scientists, as interviews by historians, and as effaced interviews by journalists of those who do not write their own stories are some ways of negotiating an "ethnological gap" (211). As ordinary people increasingly interiorize their stories through the institutions of popular memory—primarily forms of media—Lejeune looks to their reappropriation of life-knowledge and authority in ways that could transform social relations.

The concept of positionality has become increasingly important throughout narrative studies to designate how subjects are situated at particular axes through the relations of power. Foucault's analysis of "technologies of the self" as imperatives for constituting the "disciplined" self as a subject via by multiple confessional practices established a vocabulary for specifying subject positions ("Techologies of the Self"). Leigh Gilmore's nuanced reading of the "autographics" of a range of women's life narratives attends to the subject positions that narrators negotiate within the constraints of discursive regimes as they present themselves within genres that prohibit that speaking (*Autobiographics*). Issues of positionality and the geographics of identity are especially complex in narratives of de/colonization, immigration, displacement, and exile, areas of autobiography studies commanding more attention as critics such as Carole Boyce Davies, Caren Kaplan, Homi Bhabha, Frances Bartkowski, José David Saldívar, and Susan Stanford Friedman (*Mappings*) deploy new terms for subjects in process, terms such as *hybrid, border, diasporic, mestiza, nomadic, migratory, minoritized.*

Heteroglossic dialogism, the multiplicity of "tongues" through which subjectivity is enunciated, has been persuasively explored at the interfaces of orality and writing, between languages, and interdiscursively in the work of many theorists. Among critics of autobiography, Williams L. Andrews employs a Bakhtinian model to read how slave narratives enact the telling of "free" stories through dialogical shifts. Françoise Lionnet (*Autobiographical Voices*) turns to Edouard Glissant's concept of creolization to propose a theory of autobiographical textuality as a métissage or braiding of disparate voices in subjects whose cultural origins and allegiances are multiple and conflicting. And Mae Gwendolyn Henderson takes inspiration from heteroglossia and glossolalia, the practice of speaking in tongues of some African American churches, to account for the polyvocality of first-person narrative in African American women's writing.

Theorizing performativity contests the notion of autobiography as the site of authentic identity. Theorizing positionality, with an emphasis on situatedness, contests the normative notion of a universal and transcendent autobiographical subject, autonomous and free. And theorizing dialogism contests the notion that self-narration is a monologic utterance of a solitary, introspective subject. All of these concepts enable more flexible reading practices and more inclusive approaches to the field of life narrative.

Admittedly such a brief overview of critical writing that has been formative of a third wave of autobiography criticism cannot do justice to the richness and complexity of the field or the provocative terms of debate within both literary and cultural studies. Our intent is that this study provide a map for beginning to navigate these debates.

Studies in Genres of Life Narrative

There are many genres of life narrative. Appendix A lists and briefly describes fifty-two kinds of autobiographical writing, and that list could be much longer. Here we want briefly to note a few important critical texts of the last decade that have defined and explored some of these generic modes.

Although confession, memoir, and apology were noted by Francis R. Hart as three alternative modalities of autobiographical writing, focus on any one of the three may dominate in a particular critical reading. Confession has been the key modality for recent critics. Daniel B. Shea's *Spiritual Autobiography in Early America* explores the uses of confession in Puritan narrative, particularly the conversion experience, and suggests how it is a foundational discourse of American public culture. Rita Felski, in a chapter entitled "On Confession" in *Beyond Feminist Aesthetics: Feminist Literature and Social Change*, understands feminist confession as a public mode of self-presentation that constitutes feminist community and a counterknowledge founded upon the authority of experience. Leigh Gilmore, in *Autobiographics: A Feminist Theory of Women's Self-Representation*, deploys a Foucauldian critique of confessional discourse to consider the policing strategies of the West that demarcate boundaries transgressed by women writers in negotiating enunciations of a pro-scribed "I." Gilmore's *The Limits of Autobiography: Trauma, Testimony, Theory,* explores the inadequacy of confessional modes of self-narrative to contemproary acts of traumatic remembering and examines alterna-tive modes. Other studies of confession include Jeremy Tambling's *Con-fession: Sexuality, Sin, the Subject,* Susan M. Levin's *The Romantic Art of Confession: De Quincey, Musset, Sand, Lamb, Hogg, Frémy, Soulié, Janin,* and Oliver S. Buckton's *Secret Selves: Confession and Same-Sex Desire in Victorian Autobiography.*

James Olney's *Memory and Narrative: The Weave of Life-Writing* takes the narratives of Augustine, Rousseau, and Samuel Beckett as three models of confession for assessing shifts in the terms, structures, and occasions of memory in the West. Indeed, much current work on trauma, such as that of Cathy Caruth, Shoshana Felman and Dori Laub, Kelly Oliver, and Janice Haaken, considers modes of public confession as acts of witnessing in situations of both public and private crisis and theorizes traumatic memory, the limits of memory, and false memory syndrome.

Narratives of crisis, focused on injury, self-reinterpretation, and testimony, have proliferated in response to widespread illness and gen-ocidal war, to profound changes in personal life, and to the growing audience demand for personal accounts as self-help. For example, the outpouring of narratives by victims and survivors of the AIDS crisis has generated critical studies focused on the rhetoric of mourning in per-sonal narratives, as in Ross Chambers's *Facing It: AIDS Diaries and the Death of the Author.* And in *Troubling the Angels: Women Living with HIV/AIDS,* Patti Lather and Chris Smithies incorporate multiple modes of knowing about HIV/AIDS, including oral histories, critical analysis, poetic engagement with metaphors of history, and factoids, to explore how telling one's story and hearing others' stories involve an ethic of knowing and caring in the time of the pandemic. A comprehensive and far-reaching study of crisis and resolution in many modes of illness and disability is available in G. Thomas Couser's *Recovering Bodies: Illness, Disability, and Life Writing.* Surveying life narratives related to deafness, breast cancer, HIV/AIDS, and paralysis, Couser considers how these narratives, in such forms as memoirs, diaries, photo documentaries, and essays, address the stigmatizing of disability and work to reclaim bodies from cultural marginalization, including that imposed by medical practice. Similarly, Rosemarie Garland Thomson's *Freakery: Cultural Spectacles of the Extraordinary Body* has surveyed a range of narratives about several kinds of disability. In *Mirror Talk: Genres of Crisis in Contemporary Autobiography* Susanna Egan examines narratives of life and death in order to understand how, in moments of crisis and decentering, the double voicing, or mirror talk, of autobiographical acts "affects both the one who speaks and the one who listens" (25). The critical study of narratives of disability is an important focus for future work and might be expanded to take up such areas as the place of disability in postcolonial life writing and the narration of disability, recovery, and embodiment in medieval and early modern life writing, including saints' lives.

Another important genre of autobiography studies receiving recent critical attention is prison life writing. Studies by Barbara J. Harlow, notably *Barred: Women, Writing, and Political Detention*, have identified the prison as a nodal site of political repression. Building on H. Bruce Franklin's rich study (*Prison Literature in America: The Victim as Criminal and Artist*), Harlow reads prison-life narratives as interventions in national and transnational political struggles, and, at times—as in the case of Steve Biko and Ruth First—as testimonies of those who fall victim to regimes of terror.

The prison narrative has a precursor of sorts in the captivity narrative, now an energetic focus of American studies scholarship and increasingly in colonial studies internationally. Recovering the genre in out-of-print memoirs, as well as writing critical studies of its norms and dynamics, has been the work of such Americanists as Kathryn Zabelle Derounian-Stodola and James A. Levernier in *The Indian Captivity Narrative, 1550–1900*, and Paul Baepler in *White Slaves, African Masters: An Anthology of American Barbary Captivity Narratives*, and in Australia Kay Schaffer in *In the Wake of First Contact: The Eliza Fraser Stories*. Archival and interpretive work in the paradoxes of identification and reconversion in captivity narratives as a genre of public testimony is likely to rewrite the field of autobiography studies in many modern languages as literary scholars and historians jointly recover more of these narratives.

Many modes of collaborative life writing are not only being read as autobiographical but reinterpreted as arenas and occasions of a dialogical process shared among two or more voices. Studies of collaboration in Native American writing exist in the work of Arnold Krupat, Gretchen Bataille and Kathleen M. Sands, and Hertha D. Sweet Wong. Mark Sanders, in his essay, "Theorizing the Collaborative Self: The Dynamics of Contour and Content in the Dictated Autobiography," suggests how an examination of co-constructed narratives in political arenas such as those of truth commissions is coterminous with this genre and yet challenges the terms of mutuality that often were unexamined in earlier work. As Ruth Behar's *Translated Woman: Crossing the Border with Esperanza's Story* makes clear, in its shuttling between discourses of critical ethnography and first-person witnessing, the "as-told-to" narrative is a richly problematic site for future investigation.

More broadly, critics are theorizing many kinds of life writing in which the *bios* of autobiography is replaced by the *ethno-* of autoethnography. Informed by wide-ranging critiques of the investigator-informant model of ethnography as a colonizing process, critics such as Mary Louise Pratt, Françoise Lionnet, Anne E. Goldman, and Julia Watson have studied the terms of transculturation in contact zones of encounter between indigenous and metropolitan subjects. Whether tracing autobiographical inscription in such collective forms as the cookbook and the labor-organizing narrative, as Goldman does; or in the simultaneous practice and parody of ethnographic discourse within the heterogeneous testimonio, as Pratt does; or in the life narratives of emergent African women writers, as Watson does; these critics frame autoethnography less as a genre than as a situated practice of self-narration contesting the limits of person and speech.

Critics of life writing are also problematizing diary writing, once seen as a transparent activity of diurnal recording. As critics such as Robert M. Fothergill (*Private Chronicles*), Philippe Lejeune, Margo Culley (*A Day at a Time*), Suzanne Bunkers, Cynthia Huff, and Helen M. Buss in their explorations of women's private diaries suggest, recovering and reading these often unpublished life writings requires sophisticated interpretive strategies, whether the diarist was as voluminous and celebrated as Samuel Pepys or as little known as someone's grandmother.

Another genre of life writing that is beginning to be critically explored, as evidenced by the work of Laurence Buell in *The Environmental Imagination: Thoreau, Nature Writing, and the Formation of America* and the recent collection *Reading the Earth: New Directions in the Study of Literature and Environment*, edited by Michael P. Branch, is what we might think of as the ecological life narrative in which the story of the protagonist is interwoven with that of the region itself.

While travel writing is often presented as a genre distinct from autobiography, extending back to classical Greece and Rome in the West, it can in fact be read as a major mode of life narrative, in this case the reconstitution of the autobiographical subject in transit and encounter. In the last ten years there has been a virtual explosion of studies of travel narratives, including the influential work of Eric J. Leed, Georges Van Den Abbeele, Lisa Lowe (*Critical Terrains*), Dennis Porter, Mary Louise Pratt (*Imperial Eyes*), Chris Bongie, and more recently Chloe Chard and Sidonie Smith (*Moving Lives*). Because travel narratives in the West are so linked to the history of exploration, settlement, and colonization, studies of cross-cultural encounters in the contact zones around the world have explored how subjectivity is reimagined in the midst of the alien and uncanny.

As yet no single generic term has emerged as a critical concept to describe how the practices of a digitized imaginary in cyberspace life writing will differ from the analog writings of lines on the page. As Mark Poster presciently suggests, with these changes in the way writing enters the world, changes in the material structure of the trace are inevitable, as the trace becomes voice and image, in addition to alphabet. The potential for changing subjectivity of hypertextual digitized writing shakes up our notions of the figure of the author as a bounded subject creating, with copyright protection, an individual identity. Suggesting that the "author-function" will disappear in the heterotopic discourses of cyberspace, Poster suggests a new focus on links, associations, and dispersions of meaning through performances of subjectivity and collectivity.

Critical Geographies

While we have focused, in this discussion, on the theorizing of life narrative as a critical activity, such work is also embedded in many fine histories and generic studies that have emerged in the last two decades. Here we offer a survey of this work.

In historicizing American life narrative as a field both multiform and informed by intertextual debates, the book-length studies by Albert Stone, James M. Cox, Robert F. Sayre, William H. Boelhower (*Through a Glass Darkly*), G. Thomas Couser, Anne E. Goldman, Werner Sollors, and more recently those of Diane Bjorklund and Ann Fabian, and the collection of essays in Eakin's *American Autobiography: Retrospect and Prospect* are pivotal works. For American ethnic studies, the work of William L. Andrews, Frances Smith Foster, Valerie Smith, Robert B. Stepto, and Henry Louis Gates Jr. (*The Signifying Monkey*) on African American autobiography is foundational, and has been extended by the recent work of Joanne Braxton, Barbara Rodriguez, Crispin Sartwell, Kenneth Mostern, Lindon Barrett, Sandra Gunning, Ashraf H. A. Rushdy, and Samira Kawash. In studies of Native American life writing, Arnold Krupat, Dexter Fisher, and A. LaVonne Brown Ruoff have been pathbreakers, and both Krupat's and Hertha D. Sweet Wong's theorizing about the synecdochal character of collaborative life stories is informative for reading the differences of Native American writing. The considerable body of Chicano/a and Latino/a autobiographical writing has been insightfully discussed by Genaro M. Padilla, Ramón Saldívar, José David Saldívar, Sonia Saldívar-Hull, and Teresa McKenna, among others. The multiplicity of Asian Pacific American autobiographical writing has been mapped by Sau-Ling Cynthia Wong, Rey Chow, Amy Ling, Shirley Geok-lin Lim, Xiaomei Chen, and Sara Suleri, among others.

For Latin American autobiographical writing, a rich and developing field, books by Sylvia Molloy, Amy K. Kaminsky, John Beverley,

Judith Raiskin, and most recently Kristine Ibsen and Steven V. Hunsacker have begun to explore the terms of subjectivity across linguistic, cultural, and national divides, and in response to histories of exploration, conquest, settlement, and national liberation. Research into the testimonio and into such colonial forms of autobiographical inscription as the indigenous codex and the life narratives of religious are promising new areas of exploration.

Other scholars have explored the histories of life narrative in particular locales around the world. In Canada Helen M. Buss, Shirley Neuman ("Introduction"), Susanna Egan (*Mirror Talk*), Julia V. Emberley, and Terrence L. Craig are among those tracing the rise of a distinctive Canadian autobiographical writing of settlement, westward displacement, cultural conflict, bilingualism, and contemporary multiculturalism. In Australia Joy Hooton, Rosamund Dalziell, and Kay Schaffer, among others, have explored how autobiographical writing has been one venue for the reproduction of those central myths of Australian national identity such as the myth of mateship. Anne Brewster and Jennifer Sabbioni, Kay Schaffer, and Sidonie Smith, in the anthology *Indigenous Australian Voices: A Reader*, have explored how personal narrative has been a venue through which indigenous Australians have rewritten the history of encounter and state oppression as well as laid claim to alternative modes of collective identification. Recently Gillian Whitlock has comparatively investigated anglophone autobiographical practices in the British Empire, including Great Britain, Australia, Canada, South Africa, and the Caribbean.

There is, of course, a long-standing tradition of British autobiography criticism to which such eminent writers as Stephen Spender and Virginia Woolf have contributed. More recently, John Sturrock, Avrom Fleishman, Julia Swindells, Susanna Egan (*Patterns of Experience*), Michael Mascuch, and Trev Lynn Broughton have traced the encoding of life experience in British narratives, following upon the earlier work of Patricia Ann Meyer Spacks and A. O. J. Cockshut. Felicity A. Nussbaum has considered the formation of modes of autobiographical subjectivity in an emergent capitalist marketplace in the eighteenth century; Linda

H. Peterson has explored how women rework the rhetoric of conversion and spirituality (*Traditions of Victorian Women's Autobiography*); Barbara Green has explored the uses of multiple modes of autobiographical performances in the suffrage movement; and Laura Marcus has charted renegotiations of the auto/bios slash in British life writing. Studies of working-class life writing include those by Carolyn Kay Steedman, Liz Stanley, Simon Dentith, and Regenia Gagnier, who explores the formation of working-class identity in nineteenth-century British writing.

Elsewhere across the linguistic and national borders of eastern and western Europe, there is a ferment of activity in autobiography studies of life narrative. Barbara Kosta, Katherine Goodman, Jeannine Blackwell and Susanne Zantop, and Susan E. Linville have written on narratives in Germany, particularly in autobiography and film studies. Dagmar Lorenz has written on Holocaust narratives, and Andrew Plowman on "the radical subject" of recent German autobiography. Similarly in French-speaking nations, the groundbreaking historical and theoretical studies of Jean Starobinski, Michel Beaujour, and Philippe Lejeune have been augmented by studies by Leah D. Hewitt, Michael Sheringham, and Alex Hughes. Elsewhere in Europe, autobiographical traditions have been charted by Angel G. Loureiro (for Spain), Rudolf Dekker (for Holland), and Graziella Parati (for Italy). Similarly, for Slavic-language literatures, although life narrative has been less studied and its criticism less often translated into English than that of other genres, Jane Gary Harris's edited collection, *Autobiographical Statements in Twentieth-Century Russian Literature*, is a useful starting point for studying the autobiographical acts of its major writers in the context of other cultural currents.

Writing histories of criticism in the developing world is a complex proposition, as the emergence of written literatures in the Western languages of former colonial powers is a project of recent origin. But several important studies have been published in the last decade and a half. Françoise Lionnet's *Autobiographical Voices: Race, Gender, Self-Portraiture* and *Postcolonial Representation: Women, Literature, Identity* consider the logic and forms of cultural braiding (or *métissage*) in women's writing, above all in the Francophone African and Caribbean worlds. Carole Boyce Davies's *Black Women, Writing, and Identity: Migrations of the Subject* elaborates a theory of migrant subjectivity in the diasporic writing of black women in the United States, Great Britain, and the Caribbean. Similarly Winifred Woodhull, in *Transfigurations of the Maghreb: Feminism, Decolonization, and Literatures in France*, explores Francophone North African and immigrant literature as a site of nomadic subjectivity and linguistic deterritorialization more generally. And Christopher L. Miller in *Theories of Africans: Francophone Literatures and Anthropology in Africa* explores the negotiations of subjectivity in African life narratives, some fictional, which rework oral material, the idealization of the African past, and postcoloniality.

Discussions of the history of African life narrative within national or regional contexts are still relatively few, despite James Olney's early study *Tell Me Africa: An Approach to African Literature*, which called for attention to this emergent area. But studies such as Derek Attridge and Rosemary Jolly's *Writing South Africa: Literature, Apartheid, and Democracy, 1970–1995*, the work of Judith Lutge Coullie in South Africa, and essays in the special issue on African autobiography of *Research in African Literatures*, edited by Patricia Geesey, indicate a wide range of texts and issues worthy of further exploration. Comparative work on postcolonial writing and "out-law genres" has also been conducted transnationally by Françoise Lionnet and Ronnie Scharfman, coeditors of *Post/Colonial Conditions: Exiles, Migrations, and Nomadisms*, by Inderpal Grewal and Caren Kaplan in *Scattered Hegemonies: Postmodernity and Transnational Feminist Practices* and Grewal's *Home and Harem: Nation, Gender, Empire, and the Cultures of Travel*, and Kaplan's *Questions of Travel: Modern Discourses of Displacement*.

In the wake of Edward Said's *Culture and Imperialism*, studies in historical perspective on the formation and dissolution of Empire have attended to life narrative as an important site of cultural inscription. In South Asia critics such as Sara Suleri, in *The Rhetoric of English India*, and Nancy Paxton, in *Writing under the Raj: Gender, Race, and Rape in the British Colonial Imagination, 1830–1947*, trace the complex interplay of colonial language, indigenous practice, and emergent subjectivities in India and Pakistan. Though many studies exist on the autobiographical traditions of China and Japan, few have been written in or translated into English. Among those that are available are studies by Pei-Yi Wu, Wendy Larson, C. W. Watson, Richard Bowring, and Meena Sodhi.

Finally, we note the extensive history of criticism of women's life narratives accumulated over the last twenty years. The work of Estelle Jelinek and Mary G. Mason in their 1980 essays, and of Domna C. Stanton, in her 1984 collection *The Female Autograph*, inaugurated what would become a transformative body of work. Stanton, along with Nancy K. Miller ("Writing Fictions"), proposed, through their theoretically incisive readings of women's narratives, the gendered nature of the auto-biographical pact. Subsequent critics proposed in their turn ways to understand the nature of this gendered pact, among them Sidonie Smith, Felicity A. Nussbaum, Françoise Lionnet, Susan Stanford Friedman, Shari Benstock, Jeanne Perreault, Shirley Neuman, and Julia Watson. Their work has been collected in Smith and Watson's *Women, Autobiography, Theory: A Reader*, the introduction of which gives a comprehensive history of the field. Most recently, studies of women's autobiographical writing have come from Kristi Siegel, Martha Watson, Pauline Polkey, and Carol Muske-Dukes.

Autocritique and Everyday Life Writing

The boundary between criticizing and writing life narrative has been deliberately blurred in critical practice, but it is hardly a new phenomenon. Indeed Montaigne's *Essays* repeatedly exploited this boundary in creating his self-portrait. In the 1920s and early 1930s, Walter Benjamin wrote three autobiographical narratives in Germany that in a sense reformulate the modern autobiographical act by resituating the subject's relation to history, the focus also of his theoretical essays. Gerhard Richter characterizes Benjamin's narratives as "archaeological montage" (47) and notes that they "offer an experience of singularity and transgression in which the history of the self is inseparable from the history of its culture" (33). Only recently, however, have we begun to think of the criticism of life narrative as centrally implicated in its practice. In the United States a few writers have consistently defined their writing practice as "autocritique." In an essay such as "Crows Written on the Poplars: Autocritical Autobiographies," Chippewa mixed-blood writer Gerald Vizenor composes an autocritical collage by interweaving citations from scholars of autobiography with his own critique of their limited understanding of hybridized identity and his extended narrative of growing up as that intersects with his memoir of violently killing a squirrel.

In *This Bridge Called My Back*, and their narratives, *Loving in the War Years* and *Borderlands/La Frontera*, Cherríe Moraga and Gloria Anzaldúa, respectively, perform autocritical writing as a practice of mestiza identity, so that the polarity of critical and creative writing, like those of the English and Spanish languages, formal speech and dialect, Mexican and American identities, and hetero- and homosexuality, is fractured into hybrid writing. bell hooks has, over many books, made autocritique an enabling form for illuminating analytical observations about contemporary culture through examples drawn from her life. In *Bone Black: Memories of Girlhood*, she similarly uses critical concepts to interrogate the implicit norms of writing autobiography. As noted above, Nancy K. Miller, as both an eminent critic and a practitioner of autobiographical writing, has incorporated a musing, reflective narrative voice even into review essays on autobiography. Conversely, she interweaves a relational autobiographical narrative such as *Bequest and Betrayal* (on the deaths of her parents) with conceptual insights drawn from her study of the tropes and discourses of self-narrative.

H. Aram Veeser's anthology, *Confessions of the Critics: North American Critics' Autobiographical Moves*, captures the critical turn in the 1990s to personal modes of engagement with experiences inside and outside the academy. Other critics have analyzed and problematized this turn to the personal, among them Suzanne Fleischman and Herman Rapaport. Rapaport notes that, among academic practitioners of autobiographical writing as personal criticism, widely varying critical assumptions inform their work, assumptions about "situatedness, interpellation, typification, group identity, the sharability of experience, and the banality of every-day life" (49) among others.

Taking the form of autocritique to perhaps its fullest realization, Manthia Diawara, in both cinematic and written forms, interweaves critical discourse and life narrative. In *In Search of Africa* he alternates critical chapters on African American and African autobiographical writers such as Richard Wright, chapters framed as Sartrean "situations," and a travel narrative of return to his West African home after several decades in search of both a childhood friend and the prospect of a new Pan-African consciousness. In *The Country of My Skull*, South African writer Antjie Krog blends her report of testimonies from the South African Truth and Reconciliation Committee with critical essays from her perspective as journalist on the process and a personal narrative of her family's experiences of the apartheid state. In placing testimonies, analysis, and memoir side by side, Krog composes an autocritical collage in which political and personal discourses interrogate one another.

The criticism of everyday lives has been conducted by scholars and researchers from many disciplines investigating how individuals tell their life stories by borrowing from and inventing upon models of life narratives that are culturally available to them. In Great Britain the Mass-Observation project, founded by sociologist Charles Madge, anthropologist Tom Harrisson, and documentary filmmaker Humphrey Jennings in 1937, has made an extended—and still ongoing—study of the lives of ordinary people. Cultural and social historians access its archive of life stories in order to explore the multiple histories of twentieth-century Britain embedded in personal narratives. Psychologist Jerome Bruner's "Life as Narrative" is a key essay for understanding how the terms and tropes of the "life" are constitutive of the life lived in the world, and vice versa. Sociologist Ken Plummer, in *Telling Sexual Stories*, investigates how the narrators of a wide range of such stories—of abuse, incest, and rape, and HIV/AIDS narratives—negotiate cultural injunctions against telling, and how the shapes of their stories both respond to, and intervene in, the conditions of everyday life. And in *Getting a Life:*

Everyday Uses of Autobiography, Sidonie Smith and Julia Watson present a collection of essays by cultural critics on sites and occasions for which people tell, indeed often are required to tell, stories of themselves couched within the disciplinary frameworks of the institutions of public and familial life: the health history at the doctor's office (Kay K. Cook), the academic curriculum vitae (Martin A. Danahay, "Professional Subjects"), the Alcoholics Anonymous meeting (Robyn R. Warhol and Helena Michie), the television talk show (Janice Peck), or where they may strategically "forget" their identity, as in the police station (William Chaloupka).

Increasingly, scholars are turning their attention to the ways in which life stories, and life storytelling, are involved in campaigns for human rights, claims of citizenship, and disputes over property. We see this as an exciting and promising approach to the study of everyday lives. Studies of the everyday exchange of stories in civic life might explore, for instance, how life narratives may be seen as a form of personal property that can be revoked by the state. A recent U.S. District Court decision in California is a fascinating case in point. In that decision, motel handyman Cary Stayner, a convicted murderer, was sentenced to life in prison without parole, rather than the death penalty, with one provision: He must take his story of the crime to the grave to spare the victim's family any further media attention (Hanley, A-10). That is, publication of his life story was treated as part of his personal rights, subject to being legally revoked in extreme circumstances. Historically, struggles over who has rights to the use of other forms of life narratives, such as ex-slave narratives and women saints' chronicles, suggests that the ownership of one's story is less an intrinsic right and more a site of contestation than we might imagine, especially for those whose status as citizens had been either denied or revoked under law. These contemporary and historical sites of contestation suggest how complex the relationship of rights and personal narratives is, and thus how productive an area of inquiry.

The genres of autobiographical criticism discussed here are only a few of the kinds of life writing currently being produced that expand the boundaries and challenge the norms delineated by Misch and constructed in the second-wave work of Gusdorf, Hart, Weintraub, and others. They suggest how the reading of life narratives as autobiographical acts has produced a flexible and vibrant body of critical work.

The Uses of Life Narrative for Writing and Reflection: How-To's and Pedagogy

While most of this book addresses critical frameworks for reading life narrative, we want to take note of the current widespread interest in such writing. The proliferation of workshops and seminars on "writing your memoir" and the recent flood of "how-to" books attest to the growing audience for advice on shaping the memoir one has been incubating all one's life.

Of course, people read other people's narratives as prods to self-understanding, self-improvement, and self-healing. Therapists often have their clients read a life narrative as a spur to expansive self-reflection, such as Marie Cardinal's *The Words to Say It* or Hannah Green's *I Never Promised You a Rose Garden* or Barbara Gordon's *I'm Dancing as Fast as I Can*. Such narratives both model and elicit personal narratives from clients unused to putting fragments of their life experience into story form. Similarly, spiritual confessors have long urged the spiritually troubled to seek counsel by reading life narratives. Spiritual seekers turn to the struggles in the "dark night of the soul" of Teresa of Avila and John of the Cross or, in the twentieth century, Thomas Merton's *The Seven-Storey Mountain*. Or they turn to the spiritual quests for meaningful lives through social action in the autobiographies of Thomas Dooley and Dorothy Day, the rediscovery of the spiritual in Dan Wakefield's *Returning: A Spiritual Journey*, or the hybrid spiritual/sport story of basketball coach Phil Jackson, *Sacred Hoops: Spiritual Lessons of a Hardwood Warrior*. Such narratives, whether as guides to therapeutic self reflection or as spiritual counsel, direct readers to voice interiority and reconstruct their stories of questing, questioning, discovery, and renewed life, perhaps through journaling.

For such reasons how-to seminars have become popular both for those trying to discern the shape and "passages" of their life stories and those hoping to cash in on the memoir boom. Guides to writing life narrative line the "Biography" shelves of bookstores as consumers in increasing numbers join groups or spend leisure time searching for their origins and stories. How-to's offer instructions for stirring the creative juices, getting started, dealing with writer's block and crisis moments, and finding sources.

What do how-to books offer, and what larger uses might they have for teaching autobiography in the academy? While we have informally surveyed only a handful of the how-to's in books and on websites, certain methods and themes emerge, among them the following:

- The Franklin-esque motive: studying and writing one's life is useful, practically and morally, and an exercise in democratic citizenship.
- The legacy motive: writing one's life is a gift of love and memory passed on to one's posterity, although it can also threaten family harmony because of the explosiveness of "secrets."
- The psychology of discovery motive: writing one's life is a self-authorizing and empowering "journey," "dance," or encounter.

Along with thematizing motivations for writing one's narrative, "how-to" guides catalog methods for producing the story. Among the many techniques for stirring the voices for memory are journaling (Progoff), diary keeping, rereading past letters, family albums, and interviewing family members and childhood friends. Then, too, how-to's often suggest linear chronologies or kinds of topical organization for sorting and grouping the past particulars of life experience. In *The Autobiography Box: A Step-by-Step Kit for Examining the Life Worth Living*, Brian Bouldrey literally offers an owner's manual for assembling one's life narrative. This boxed set consists of four sets of cards to prompt specific ways of accomplishing the life narrator's tasks: to remember, discover, dramatize, and structure one's ordinary experience into an organized narrative that can take its place alongside published works of the memoir boom. Typically, the guides pay less attention to audience, since they presume their readers are writing private memoirs. Some guides, such as Bill Roorbach's *Writing Life Stories*, aimed at students and budding professional writers, discuss markets for memoir manuscripts in journals and publishing houses.

As Lejeune has observed for France, many memoirs of ordinary citizens are published by vanity presses ("Autobiography of Those Who Do Not Write," 220–23). Nor are such publications necessarily trivial or inconsequential. The collaborative memoir of Mary Ellicott Arnold and Mabel Reed, entitled *In the Land of the Grasshopper Song: A Story of Two Girls in Indian Country in 1908–1909*, is a case in point. First composed in rural California while the two women were teaching nonassimilated Native Americans in the Siskiyou Mountains, and compiled in the early 1940s, *Grasshopper Song* was published by Vantage Press in 1957, and then "discovered" by National Public Radio in the 1990s as a rich collaborative life narrative. Unquestionably, many personal narratives with larger cultural and historical consequences remain to be "discovered," or compiled from the diaries of ancestors, as Suzanne Bunkers suggests, or interwoven with familial stories, as Janet Campbell Hale and Norma Elia Cantú have done.

What are the implications for pedagogy of using everyday life narrative? Writing life narrative is now much practiced in composition courses, as a practice for encouraging and authorizing student writers and exploring alternative modes of critical investigation. And, as we know, composition courses underwent a pedagogical revolution when life narrative was introduced to rethink the norms of the critical essay and composition theory itself, as Linda Brodkey has argued. In literature courses exercises in writing life narrative have encouraged students to become more sensitive, sophisticated, and patient readers of others' and their own personal narratives. In courses in such fields as ethnic studies and women's studies, the study of personal narratives or ethnographies of relatives serves a larger purpose of valorizing the lives of ordinary, often marginalized subjects.

A new generation of critic/theorists of autobiographical acts and practices has turned to the educational and political uses of autobiographical narrating, particularly autobiographical narrating in the academy. Cynthia G. Franklin has studied narratives that construct communities of identity in various political contexts, including the classroom. Discreetly writing herself into her critiques of the "exclusionary logic and divisiveness of existing (identities)," she practices a personalized scholarship without recourse to personal criticism.

And in her recent study of sites of the autobiographical on college campuses, Wendy Hesford has explored how extensively autobiographical practices are engaged in college settings to legitimate students. Noting how struggles over identity-based discourses fuel a range of debates in and out of the classroom, Hesford observes: "Autobiography is not an unequivocally empowering medium, but it does have the pedagogical potential of initiating critical reflexivity about self-positioning" (95). Hesford's metatextual process asks students to reflect on multiple constructions of difference in their own writing. In this way they move toward a multicultural literacy that makes them critically aware of their own self-positionings (59–60).

Conclusion

Of course, this brief review of autobiography criticism of the last half century is itself a critical fiction made from a welter of individual theories. As Spengemann reminds us, there has been no such unilinear progression "from facticity, to psychology, to textuality" (16). Multiple approaches to life narrative coexist in a productive ferment. The proliferation of autobiographical texts, subjects, modes, and acts generates new reading strategies and new scholarly projects. And so critics and theorists will continue to turn their attention to many kinds of life narratives long considered marginal and excluded from the canon of autobiography, even as they rethink canonical texts. Such work in redefining the contexts of narrative may lead us to regard life narratives as rhetorical acts situated in the history of specific communities. Understanding the constitutive processes of autobiographical subjectivity and the components of any particular autobiographical act—those occasions, sites, autobiographical "I"s, others, addressees, structuring modes of self-inquiry, patterns of emplotment, media, and audiences—in turn complicate and enrich the way we understand the stories we read and the way we tell stories about ourselves.

CHAPTER 7

A Tool Kit:
Twenty Strategies for Reading
Life Narratives

You pick up a memoir in your local bookstore that looks interesting and read the opening page. Or you're asked to read a well-known auto-biography for a college course or exam. Or you come upon a personal narrative in an archive you're perusing for a history project. Or you find yourself a captive listener at a family gathering during which people regale one another with stories of the past.

Given the complexity of autobiographical acts that we have charted in chapters 2 and 3, what kind of questions might you ask as you become immersed in these autobiographical narratives? *How exactly might you read them?*

In this chapter we present you with a "tool kit" for approaching and engaging autobiographical or self-referential texts. The sets of questions in twenty categories offer entering points and strategies for addressing the burgeoning array of life narratives available to us today. They might also generate points of departure for writing your own autobiographical narrative.

Authorship and the Historical Moment
What kinds of historical knowledge can be brought to bear when read-ing a life narrative?

First, there is the history of the cultural meaning of "authorship." What did it mean to be an "author" at *the historical moment* in which the narrative was *written, published, and circulated?* We know, for instance, that the notion of authorship changed radically when copyright became a legal requirement in the early nineteenth century. The legal concept of copyright implies that people hold a proprietary interest in their own stories. This new relationship to the personal story is radically different from earlier relationships. When a medieval mystic such as Margery Kempe dictated her narrative to an amanuensis, she didn't understand herself as an "author" with ownership rights in her story. She was, rather, a Christian supplicant before God and his earthly authorities.

Second, we might ask what cultural meanings a narrative acquired when it was written or published. Were there religious, juridical, political, and/or other cultural institutions invested in particular kinds of life narratives at this historical moment? Another way to think about these historical questions is to ask what kind of investments people have had in their own personal narratives and in other people's personal narratives. Why might it have been important to narrate to oneself a personal story, or to make it public? Who else might have had an investment in this particular story or in this kind of story?

Third, we might also ask how larger historical and cultural conjunctions and shifts bear upon the composing and publication of a particular narrative; that is, how did the narrative transform history? For instance, narratives by indigenous Australians of the "Stolen Generation" have been crucial to the reconsideration of the history of state policies through which Aboriginal children were "stolen" from their families and communities in order to enforce assimilationist priorities.

Finally, we can historicize present practices by asking what kinds of narratives get published today. That is, who gets published and why? What political, social, cultural, linguistic, and economic forces affect publication and international circulation today?

The History of Reading Publics

The *reading public* is not a static entity but a collectivity with sharply differing competencies, interests, and needs. We may ask: Who made up the reading public or consumers of the life narrative at the time it was written? Who might have heard the story recounted? Who would have been literate and what would the cultural meaning of literacy have been? Think of the reading public in expansive terms. Who would have purchased or borrowed the book? Who heard the story as it circulated by word of mouth? What roles might groups such as clubs, libraries, or talk shows have played in the circulation of the narrative? What evidence is available about the kinds of books people were reading at this time or what the author was reading while writing? Or, if there is little evidence about the text, are there other books or kinds of books you might hypothesize that the writer was reading? These can be difficult questions to answer because of the kind of research required; but they can yield fascinating discoveries.

Books with an extended printing history may suggest changing cultural responses to a narrative that materialize in different editions. The captivity narrative of Mary Rowlandson, for example, originally published in 1682, has a long history of editions, spanning over three hundred years. Comparing several editions of a text such as the Rowlandson narrative may reveal changes in text, illustrations, the preface, and the afterword. In looking at the history of publication, you might ask the following questions. What differences are noticeable in successive editions of the narrative—changes in book size, typeface, use of illustrations, design, quality of paper, cover page, exact title, and so on? Have there been changes in the content or the addition of introductions, prefaces, appendixes? How has the narrative been edited at the micro- or macro-level? Who issued the various editions? Where were they published? What historical factors might account for these changes? What distinguishes the different historical moments of the multiple editions? Can you discern shifting audiences for, and cultural uses of, life narrative through the history of this book? Finally, how did this narrative come into your hands? Where might it go after leaving your hands?

The Autobiographical "I"

How may you distinguish among the historical, narrating, narrated, and ideological "I"s of the text? (See chapter 3.) What is the position of the *historical person writing the autobiography* within her cultural world? For instance, is she an outsider, a prominent figure, an immigrant or someone in exile, a child? If an outsider, what kind of outsider is she? What kinds of difference are significant to her identity in terms of gender, racial or ethnic identity, class, sexuality, occupation, legal status (e.g., criminal, slave, captive)?

How would you describe the *narrating "I"*? What kind of tone comes through the narrative voice? Is it defensive, ironic, romantic, self-important, self-critical, transgressive? What kind of story does the narrator seek to tell about himself? How would you describe the gap between the narrating "I" or narrator and the narrated "I"? Is the *narrated "I"* in the text a less sophisticated figure than the narrator? What kind of attention does the narrator pay to the younger, or more naive or successful, persona or version of himself? Are there multiple narrated "I"s?

There are also important questions about the historical notion of personhood and the meaning of lives at the time of writing—that is, the *ideological notion of the "I"* affecting the self-narrator. How do changing notions of "I"-ness or personhood affect the self-narrative you are reading and interpreting? How is the life cycle understood? The relationship of an individual to the collectivity? The relationship of an individual to history and time? What kinds of public roles seem important and privileged?

Identity

What *models of identity* were culturally available to the narrator at her particular historical moment? What models of identity are used (recall the distinction between the person writing, the narrator, and the narrated "I") to represent the subject? What are the features or characteristics of the models of identity included in this self-representation? What qualities or experiences seem to have been excluded in conforming to particular models of identity? Are there several identities in succession or alternation within the narrative text?

How does the narrator negotiate fictions of identity and resistances to the constraints of a given identity in presenting her- or himself as a gendered subject, or a racialized subject, or an ethnic subject? Does one difference dominate or structure the narrative at all times? Or is there a multiplication of identities? Where do you find evidence of conflicting models of identity at work in the text? What's the significance of these contradictions and conflicts? Does the narrator seem to be aware of the conflicts? If identity is seen as conflictual, is this thematized in the narrative? If the narrator identifies himself as having multiply marked identities, what holds these differences in some kind of dynamic tension? How can we productively, rather than reductively, describe this multiplicity of identities?

Narrative Plotting and Modes

What *narrative plottings or patterns* are used to structure the self-narrative? Think about the pattern of action and ask yourself: is its generic pattern that of the Bildungsroman, a story of development in the social world? A confessional self examination? A coming to artistic self-consciousness? A story of conversion through fall and enlightenment? A story of individual self-making? A call to action? A narrative of the individual's realization that she is embedded in a larger collective? Are there multiple plottings in the text or does one pattern dominate? Where are the shifts in plotting? And what are the effects of those shifts? How does the narrative begin? How does it conclude?

What are the histories of the narrative plottings identified? That is, why are or were they available to the self-narrator? Where, culturally and historically, do the narratives employed come from? Which narratives come from the dominant culture and which from alternative or diverse cultural sources? Consider the social locations of these stories— schools, religious faiths, political beliefs and practices, family history, work or apprenticeship, cultural stereotypes. Does the life narrative resemble and become recognizable through other kinds of writing current at the time (novels, journalism, letters)?

Consider carefully the relationship between narrative plotting and models of identity. For example, a narrative of the self-made man requires a plotting that takes the narrative subject first through an apprenticeship and then through successive stages of public accomplishment and validation.

Think as well about ways in which the possibilities of life story-telling are drawn from and may incorporate a variety of fixed forms and media into the plotting. What forms, or organizing principles, are employed—for instance, lyric poem, fable, letter, essay, meditation, or testimony? Are visual images such as photographs and illustrations embedded in the narrative to tell the story and involve the reader? What are the effects of these images? What possibilities and constraints do each of these forms enable or disable? The fable, for instance, allows the individual "I" to be understood as an allegorical type of human aspiration. The meditation turns the attention away from what an "I" has done in the world and toward the meaning of a precise moment in a larger spiritual history of the individual. The photo at once gives flesh to the narrator, embodying her for the reader, and creates a phantom narrator, thereby dematerializing her.

Temporality

Can you identify the time of the telling, that is, the narrative moment? At what stage in his life does the narrator compose the text? Publish it? Does the narrator speak directly about the act of telling his story, that is, does he *situate the moment* of its telling? Does the narrator tell the story at one fixed moment, or are there two or more moments of telling? What characterizes these moments of telling? How are they different from or similar to one another? How do narrative tone and narrative intention shift with the shifts in historical moments or times in the narrator's life cycle? If the narrator has written or voiced a series of autobiographical texts, are the same events and life experiences narrated from successive, perhaps conflicting, perspectives? Or are successive stages of the life chronicled?

It may be helpful to contrast the time of writing with the time-span of the narrative. Consider, for instance, how the times of past, present, and future are organized in the telling of the story: Does the narrative relate a continuous chronology from birth to adolescence to adulthood? Or does the narrative begin "in the middle" and use flash-backs and flash-forwards? How much concern is there for organizing the narrative through chronology? If the narrative is discontinuous or if it skips over long periods of time, what effects do these gaps have on the story produced? Why might the narrator have played with or manipulated chronological or historical time in these ways?

Audience and Addressee

An autobiographical narrative may address *multiple audiences*. Is there a person or persons to whom this text is explicitly addressed, perhaps in the dedication, or at a crucial moment in the narrative? Why might the narrator explicitly name and address a specific reader? Is there an implicit audience addressed? What kind of general reader does the text seem to be addressing? Another way of framing this question is to ask, what kind of reader does the text ask you to be? For instance, are you posited as a sympathetic and forgiving reader, a celebrity maker, a secret sharer or friend, a confessor or therapist, a student? Where does the text instruct you to be that kind of reader? Are there instructions for reading encoded in a preface or embedded in the narrative?

Coherence and Closure

Consider what claims the narrating "I" makes to a coherent story. Does the narrator explicitly assert the coherence of his or her story? Are there moments when that *impression of narrative coherence* breaks down in the text? Consider digressions, omissions, contradictions, gaps, and silences about certain things. How does noting this silence or gap affect your reading of the narrative of the historical person? How does a gap affect your understanding of the kind of "I" the narrator wants to project? Consider as well where multiple and conflicting voices emerge in the narrative (see "Voice" later in this chapter). How do you account for a proliferation of voices at some points? What happens to them?

You might also look at the narrative's *closure*. In life narrative the narrative, by definition, concludes prior to the death of the historical person; none of us can narrate beyond the end of our lives or know the shape of that end in advance. Does the ending seem to bring the narrative to a tidy closure and, if so, how? Does it seem to be a permanent closure? What alternative possibilities for closure might other threads of the narrative suggest?

Memory

Distinctions can be made about the kinds and *meanings of remembering*. What acts of remembering are emphasized? And what times of remembering—childhood? courting? "firsts"? What triggers remembering in general, and particular memories? What feelings seem to permeate various kinds of memories in the text? Does the narrator always remember what he seeks to? Or does the narrator call attention to things forgotten, times irretrievable? Does the narrator make the very act of remembering a significant theme within the narrative? That is, how self-reflexive is the narrator about the problem of remembering?

What means of accessing memory are incorporated in the text? What are the sources of remembering? Are they personal (dreams, family albums, photos, objects, family stories, genealogy)? Are they public (documents, historical events, collective rituals)? Try to identify and distinguish sources of memory in the text. What is the relationship of personal to public forms of remembrance in the narrative? If one or the other predominates, how is it related to the life narrative's audiences and purposes?

Trauma and Scriptotherapy

Does the narrative engage issues involved in *traumatic or obsessive memory* to find ways of telling about events and sufferings that defy language and understanding? Does the narrator struggle to find words to speak the unspeakable? Are those traumatic memories of a personal and/or political sort? Consider how the narrator deals with trauma and the resultant obsessional memory. Does it come to the fore fragmentarily, repeatedly, throughout the narrative? Does it seem to be, indeed can it be, resolved in any way? What kind of understanding seems to be achieved?

Does the narrator discuss the therapeutic effects of writing in the text? Is the therapeutic value of writing itself a major theme? Does the process of writing seem to have changed the narrating "I" and the life story itself? Does the act of reading a narrative of trauma have therapeutic effects on the reader? Where and in what ways does the narrator offer the reader a possibility of community in identifying with the narrator? Where and in what ways does the narrator ask the reader to see his/her own identity differently?

Evidence

How does the narrator win the reader's belief, and seek to have the "truth" of the narrative validated? What *kinds of evidence* does the narrator incorporate into her text to persuade the reader of the narrative's claims to truth? How does the narrator authenticate certain truth claims or justify writing and publicizing a personal story? What kinds of authority does that evidence carry? That of personal memory? Dreams? Religious visitations? The testimony of others? What about "objective" evidence, such as photos and documents? References to historical events or places? The authority of other narratives? Note when particular kinds of evidence are introduced into the text. Why and with what effects might evidence from an authority be placed strategically at one point, and not another?

Try to be attentive to your responses to the narrating "I"'s bids for your attention. Is your trust in this story or the storyteller ever undermined? And how does that occur? Are there statements or ellipses in the text that conflict with other parts of the narrative, causing you to doubt it? What's at stake for the narrator in persuading you of the truth of his story? What's at stake historically (in the larger society) in having this text accepted as a "truthful" account of a life? What difference would it make to learn that the narrative is a fabrication?

Authority and Authenticity

We expect particular kinds of stories to be told by those who have a direct and personal knowledge of that experience. We also have notions about whose life is important, whose life might be of interest to a broader public, and what experiences "count" as significant. In these expectations we imply a set of questions to raise about life narratives.

Does the narrator address the issue of *authority and authenticity*, that is, the "right" to speak this story, directly in the narrative? Does the narrator seem to be troubled by the act of telling the story? How does the narrator assert, or imply, or enact the authority to tell her story? And what about the transgressive aspects of public exposure? How does the narrator normalize or moderate them? Does she have recourse to an authority figure who introduces the text or is prominently cited in the text as a source of authorization? Does the narrator incorporate the biography of an authorizing figure into her text? At what points in the narrative must the narrating "I" reassert itself? How is it reasserted? By the end of the narrative, has the telling seemed to authorize the teller?

Voice

While there is one narrator, the *voices of the narrator* may be many. Consider whether there seems to be one voice dominating the narrative or multiple and conflicting voices. That is, is the text monovocal or polyvocal? If one voice dominates throughout the narrative, where and how do other voices emerge? How does the narrating "I" contain or curtail them? If there are multiple voices, when do they emerge and when disappear? Why? Is there a blending or an unresolved tension of voices in the narrative? Is a relationship posited between the individual narrator's voice and the collective voice of some larger political community? What values and discourses are identified with that larger collectivity? Is more than one group or collectivity invoked in the text, each with distinct values and languages? What form does that incorporation take? For instance, reported dialogue or explicit memories?

Consider also how voice itself is thematized. Does the narrator explicitly call attention to issues of voice in the text? Are speech and/or silence thematized? What happens at the end of the narrative to multiple voices? Is there a closure to these multiple voices?

Experience

How and when is an appeal to the authority of *experience* made in the text? Is that appeal to authority gendered? Is it made on the basis of sexual, or ethnic, or racial, or religious, or national identity claims? Are there any indications that the narrator doubts what claims can be made, based on the authority of experience?

Can you identify passages in the text where the narrator reflects upon the very act of "reading" his own past? Or upon the interpretive schema he brings to bear on that experience? Does the narrator critique his ability to understand the experiences of the past at any points in the text?

Do the different interpretations of an experience in narratives written at different times by the same person signal stages of, or changes in, the overall pattern and beliefs of the autobiographical story? Do the changes from one text to a "sequel" signal that the interpretation of experience is specific to a particular historical moment? Do such changes signal a shift in thinking about the narrator's belief system, or the nature of memory, or a cultural shift in the stories tellable at that historical moment?

The narrator is not the only one engaged in interpreting what constitutes experience. We as readers are also historically embedded, our understanding of what counts as experience historically situated. How does your historical situation as a reader affect the legibility or readability of experience in the text?

Body and Embodiment

Several questions can be posed of a life narrative that bring *embodiment* into focus. Precisely when and where does the body become visible in the narrative? Which part, or functions, or feelings of the body? How does it become visible? What does that visibility mean? How are the narrator's body and its visibility tied to the community from which the narrator comes? In other words, how is the life of the real person outside the text affected by the visibility of his body?

What cultural meanings are attached to the narrator's body outside the text? Do particular bodily processes take on significance? Does the body, or parts of it, vanish from the narrative at some point? Are there bodies other than the narrator's that the narrator encounters, or labels, or acts upon, or assigns meaning to in the course of the narrative? Is the body fetishized, that is, is it ritualized and eroticized? Is the body a locus of desire, or an impediment to the circulation of desire? What's the relationship between the material body of a narrating "I" and the body politic? How is the body represented as a site of sensuality and emotion? As a site of knowledge and knowledge-production? As a site of labor, disease, disability? Does writing the life narrative seem to have a therapeutic function?

Agency

People tell stories of their lives through the cultural scripts available to them, and they are governed by cultural strictures about self-presentation in public. Given these constraints, how do people change the narratives or write back to the cultural stories that have scripted them as particular kinds of subjects? How is this "writing back," this changing of the terms of one's representation, a strategy for *gaining agency*? Do you find passages in the text where the narrator seems to be reproducing certain cultural scripts of identity? Do you find passages where the narrator seems to be contradicting or interrupting cultural scripts of identity? Is the narrator self-conscious about reproducing or interrupting cultural scripts?

Similarly, how do narrators negotiate strictures about telling certain kinds of stories? How, for instance, do particular women write around cultural strictures about female duty, virtue, and modesty when they are engaged in the act of telling their life stories for publication? How do postcolonial subjects write back to the empire that formerly colonized them as less than human, as childlike? That is, are there strategic means of writing through the narratives that have been used to fix colonial subjects toward a new or revised narrative of possibility? Are the tropes and formulas for individualizing an "I" associated with the colonizer's domination? Can the stories of empire be re-formed (or deformed)? Do such narrators speak in multiple voices, employ diverse strategies, or alternate among several audiences as they negotiate their story of de/colonization? What language or languages does the narrator use to tell her story? Is the political significance of language thematized in the text?

Relationality

What others inhabit the text? Is there a significant other posited in the text through whom, to whom, or about whom the life narrative is narrated? Who or what is that other—a family member, friend, mentor, lover, or even a divine force? To what extent is the knowledge of that relation made apparent to the reader? Do we hear the voices of this other (or these others) explicitly in the text, or implicitly? When do the voices of the other emerge? What kind of investment does the narrator seem to have in this someone or something and how does that investment affect the interpretation that the narrator makes of the life? What is the impact of this *relationality* upon your understanding of the rhetorical "I" or the narrator's subjectivity?

Knowledge and Self-knowledge

It is helpful to delineate processes or methods of *knowledge production*. Consider whether the narrative takes up a formal self-interrogation, for example, a formal "examination of conscience." Does the narrator have a method for interpreting dreams or particular experiences? Does the narrative give space to multiple kinds of knowledge—intuitive, irrational, supernatural, mystical, symbolic? How does the narrative interrogate cultural forms of knowledge valued at the historical moment of writing? What relationship does the narrating "I" make between knowledge of the world or of others and self-knowledge? Does the narrative itself generate alternative sources of knowledge? Does the act of narrating his life bring the autobiographical narrator to different ways of knowing that life? What kind of knowledge could the reading of the life narrative produce for readers?

Collaborative Autobiography

While readers cannot resolve either the psychodynamics or the politics of collaborative life writing, several questions arise about the *terms of collaboration*. Is the narrative a product of more than one person? What kind of collaborative involvement has there been? Is this an "as-told-to" or ghostwritten narrative? Has there been an editor, a transcriber, an amanuensis, or an interviewer involved in the project? What role has each person played in the making of the narrative, and what are your sources for knowing this? Who is presented as speaking in the narrative? To put it another way, who says "I," whose voice do you hear in the narrative? How has the editor or transcriber made her presence felt in the narrative, or, on the contrary, tried to efface her role in producing the narrative? Is there a preface, framing story, or notes that attend to the relationship between narrator/informant and editor/collaborator within the text? Does the plotting or presentational format of the narrative indicate problems or inequities in the collaborative relationship? What are the differences between the narrator and the editor or amanuensis? And what's at stake politically in those differences? Who has benefited socially or financially from the telling of the story?

Ethics

The ethical issues of writing life narrative are many; that is, real consequences upon the writer's or other people's lives may ensue from publishing a narrative and from reading it. Are there revelations in the narrative that might be hurtful or embarrassing to living people—the writer's family, friends, colleagues—or that might compromise other people's reputations? Where does the narrator signal that something he has divulged is potentially compromising or transgressive? What justifications does the narrator give for publicizing such intimate and potentially compromising details of personal life or the lives of others? What are the cultural conventions at the historical moment of writing that set established limits to self-revelation? What purposes or motives might the narrating "I" have in violating those norms?

There is also an ethics of readership. As readers, we may feel uneasy about reading narratives of radical suffering, difference, or self-disclosure. What is ethically involved, for the reader, in engaging, for example, a narrative of profound suffering? How is your own ethical sense differently addressed in such a life narrative than it would be in, say, a novel? What difference is there in the kind of story that is told? In your assessment of the narrator?

Conclusion

This "tool kit" of questions may seem daunting. We have purposely multiplied the questions that you can ask of any life narrative. Probably few texts would sustain examination through all of these topics; and certainly, some questions are better suited to some texts or some readers. But if you habitually read in terms of, say, reader response, you may find it illuminating to take up the question of embodiment or of agency in narrative. In the multiple plottings, separate voices, divergent memories, and diverse audiences that even apparently uncomplicated life narratives invite, there is a world of identities and stories to engage.

Appendixes

A. Fifty-two Genres of Life Narrative

B. Group and Classroom Projects

C. Internet Resources

D. Journals

Fifty-two Genres of Life Narrative

As autobiographical narrators write their stories, they assign meaning to events, behaviors, and psychological processes that differ widely over time, place, belief system, and social position. As subjects of historically and culturally specific understandings of memory, experience, identity, embodiment, and agency, they both reproduce the various ways in which they have been culturally read and critique the limits of those cultural modes of self-narrating. Through reading their lives within and against the terms of life narrative, they shift those terms and invite different ways of being read. That is, autobiographical subjects register, consciously and unconsciously, their complicity with and resistance to the terms of cultural self-locating they inherit. In the contexts of those tensions they give shape to alternative modes of address, each with its own defining characteristics. Established generic modes mutate and new generic possibilities emerge.

While it is impossible to comprehensively survey the numerous autobiographical modes produced over centuries, this appendix offers a glossary of selected genres of life narrative, with brief definitions of their features. Many of these genres are discussed more extensively in the preceding chapters.

Apology. A form of self-presentation as self-defense against the allegations or attacks of others, an apology justifies one's own deeds, beliefs, and way of life. Typically, the formal genre of the apology admits wrong-doing or expresses regret primarily to excuse its speaker. The mode is famously employed by Socrates in Plato's *Apology* and by Montaigne in the "Apology for Raimond Sebond." Apology is both a genre in itself and, as Francis Hart notes, a major stance of self-presentation in personal narratives, and often in the autobiographical writings of statesmen. Former Secretary of Defense Robert S. McNamara, for instance, writes a justification of his positions and role during the Vietnam War in his 1995 *In Retrospect*. Women writing in the mode of apology often mount a defense of women's intellectual and moral equality, as do Mary Wollstonecraft in *A Vindication of the Rights of Women* and Sor Juana Inés de la Cruz in *The Response*.

Autobiographics. Leigh Gilmore proposed the term *autobiographics* to suggest how many women's life narratives transgress received genre norms. She defines autobiographics as "those changing elements of the contradictory discourses and practices of truth and identity" and explores how the autobiographical is constituted in a wide range of women's personal narratives (*Autobiographics*, 13).

Auto/biography, or a/b. This acronym signals the interrelatedness of autobiographical narrative and biography. Although the slash marks their fluid boundary, they are in several senses different, even opposed, forms (see chapter 1). The term also designates a mode of the autobiographical that inserts biography/ies within an autobiography, or the converse, a personal narrative within a biography. Older instances of this form include Margaret Cavendish's biography of her husband to which she appended her own brief autobiographical narrative. More recent instances include John Edgar Wideman's *Brothers and Keepers*, in which Wideman's biographical narrative of his imprisoned brother is entwined with his own memory of growing up in the harsh urban environment of Pittsburgh. While earlier forms tended to distinguish biography from autobiography, contemporary writers often intermix biographical and autobiographical narrating into a "relational" story. (See *Relational autobiography*.)

Autobiography in the second person. In this style of address the narrating "I" puts the narrated "I" in the second person as "you" and conflates or confounds that "you" with the reader, though it is also understood as the subject talking to her- or himself. For example, in *Patterns of Childhood,* Christa Wolf often uses the second person to address both her childhood memories and those of Germans during the Hitler years. In *Wasted,* Marya Hornbacher shifts into "you" to insist on her reader's identification with her descent into the dark night of the anorexic's self-erasure, personalizing the generalized pattern of the anorexic's struggle with her diminishing body and absorbing hungers.

Autobiography in the third person. Yet another style of address, here the narrating "I" refers to the narrated "I" in the third person as he or she. Philippe Lejeune characterizes this as a situation in which one narrator pretends to be two. Another way to describe this style is to understand the "I" as an implied narrator ventriloquating the "he" or "she." But why have recourse to autobiography in the third person? Jean Starobinski suggests that "though seemingly a modest form, autobiographical narrative in the third person accumulates and makes compatible events glorifying the hero who refuses to speak in his own name" (77). In this style, the narrator seems to take on "the impersonal role of historian" (77), presenting the protagonist in the third person. But the covert identification of the author and third-person pronoun belies this apparent objectivity. And, as the third-person self-presentation of Henry Adams in *The Education of Henry Adams* suggests, the role of an apparent self-historian may be ironic and self-deprecating, rather than heroic.

Autoethnography. In the autoethnographic mode of life narrative, according to Mary Louise Pratt, "colonized subjects undertake to represent themselves in ways that engage with the colonizer's own terms" (*Imperial Eyes,* 7). Pratt argues that indigenous or oppressed subjects, in taking up writing, may both collaborate with and appropriate a colonizer's (or dominant culture's) discursive models, thereby "transculturating" them into indigenous idioms and producing hybrid forms of collectivized life narrative. Autoethnography emphasizes "how subjects are constituted in and by their relations to each other" in "the contact zone" of cultural encounter (7), and how the identities of dominant and subordinated subjects interlock and interact despite histories of radically uneven power relations. The concept of autoethnography is related to such terms as "auto-anthropology," defined by Marilyn Strathern as "anthropology carried out in the social context which produced it" and "self ethnographic texts" as defined by David Hayano. These and other related concepts, such as the "native ethnography," the study of one's own group, and "ethnographic autobiography," a life narrative of ethnographic interest, are discussed in detail by Deborah Reed-Danahay (1–9).

Autofiction. This is the French term for autobiographical fiction, or fictional narrative in the first-person mode. Ultimately, the attempt to distinguish "autobiography" from "autobiographical fiction" may, as Paul Jay argues, be "pointless" (16) "for if by 'fictional' we mean 'made up,' 'created,' or 'imagined'—something, that is, which is literary and not 'real'—then we have merely defined the ontological status of any text, autobiographical or not" (16). Despite the difficulty of fixing the boundary between fiction and autobiography, the reader comes to an autobiographical text with the expectation that the protagonist is a person living in the experiential world, not a fictional character, and that the narrative will be a transparent, truthful view of that world. But, as the autofiction of Roland Barthes in *Roland Barthes by Roland Barthes* (1975) and others in France in the 1970s suggests, no definitive truth about the past self may be available. The referential "real" assumed to be "outside" a text cannot be written; the subject is inescapably an unstable fiction; and the autobiography-fiction boundary remains illusory. While autobiographical storytelling employs fictional tactics and genres, however, autofiction uses textual markers that signal a deliberate, often ironic, interplay between the two modes.

Autography. Jeanne Perreault used this term to characterize the instability of both the "I" and the category "woman" in feminist narratives.

"In autography," she suggests, "I find a writing whose affect is to bring into being a 'self' that the writer names 'I,' but whose parameters and boundaries resist the monadic" (2). That is, in autobiography the collective "we" of feminist communities is seen as constitutive of a written "I" in continuous interplay with that community. Autography is also used by H. Porter Abbott to characterize the ways in which Samuel Beckett interweaves first-person voices and issues of self-reference into his fictional narratives.

Autogynography. Domna C. Stanton's influential essay, "Autogynography: Is the Subject Different?," proposed this term to suggest the centrality of gendered subjectivity to the literary production of self-referential acts. Although Stanton offers a postmodern critique of the unexamined belief in referentiality, she argues that the textuality of the psychic splitting of woman's subjectivity must be located in her "different status in the symbolic order." And she concludes that women's "gendered narrative involved a different plotting and configuration of the split subject" (16). Stanton notes that, at the moment of second-wave feminism in which she was writing, "the gender of the author" "did make a difference" because the refusal of the referential status of the signature threatened to perpetuate "female anonymity" (18–19).

Autopathography. G. Thomas Couser first used this term to characterize personal narratives about illness or disability that contest cultural discourses stigmatizing the writer as abnormal, aberrant, or in some sense pathological. Couser has suggested that such narratives be seen, instead, as "antipathological" because "in my experience the impulse to write a first-person illness narrative is often the impulse to depathologize one's condition" (Couser, correspondence). The term *autopathography,* however, remains useful to distinguish first-person illness narratives from those told by another, in the third person. Its focus is typically not on the medical condition or details of treatment. Rather, it critiques social constructions of the disabled body and incorporates a counternarrative of survival and empowerment that reclaims the individual's or a loved one's body from the social stigmatization and the impersonalization of medical discourse. (See also Anne Hunsaker Hawkins on pathography.)

Autothanatography. This term has recently been applied to autobiographical texts that confront illness and death by performing a life at a limit of its own, or another's, undoing. Nancy K. Miller suggests that "autobiography—identity through alterity—is also writing against death twice: the other's and one's own." For Miller, in a sense "every autobiography, we might say, is also an autothanatography," since the prospect of nonexistence looms inescapably ("Representing Others," 12). Susanna Egan, in an extended treatment of autothanatography, focuses on how the attention of recent life narrators to issues of terminal illness "intensifies the rendition of lived experience, the immediacy of crisis, and the revealing processes of self-understanding" in the process of dying (*Mirror Talk*, 200). AIDS-related autothanatography, Egan notes, confronts death head on: "Death writing becomes preeminently life writing, and a bid to take charge of how that life writing is read" (207). It is "part of a complex claiming of agency" that attempts to connect the organic to the symbolic (208). At the zero-degree of both life and autobiography, with the death of the writing, or visual, or filmic life narrator, "the subject becomes an object entirely exposed to being read, entirely dependent on its reader for constructions of meaning" (212). Indeed, the narrative may be completed by another after the subject's death, as was Tom Joslin's film *Silverlake Life: The View from Here* (214). Egan suggests that even in monologic autothanatographies, such as Audre Lorde's *The Cancer Journals* and *a burst of light*, the text is dialogic, the voice polyphonic, in integrating the anticipation of death into living (215). Making a record of living in a text that outlives the life, autothanatographies intensively "focus on illness, pain, and imminent death as crucial to the processes of that life" (224).

Autotopography. This term was coined by Jennifer A. Gonzáles to define how a person's integral objects become, over time, so imprinted with the "psychic body" that they serve as autobiographical objects. The personal objects may be serviceable, such as clothing or furniture; but they may also be physical extensions of the mind—photographs, heirlooms, souvenirs, icons, and so forth: "These personal objects can be seen to form a syntagmatic array of physical signs in a spatial representation of identity" (133). Organized into collections, such material memory landscapes might be as elaborate as a home altar or as informal as a display of memorabilia. Autotopographies are invested with multiple and shifting associative meanings; they are idiosyncratic and flexible, although their materiality prevents free-floating signification (144). The autotopography may act either as a revelation or as a kind of screen memory to aid the forgetting of a traumatic moment. An autotopography can also be a space of utopian identification and mythic history, idealizing the subjectivity that is recreated through the material evidence of artifacts (145). Finally, an autotopography may be thought of as a "countersite" to both resist and converse with mass-media images. It draws from life events and cultural identity to build a self-representation as a material and tactical act of personal reflection (147).

Bildungsroman. Traditionally the Bildungsroman has been regarded as the novel of development and social formation of a young man, as in Dickens's *Great Expectations.* This "apprenticeship novel," argues C. Hugh Holman, "recounts the youth and young manhood of a sensitive protagonist who is attempting to learn the nature of the world, discover its meaning and pattern, and acquire a philosophy of life and 'the art of living'" (31). The plot of development may involve escape from a repressive family, schooling, and a journey into the wide world of urban life where encounters with a series of mentors, romantic involvements, and entrepreneurial ventures lead the protagonist to reevaluate assumptions. The Bildungsroman culminates in the acceptance of one's constrained social role in the bourgeois social order, usually requiring the renunciation of some ideal or passion and the embrace of heteronormative social arrangements.

And yet the form of the Bildungsroman has been taken up more recently by women and other disenfranchised persons to consolidate a sense of emerging identity and an increased place in public life. The

Bildungsroman can also be used negatively as a norm of assimilation into the dominant culture that is unattainable and must be relinquished, or that produces alienation from the home community. In much women's writing, its plot of development culminates not in integration but in an awakening to gender-based limitations (see Fuderer, 1–6).

Biomythography. This term was coined by Audre Lorde to signal how the re-creation of meaning in one's life is invested in writing that renegotiates cultural invisibility. Lorde redefines life writing as a biography of the mythic self (see Raynaud, "Nutmeg Nestled Inside Its Covering of Mace"), a self she discovers in imaginatively affiliating with a mythic community of other lesbian women. In *Zami: A New Spelling of My Name*, Lorde uses the term to refer to an affiliation with her mother's place of origin and a sisterhood of lesbian friends. In *The Cancer Journals,* she exemplifies it by combining journal entries and analytical essays to reconstitute herself as an empowered Amazon, a one-breasted warrior/survivor of cancer.

Captivity narrative. An overarching term for any narrative told by someone who is, or has been, held captive by some capturing group. This category includes Indian captivity narratives, slave narratives, spiritual autobiographies, UFO stories, convent captivity stories, and narratives of seduction. Indian captivity narratives, the stories of non-Indians captured by indigenous peoples, have since the sixteenth century numbered in the thousands, many written by or about women. They were produced predominantly in what is now the United States, though some were produced in Canada and Australia and some published in languages other than English. According to Kathryn Zabelle Derounian-Stodola, "the Indian captivity narrative concerns the capture of an individual or several family members ... and its plot is most commonly resolved with the captive's escape, ransom, transculturation, or death" (xi).

Case study. This term designates a life narrative that is gathered into a dossier in order to make a diagnosis and identification of a disease or disorder.

This mode of life-reporting is often associated with Freud's extended analyses of the cases of various patients with symptoms such as hysteria and gender-identity disorder. The treatment begins with the patient's producing of a story of unhappiness and illness. The unsatisfactory nature of this first narrative usually lets the analyst "see his way about the case" (66) in gaps, hesitations, inconclusiveness, and changes in dates, times, and places. That is, the narrator/patient presents clues to another story she is unable to tell. Freud's emphasis is on making, with the patient, a new and coherent narrative that, in giving the patient possession of a past life, enables her to own her own story. Another sense of the case study is discussed in *Landscape for a Good Woman* by Carolyn Kay Steedman, who critiques its ability to embed gendered social history in the story of rural working-class British mothers (130–31).

Chronicle. A form used in classical, medieval, Renaissance, and modern times involving a first-hand account of the history of one's time, and often incorporating earlier histories. The chronicle is connected as a loosely linked series of encounters and exploits.

Collaborative life narrative. A term that indicates the production of an autobiographical text by more than one person through one of the following processes: the as-told-to narrative in which an informant tells an interviewer the story of her life; the ghostwritten narrative of a celebrity recorded, edited, and perhaps even expanded by an interviewer; a coproduced or collectively produced narrative in which individual speakers are not specified or in which one speaker is identified as representative of the group. Collaborative narratives are multiply mediated by the interviewer and editor, and often two or more parties are included in the production of the published story, particularly when translation is required. In collaborations, despite assurances of coproduction, power relations between the teller and recorder/editor are often asymmetrical, with the literarily skilled editor controlling the disposition of the informant's narrative material.

Confession. An oral or written narrative, the confession is addressed to an interlocutor who listens, judges, and has the power to absolve. Confession was originally doubly addressed, to God and to a confessor. Since Augustine's narrative, the double address of the confession has been directed to God and the human reader who needs a narrative explanation of sinfulness and redemption. As Stephen Spender argues in "Confessions and Autobiography," the penitent's "purpose is to tell the exact truth about the person whom he knows most intimately . . . himself. His only criterion is naked truth: and usually his truth is naked without being altogether true" (118). Further, he adds, "all confessions are from subject to object, from the individual to the community or creed. Even the most shamelessly revealed inner life pleads its cause before the moral system of an outer, objective life" (120). Confessional life narrative may be a record of some kind of error transformed; it may also be the narrator's attempt to reaffirm communal values or justify their absence (121). Foucault has written extensively on how confession in the West has served to discipline subjects by managing illegitimate desire and producing knowledge about sexuality (*History of Sexuality*, 58). His analysis has been productively applied to contemporary modes of the confessional such as talk shows, where people's obsessive confessing ritually enacts disorderly desires and behaviors, as well as their containment by the format of the talk show itself (see Peck).

Conversion narrative. This narrative mode is structured around a radical transformation from a faulty "before" self to an enlightened "after" self. The typical pattern involves a fall into a troubled and sensorily confused "dark night of the soul," followed by a moment of revelation, a life and death struggle, a process of reeducation, and a journey to a "new Jerusalem" or site of membership in an enlightened community of like believers. Conversion experiences as varied as those recounted in Frederick Douglass's *Narrative*, Malcolm X's *Autobiography*, John Bunyan's *The Pilgrim's Progress*, e. e. cummings' *The Enormous Room*, and Alcoholics Anonymous narratives share these paradigmatic features.

Diary. A form of periodic life writing, the diary records dailiness in accounts and observations of emotional responses. While diaries may seem incoherent or haphazard in their preoccupations, they "gather force by accretion of experience, always chronological" (Roorbach, 163). And through the force of that accretion, the diarist's voice takes on a recognizable narrative persona (Culley, *A Day at a Time*, 12). Culley also notes that unlike many oral forms of self-presentation, the self-constructions in the pages of a diary are fixed in time and space, available to the diarist for later viewing, and for comment or emendation (20). In effect, then, the diary is fragmented, revisionary, in process. The immediacy of the genre derives from the diarist's lack of foreknowledge about outcomes of the plot of his life which creates a "series of surprises to writer and reader alike" (21). Some critics distinguish diary from journal by noting that the journal tends to be more a public record and thus less intimate than the diary.

Philippe Lejeune, who does not make a distinction between the diary and the journal, regards diary writing as "an immense field, as yet largely unexplored" and "a social outcast, of no fixed theoretical address" ("Practice of the Private Journal," 202). Lejeune has devoted several books and essays to diaries in the last decade, particularly the French diaries of ordinary people, of girls in the nineteenth century, and of Anne Frank. He asserts that these studies have, in his eyes, "erased the dichotomy between journal and autobiography" (201). Lejeune observes that "the private diary is a practice ... a way of life, whose result is often obscure and does not reflect the life as an autobiographical narrative would do" (187). It has a wide range of functions and forms and may incorporate many kinds of writings, drawings, documents, and objects (191). Perhaps never truly "sincere" or secret, the diary is "motivated by a search for communication, by a will to persuasion" (192). Lejeune suggests several directions for future research: on who keeps diaries and attitudes about them; how one reads another's and one's own journal; and the rights and duties of the diarist. He also calls for the creation of a comprehensive list of journals that have been published or archived and exhibits of private diaries (198–200).

Ecobiography. We propose this term for narratives that interweave the story of a protagonist with the story of the fortunes, conditions, geography, and ecology of a region, and reflect on their connection (and perhaps its failure) as a significant feature of the writing. Terry Tempest Williams's *Refuge* is a case in point. (For explorations of ecology and narrative, see Dana Phillips on "ecocriticism, literary theory, and the truth of ecology," Lawrence Buell on "the environmental imagination," and *The Ecocritism Reader: Landmarks in Literary Ecology*, edited by Cheryll Glotfelty and Harold Fromm.)

Ethnic life narrative. A mode of autobiographical narrative, emergent in ethnic communities within or across nations, that negotiates ethnic identification around multiple pasts and "multiple, provisional axes of organization" (Sau-Ling Cynthia Wong, "Immigrant Autobiography," 160). Within this larger category critics have differentiated immigrant from exile narratives. William Boelhower, following Werner Sollors, presents a trans-ethnic schema of descent and consent through which to read immigrant narratives ("The Making of Ethnic Autobiography"). Sau-Ling Cynthia Wong, critiquing Boelhower's universal ascription of these patterns across ethnic and generational lines, suggests that such a scheme telescopes the experience of different generations into one universal pattern of transindividual ethnic subjectivity and fails to account for generational differences in the mediations of memory and "the historical particularities of various ethnic groups" (160). Narratives of exile inscribe a nomadic subject, set in motion for a variety of reasons and now inhabiting cultural borderlands, who may or may not return "home," but who necessarily negotiates cultural spaces of the in-between where "hybrid, unstable identities" are rendered palpable through the negotiation "between conflicting traditions—linguistic, social, ideological" (Woodhull, 100).

Ethnocriticism. A term proposed by Arnold Krupat for studying Native American and other indigenous cultural productions, particularly life narratives, that methodologically fuse a mixture of anthropology, history, and critical theory. Its focus, Krupat argues, is properly on the frontier, understood as a "shifting space in which two cultures encounter one another," a kind of unmappable social setting in which peoples of different identities meet, though relations in this hemisphere are inevitably within a context of dominant imperialism (*Ethnocriticism*, 4–5). Ethnocriticism "seeks to traverse rather than occupy a great variety of 'middle grounds'" in critical positions (25). Its focus on borders and boundary crossings, the "in-betweenness" of transcultural processes, is expressed in the rhetorical figure of the oxymoron as a process of meaning-making through apparent contradiction (28). Krupat argues that ethnocriticism is situated as a relativist mode of analytic discourse positioned at multiple "frontiers" of historical and cultural encounter. Unlike postmodernist theory, it pursues a form of strategic essentialism (6–8).

In a somewhat similar vein, Georges E. Sioui has proposed the term *Amerindian autohistory* as a method for enabling a process of what he terms "reverse assimilation." Scholars should study the correspondences of Amerindian and non-Amerindian sources to identify what is original in Native American culture and make Euroamerican immigrants aware of their potential "Americity" if they attend to the model offered by Native people (xxiii).

Genealogy. A method for charting family history, genealogy locates, charts, and authenticates identity by constructing a family tree of descent. Its key concept is the "pedigree" of ancestral evidence based on documents and generational history and verified through fixed protocols, such as trees and charts. Genealogical projects recover the recorded past, which they can verify as an official past. They are interested in the objective documentation of relationship, not in the subjective stories people remember. (See J. Watson, "Ordering the Family.")

Heterobiography. A term coined by Philippe Lejeune to describe collaborative or as-told-to life narratives as the inverse of what occurs in autobiography in the third person. In third-person narrative there is a narrator who pretends to be another; in heterobiography there are "two who pretend to be only one" (Lejeune, "Autobiography of Those Who Do Not Write," 264 n. 10). Lejeune also explores the concepts of "auto-ethnology" and the "ethnobiographer" in considering how they redirect the practice of life narrative away from the control of the ethnographer to informants, "those who do not write."

Journal. A form of life writing that records events and occurrences, as in Daniel Defoe's *A Journal of the Plague Year*. Some critics distinguish diary from journal by characterizing the journal as a chronicle of public record that is less intimate than the diary. Lejeune, however, does not distinguish between diary and journal, but uses the terms interchangeably. (See the "Diary" entry and Lejeune, "Practice of the Private Journal.")

Journaling. This is the practice of regular, free life writing, emphasized in the journal-writing workshops Ira Progoff has organized and written about.

Letters. A mode of directed, and dated, correspondence with a specific addressee and signatory, letters seem to be private writings, but in the late eighteenth century they began to be understood as both private correspondence expressing the inner feelings of the writing subject and as public documents to be shared within a literary circle. Bernhard Siegert argues that, at that moment, "every self thus became the subject of its own discourse a priori," and the subject was presumed to precede its representation, circulating as its property in the mail (n.p.). Letters become vehicles through which information is circulated, social roles enacted, relationships secured, often in a paradoxical mix of intimacy and formality. And they are highly stylized in terms of conventions of politeness and modes of conveying information that are implicated in ideologies of gender, ethnicity, class, and nationality. Often letters remain unpublished. But some famous correspondences, such as those of Abelard and Héloïse, Lady Mary Wortley Montagu to friends, and Hester Lynch Piozzi (Thrale) and Samuel Johnson, have been published and critically studied for their interactional modes of self-presentation.

Life writing. An overarching term used for a variety of nonfictional modes of writing that claim to engage the shaping of someone's life. The writing of one's own life is autobiographical, the writing of another's biographical; but that boundary is sometimes permeable. (See *Relational autobiography*.)

Life narrative. A term distinguishing the writing of one's own life from that of another's. (See *Relational autobiography*.) Our understanding of the acts and practices of narrating one's life, which calls into question a narrowed definition associated with what we've termed *canonical* or *traditional autobiography* in chapter 5, encompasses this broader term life narrative for the writing of one's own life.

Meditation. A prominent form of self-reflexive writing during the Protestant Reformation of the sixteenth and seventeenth centuries. According to Louis Lohr Martz, the "meditation" is a rigorous exercise in self-contemplation whose aim "is the state of devotion" (15). When the meditation is put into literary form, its emphasis is on "a process of the mind rather than a particular subject-matter" (324) as the narrator seeks "the work of special grace" (16). The history of self-reflexive meditation in nonfictional prose can be traced through Montaigne's *Essays,* Donne's sermons, Browne's "Religio Medici," Pascal's *Pensés,* Francis de Sales's *An Introduction to a Devout Life,* Teresa of Avila's *Interior Castle,* and, more recently, Thoreau's *Walden* and Yeats's *A Vision.* Poetry as well offers occasions for meditation, as in the poetry of Gerard Manley Hopkins, Emily Dickinson, Paul Valéry, Rainer Maria Rilke, Wallace Stevens, and T. S. Eliot. The meditative poem, writes Martz, "is a work that creates an interior drama of the mind; this dramatic action is usually (though not always) created by some form of self-address, in which the mind grasps firmly a problem or situation deliberately evoked by the memory, brings it forward toward the full light of consciousness, and concludes with a moment of illumination, where the speaker's self has, for a time, found an answer to its conflicts" (330). Meditative discourse is interwoven in many life narratives and is prominent in such texts as Thomas Merton's *The Seven-Storey Mountain* and Dorothy Day's *The Long Loneliness*.

Memoir. A mode of life narrative that historically situates the subject in a social environment, as either observer or participant; the memoir directs attention more toward the lives and actions of others than to the narrator. Memoirs have been published in many contexts. Domestic memoirs, written as private narratives, focus on accounts of family life. Secular memoirs, written by public figures such as diplomats and soldiers, emphasize life in the public sphere, chronicling professional careers and activities of historical import. In contemporary parlance *autobiography* and *memoir* are used interchangeably. But distinctions are relevant. As Lee Quinby notes, "[W]hereas autobiography promotes an 'I' that shares with confessional discourse an assumed interiority and an ethical mandate to examine that interiority, memoirs promote an 'I' that is explicitly constituted in the reports of the utterances and proceedings of others. The 'I' or subjectivity produced in memoirs is externalized and … dialogical" ("Subject of Memoirs," 299). For Nancy K. Miller "memoir is fashionably postmodern, since it hesitates to define the boundaries between private and public, subject and object." Central for Miller is the etymological root of the word in the double act of recalling and recording: "To record means literally to call to mind, to call up from the heart. At the same time, record means to set down in writing, to make official. What resides in the province of the heart is also what is exhibited in the public space of the world" (*Bequest and Betrayal*, 43).

Oral history. In this technique for gathering a story, an interviewer listens to, records, shapes, and edits the life story of another. In oral history the one who speaks is not the one who writes, and the one who writes is often an absent presence in the text who nonetheless controls its narrative. Oral history is, then, a mediated form of personal narrative that depends on an interviewer who intervenes to collect and assemble a version of the stories that are situated and changing. Sherna Berger Gluck and Daphne

Patai, together and separately, have published oral histories and given suggestions on how to conduct them.

Otobiography. Jacques Derrida proposed this term in a lecture and discussion on Nietzsche and the politics of the proper name. In this lecture Derrida deconstructs the "problematic of the biographical within philosophy" by recuperating the signature in the discourse of Hegel, where it is apparently subordinated, and asserting its deferral in Nietzsche, where it seems writ large (56–57). Exploring "the difference in the ear," Derrida transforms *auto* into *oto*, asserting that "The ear of the other says me to me and constitutes the autos of my autobiography." That is, the autobiographical signature (the proper name) in a sense is activated on the addressee's side, in its hearing and apprehension; and further, "the structure of textuality" itself is testamentary, entrusted to the other (50–51). Nietzsche notes, of Derrida, "When he writes himself to himself, he writes himself to the other who is infinitely far away and who is supposed to send his signature back to him." His self-relation is inescapably deferred by "the necessity of this detour through the other in the form of the eternal return" (88). Finally, the autobiographical is the fort-da of self-relation, "the effect of a process of ex-appropriation which produces only perspectives, readings without truth, differences, intersections of affect, a whole 'history' whose very possibility has to be disinscribed and reinscribed" (74).

Oughtabiography. Coined by Chon Noriega, this term designates life narratives focused on all the things one should have done (personal communication). As a discourse of regret and remorse, oughtabiography is woven through many narratives—of, for example, Rousseau, Henry Adams, Robert Burton. A sustained study, however, has not yet been undertaken.

Periautography. This term is used by James Olney to mean "writing about or around the self" as one mode of life narrative he takes up in *Memory and Narrative.* He notes that the term was first used in the seventeenth century by Count Gian Artico di Porcia, who proposed that Italian scholars write their memoirs to benefit the young, a call to which Vico responded with a new mode of autobiography. Olney states, "What I like about the term 'periautography' . . . is precisely its indefinition and lack of generic rigor, its comfortably loose fit and generous adaptability" (xv).

Personal essay. A mode of writing that is literally a self-trying-out, the personal essay is a testing ("assay") of one's own intellectual, emotional, and physiological responses to a given topic. Since its development by Montaigne as a form of self-exploration engaging received wisdom, the essay has been a site of self-creation through giving one's perspective on the thoughts of others.

Poetic autobiography. A mode of the lyric distinguished, according to James Olney, not by content but by "the formal device of recapitulation and recall" ("Some Versions of Memory," 252). It may appear that all lyric poetry is life narrative in that the speaker of the lyric inscribes a subjective self as he or she explores emotions, vision, and intellectual states. We need, however, to distinguish certain kinds of lyrics that announce themselves as "autobiography" from lyric as an umbrella term for many forms of poetic self-inscription. Exploring texts he calls poetic autobiographies, such as T. S. Eliot's *Four Quartets* and Paul Valéry's *The Young Fate*, Olney argues that what characterizes the lyric as autobiography includes extended engagement with the uses of memory, "the web of reverie," and internal states of consciousness. Since the early nineteenth century, he notes, autobiography in poetry has centered on a sustained exploration of "the consciousness of consciousness" and "the growth of a poet's mind," as in, for example, Wordsworth's *The Prelude; or, Growth of a Poet's Mind.* The broader question of lyrical life narrative needs further study, but is suggested in works such as Robert Lowell's *Life Studies,* Adrienne Rich's *Diving into the Wreck,* A. R. Ammons's *Tape for the Turn of the Year,* John Ashbery's *Self-Portrait in a Convex Mirror,* and Anne Sexton's *Live or Die.*

Prison narratives. A mode of captivity narrative written during or after incarceration, writings from prison often become occasions for prisoners to inscribe themselves as fully human in the midst of a system designed to dehumanize them and to render them anonymous and passive. Additionally, H. Bruce Franklin suggests, "most current autobiographical writing from prison intends to show the readers that the author's individual experience is not unique or even extraordinary" (250). Barbara Harlow distinguishes two categories of prisoners—common law and political detainees—but insists that they cannot be sharply distinguished ("From a Woman's Prison," 457). She also suggests that these narratives emerge from political and social repression in the contemporary Third World. In the case of prisoners identifying themselves as detainees, she notes, "their personal itineraries, which have taken them through struggle, interrogation, incarceration, and, in many cases, physical torture, are attested to in their own narratives as part of a historical agenda, a collective enterprise" (455). (See also Harlow's *Barred.*) Such life narratives as Ruth First's *117 Days,* Jacobo Timerman's *Prisoner without a Name, Cell without a Number,* and Breyten Breytenbach's *The True Confessions of an Albino Terrorist* are centrally concerned with narrating the shifts in consciousness occasioned by imprisonment.

Relational autobiography. This term was proposed by Susan Stanford Friedman in 1985 to characterize the model of selfhood in women's autobiographical writing, against the autonomous individual posited by Gusdorf, as interdependent and identified with a community. Drawing on Sheila Rowbotham's historical model (in *Woman's Consciousness, Man's World*) and Carol Gilligan's psychoanalytic model (in *In a Different Voice*), Friedman argued that women's narratives assert a "sense of shared identity with other women, an aspect of identification that exists in tension with a sense of their own uniqueness" (44). And they do so across "fluid boundaries" between self and an Other or others. More recently, both Nancy K. Miller and Paul John Eakin have challenged the notion that only women's life narratives are relational by turning to Jessica Benjamin's theory that in childhood development both relational and autonomous tendencies occur and are intertwined in processes of individuation. For example, Eakin argues that "because the assertion of autonomy is dependent on this dynamic of recognition [of the intersubjectivity of identity], identity is necessarily relational" (*How Our Lives Become Stories*, 52). That is, an integrated gender identity would express what are conventionally viewed as both masculine and feminine aspects of selfhood. Smith and Watson, in *Women, Autobiography, Theory: A Reader*, discuss further ramifications of this relationality.

Scriptotherapy. A term proposed by Suzette Henke to signal the ways in which autobiographical writing functions as a mode of self-healing, scriptotherapy includes the processes of both "writing out and writing through traumatic experience in the mode of therapeutic re-enactment" (n.p.). Henke attends to several twentieth-century women's life narratives that focus on such childhood trauma as incest and abuse, which adult narrators—for example, Anaïs Nin and Sylvia Fraser—record in order to both heal themselves and reconfigure selves deformed by earlier abuse.

Self-help narrative. This genre of everyday narrative requires people to publicly tell stories of some form of addiction or dependency from which they are seeking recovery. The formulaic pattern of the self-help narrative involves a fall into dissolution and self-indulgence, alienation from a community, "hitting bottom," recognition of the need for help, renunciation of the substance or behavior, and, with trust in a higher power, recovery of a truer postaddiction self. Charlotte Linde describes how this formula reflects a "coherence system" involving "systems of assumptions about the world that speakers use to make events and evaluations coherent" (11). For instance, in Alcoholics Anonymous narratives, as Robyn R. Warhol and Helena Michie argue, "a powerful master narrative shapes the life story of each recovering alcoholic, an autobiography-in-common that comes to constitute a collective identity for sober persons" (328).

Self-portrait (in French, *autoportrait*). Primarily this term is used for an artist's painted, photographed, drawn, or printed portrait of him- or herself. But in literary studies, *self-portrait* has been used to distinguish the present-oriented from the retrospectively oriented autobiographical narrative. William L. Howarth argued that "an autobiography is a self-portrait" (85), and explored analogies between Renaissance self-portraits and autobiographies throughout Western history. But later theorists challenged this analogy between visual and written self-portraiture.

Michel Beaujour, insisting that the literary self-portrait as an act of "painting" oneself is inescapably metaphorical, not literal, defines verbal self-portraiture as "focused on the present of writing rather than the remembrance of the past and referring all things to the speaking subject and his perceptions" (340). In the self-portrait, according to Beaujour, the intent is not so much to reconstitute the subject of history in a remembered past, as to meditate upon the processes of self-writing itself. Here the narrating "I" as agent of discourse is concentrated in a present in which the self can never be fixed. Montaigne, Nietzsche, Leiris, and, for Françoise Lionnet, Zora Neale Hurston as well, could be considered self-portraitists.

In contemporary French studies, Candace Lang has argued that the literary self-portrait is not a memoir but a genre of postmodern autobiography, with Roland Barthes its best known practitioner. Lang characterizes *Roland Barthes* by Roland Barthes as a text of fragments from Barthes's previous writings, combined with fragmentary comments on those fragments (*Irony/Humor*, 165–72). Eakin notes that Barthes "explicitly disavows any connection between the 'I' of his text and any self anchored in an extratextual realm of biographical reference" (*How Our Lives Become Stories*, 137), but also insists that Barthes's seeming refusal of reference is anchored in an interpersonal discourse with his mother that "fosters the emergence of the extended self and its store of autobiographical memories" (139).

Serial autobiography. Designates an autobiographical work often published in multiple volumes (or films, videos, artworks). Although some writers may consider these as "chapters" in an ongoing life story, many significantly revise their narratives from the perspectives of different times of writing.

In such autobiographical writers as Mary McCarthy and Frederick Douglass, for example, the emphasis falls on dramatically different moments and interpretations of their significance as they publish their life narratives during youth and middle age. Seriality in relation to memory and the terms of various autobiographical genres calls for more sustained study.

Slave narrative. A mode of life narrative written by a fugitive or freed ex-slave about captivity, oppression—physical, economic, and emotional—and escape from bondage into some form of "freedom." In the United States slave narratives were usually antebellum (published before the Civil War), though the dates of enslavement differ in different nations, and some narratives are published well into the twentieth century (e.g., *The Autobiography of a Runaway Slave*, the life narrative of Esteban Montejo, enslaved in Cuba, as told to Miguel Barnet, was first published in Spanish in 1966). Frances Smith Foster notes that U.S. slave narratives were a popular form; hundreds were published, and some went through many editions and sold thousands of copies. The form has also generated a rich critical literature and been influential for the development of later African American narrative forms, as Robert B. Stepto notes in describing four modes of slave narratives—eclectic, integrated, generic, and authenticating.

Olney describes ten conventions characteristic of slave narratives, including, among others, the narrative's engraved, signed portrait; a title page asserting the narrative was written by the ex-slave; testimonials and prefatory material by white abolitionists; a beginning, "I was born"; accounts of whippings by cruel masters and mistresses and a slave's resistance to them; an account of the slave's difficulties in learning to read and write; denunciations of Christian slaveholders as the cruelest; accounts of successful effort(s) to escape; and the choice of a new last name ("'I Was Born,'" 152–53). Because the ability of ex-slaves to become literate was often contested, several narratives were denounced as inauthentic, for example, Harriet Jacobs's *Incidents in the Life of a Slave Girl* (later shown by Jean Fagan Yellin to have been authored by Jacobs under the pseudonym Linda Brent). The narratives of ex-slaves importantly challenge myths of the slave system promulgated in the plantation culture of Southern literature and history and, according to William L. Andrews, "create a composite portrait of the slave experience by blending the life story of many former slaves into a single overarching narrative pattern" (Andrews paraphrasing Nichols). Recently Samira Kawash has called for rethinking concepts of the slave narrative because the "freedom" promised in emancipation from slavery as a negation of the slave as property is interrogated in many of these narratives as incomplete, since ex-slaves were unable to claim the property rights of liberal citizen subjects (50).

Spiritual life narrative. This mode of writing traces the narrator's emerging consciousness back to "the acquisition of some sort of saving knowledge and to an awakening of an awareness within" regarding a transcendental power (Andrews, *Sisters of the Spirit*, 1). Spiritual life narrative typically unfolds as a journey through sin and damnation to a sense of spiritual fulfillment and arrival in a place of sustaining belief. Sometimes the journey motivates rededication, intensification, or clarification of spiritual beliefs and values. The pattern of conversion and its aftermath is a traditional feature of spiritual life narratives. (See *Conversion narrative.*)

Survivor narrative. This term designates narratives by survivors of traumatic, abusive, or genocidal experience. Linda Martin Alcoff and Laura Gray-Rosendale propose this term to distinguish the political utility of self-referential discourse from the more limited discourse of confession. They note that, while "survivor discourse and the tactic of speaking out may often involve a confessional mode of speech, including personal disclosure, autobiographical narrative, and the expression of feelings and emotions" (213), effective voicing of certain kinds of trauma must go beyond the confessional to acts of witnessing. The confessional mode, they suggest, focuses attention on a victim's psychological state rather than the perpetrator's act and invests power in a confessor as interpreter and judge, stripping the survivor of authority and agency (213).

Victims must be remade as survivors through acts of speaking out, telling their stories in ways that move beyond a concentration on personal feelings to testimony that critiques larger cultural forces. "What we need is not to confess, but to witness" (220).

Testimonio. The term in Spanish literally means "testimony" and connotes an act of testifying or bearing witness legally or religiously. John Beverley defines *testimonio* as "a novel or novella-length narrative in book or pamphlet ... form, told in the first person by a narrator who is also the real protagonist or witness of the events he or she recounts, and whose unit of narration is usually a 'life' or a significant life experience" ("Margin at the Center," 92–93). In testimonio, the narrator intends to communicate the situation of a group's oppression, struggle, or imprisonment, to claim some agency in the act of narrating, and to call upon readers to respond actively in judging the crisis. Its primary concern is sincerity of intention, not the text's literariness (94). And its ideological thrust is the "affirmation of the individual self in a collective mode" (97).

Trauma narrative. A mode of writing the unspeakable. Nancy Ziegenmeyer and Larkin Warren define what it means to witness in the following terms: "to speak out, to name the unnameable, to turn and face it down" (218). But speaking the unspeakable involves the narrator in a struggle with memory and its belatedness, for, as Cathy Caruth notes, "the experience of trauma ... would thus seem to consist ... in an inherent latency within the experience itself" (7–8). This latency of traumatic memory, and the way in which "to be traumatized is precisely to be possessed by an image or event," manifests itself in the psychic delay of memory's temporality and the crisis of its truth (4–5). As Caruth asserts, "the fundamental dislocation implied by all traumatic experience" lies in "both its testimony to the event and to the impossibility of its direct access" (9). Leigh Gilmore, discussing recent studies on trauma by Caruth and Felman and Laub, notes that "the subject of trauma refers to both a person struggling to make sense of an overwhelming experience in a particular context and the unspeakability of trauma itself, its resistance to representation" (*Limits of Autobiography*, 46). Observing that the Greek root of *trauma* is "wound," Gilmore stresses in the experience of trauma its self-altering or self-shattering character and the centrality of difficulties in attempting to articulate it (6).

Travel narrative. This broad term encompasses multiple forms: travelogue, travel journal, (pseudo)ethnography, adventure narrative, quest, letter home, narrative of exotic escape. Travel narratives have a long history, extending in the West back to the Greeks and Romans. Travel narratives are usually written in the first person and focus, in progress or retrospectively, on a journey. Subordinating other aspects of the writer's life, they typically chronicle or reconstruct the narrator's experience of displacement, encounter, and travail and his or her observations of the unknown, the foreign, the uncanny. In this way they become occasions for both the reimagining and the misrecognizing of identity (Bartkowski, xix), and for resituating the mobile subject in relation to home and its ideological norms.

Witnessing. As an act of being present to observe or to give testimony on something, witnessing is relevant to issues of how subjects respond to trauma. Kelly Oliver notes, "Witnessing has the double sense of testifying to something that you have seen with your own eyes and bearing witness to something that you cannot see" (18). Thus an eyewitness is judged by the accuracy of her testimony based on first-hand knowledge, while bearing witness implies a stance toward "something beyond recognition that can't be seen" (16). Oliver emphasizes that witnessing is an act addressed to another, real or imagined, with the possibility of response. The two senses of witnessing are inevitably in a tension that Oliver argues may be productive for getting beyond the repetition of trauma to a more humane, ethically informed future (17–18).

Group and Classroom Projects

We offer here ideas for classroom projects. They are meant to be suggestive, not prescriptive, and are organized in no particular way.

Do a collective investigation of websites about identity and generate a list of their characteristics. Note the proportion of visual to written text in them and the extent of hypertext organization, with an eye to generational and other differences.

Compile a website on life narratives in an area that interests you, such as a particular sport, a kind of self-help, or set of ethnic or national stories.

Visit Jennicam.com or a similar website for one week and report back on the autobiographical acts that it performs. How do you distinguish such a "real-time" site from someone simply living his or her daily life?

Find a book that compiles multiple testimonies about a particular life experience, such as Studs Terkel's *Working*, or Victoria Morris Byerly's *Hard Times Cotton Mill Girls*, or collections of sexual-abuse narratives, AIDS narratives, oral interviews, or testimonies on giving birth. What narrative strategies are employed in the narratives of this particular experience? What collective patterns emerge? What positioning do these people share that makes them a collective? What cultural work does the volume do? Is there any evidence within the narratives about how the narrators/speakers would like their narratives to be used? Can you find any information about how their narratives have been used? What role has the oral interviewer or collector played, and how do you evaluate its significance?

In a small group or a pair go to a particular place to observe how people tell stories about themselves. Examples of such sites include a recovery group, a senior citizens' group, a genealogy project. Who are the coaxers and what kinds of stories do they prompt people to tell? How do particular people narrate their stories? What group rituals organize the telling of the stories (before, during, and after)? Use the material provided by one of these sites to analyze the kinds of coaxer-teller relationships they construct and their long-term aims.

Target a particular talk show. Watch and take notes on it for a period of time. Do an analysis of the way the talk-show format structures people's telling of personal stories and the kinds of stories that are elicited and rewarded.

Gather several kinds of data forms that request autobiographical information and analyze the life narratives they call forth. Here are some examples: medical history forms, social-service client forms, applications to graduate school, résumé guidelines, job applications.

In an election year, collect and analyze the political speeches given by one or a few candidates. Make a video that shows their use of autobiographical narratives. To what uses do candidates running for office put their life stories?

Write a personal narrative of a particular part of your body as both seen from the outside and felt from the inside. Imagine yourself as that body part and speak in its "voice."

Read a life narrative of both a male sports figure and a female sports figure. Compare and contrast the kinds of stories they tell about some of the following: experiences, role models, training methods, view of physical and emotional conflict, relation to other team members, long-term goals, sense of their own bodies. Consider also to what extent gendered differences intersect differences of ethnicity, race, sexuality, or cultural location.

Watch a particular music group on a network such as MTV or Black Entertainment Network. Analyze the ways in which the group's performance and lyrics inflect its enactment of a "life" narrative.

In a discussion group, develop a set of questions to be asked in oral interviews around a particular aspect of life experience. Examples might include the following: becoming an American, being a young girl in different decades, rewards and conflicts of professional identity, familial versus regional versus national identities, being a medical patient, attitudes toward the body. Interview one or more people about this topic, then write up the oral interview. Attach to it a critique that explores the process of doing the interview and developing the essay. Try to reflect on what issues are involved in one person soliciting and editing another person's life narrative.

Write a narrative of your own childhood, then research the history of childhood at the time of your childhood. Rework your autobiographical narrative to reflect and/or critically evaluate the historical moment of its place and time.

Take a family album and find a selection of six to eight photos that seem particularly revealing of what characterizes your family. Write the narrative that the photos seem to tell. Contrast that story with your memory of particular events that were photographed. You may also want to interview one or more family members about their memories of the events—but be sure to record your own story first.

Go to a shopping mall and watch people go by for a few hours. Observe what you would call the "identity markers" that people use to communicate a story about themselves. Identity markers might include clothing, objects, hairstyles and jewelry, body markings, and body language. The size of the groups they are with may support this story, or tell another.

Similarly, go to a shopping mall, but try to listen to the stories people are telling one another as they walk by you. What kinds of stories do you hear and how would you complete one or two particular stories? Write up a narrative based on these fragments of others' stories that extends or speculates on their identities.

Using the personal ad section of your local alternative newspaper, pick out and contrast the self-presentation in several ads. Identify the autobiographical markers of each ad as aspects of an ideal person that each narrator is trying to construct. How well does each succeed in making a coherent portrait of a prospective "date"?

Write three forms of self-advertisement: your own personal ad; your job letter after graduation; and your obituary. Contrast the self-presentations in all three and discuss how their intended audiences shaped what you put in or left out.

Assemble a collective work history of your family. Or its collective educational history. Or a narrative of your family origins over three generations. What narratives about larger sociocultural forces and events does this collective history point to?

In group work brainstorm why someone would write a life narrative. What are some occasions, passages, transitions, losses, realizations, rationales, conditions that might motivate someone to write a story of her or his life?

Make a list of life narratives you've read. What famous people do you know about through their autobiographical writing? Make a list of people whose life stories you'd like to read. In what ways do life narratives introduce you to people you've never met?

Pick a historical figure who has written a life narrative and about whom one or more biographies have been written. Read the life narrative and biographies against one another and explore the different kinds of subjects represented in the two modes of life writing.

Is there a storyteller in your family on whom people rely to tell and to keep the family stories together? What are the characteristics of that person's stories? How do particular family members respond to the storyteller and to the stories told?

What memorable stories are preserved within your family? Within your community? Within your region/nation? Who is expected to tell their stories within the family, within the community, within the region/nation?

If you have seen any painted or photographed self-portraits, what makes a visual self-portrait seem different than the image made of that person by some other artist or photographer?

Look at the beginnings of three or four life narratives. Describe when and how the narrators begin their stories. Do they begin at the beginning, middle, or end of their lives? If you were to start your autobiography in some way other than "I was born," what are two or three possible points of departure?

Write an autobiographical paragraph about yourself in the third person. Then after a few hours rewrite it in the first person. Note the kinds of changes you made in it.

Take your autobiographical paragraph and recast it for three audiences:

the audience of a personal ad, readers of a college application essay, and the audience for an election speech.

Imagine for a moment what kind of story you would tell about yourself in another ten years. Write a set of notes about it. Then, at a later date, consider how it contrasts with how you now see yourself.

What books or kinds of books that you've read might provide you with models for or ways to tell a story of your life? Name and describe a few of these texts.

When you read a narrative of someone else's life or listen to someone's self-narrative, what interests you most about it? What kinds of questions do you begin to ask about the story? About the teller?

Gather three of four editions of a life narrative republished at separate historical moments. Some examples of often-published autobiographical narratives include those of Franklin, Rowlandson, Jemison, Douglass, and Twain. Analyze the way the story is "framed" and introduced in each of the republications. What physical differences are visible in the presentations? What might account for these differences?

Internet Resources

The Internet is always in flux, with new sites continually being created and old ones abandoned. To find other related sites with a search engine, try entering the key words "writing autobiography," "autobiography studies," "autobiographical studies," "life writing," "online journals," "memoirs," "diary," "ethnography," "oral history," and "life narrative."[1]

"American Life Histories: Manuscripts from the Federal Writer's Project, 1936–1940." A Library of Congress site that provides access to over 2,900 life histories collected by interviewers in the late 1930s.
http://memory.loc.gov/ammem/wpaintro/wpahome.html

"Autobiographical/Biographical Webs, by Elayne Zalis." Provides categories of links for Online Diaries/Journals, Self-Representations, Letters, Travelogs, Biographies (General, Literary), and Memorials/Tributes.
http://www.beyondwriting.com/autobio.htm

"Autopacte." A French-language site maintained by Philippe Lejeune that provides an extensive bibliography of resources relating to autobiography studies.
http://worldserver.oleane.com/autopact/

"California as I Saw It: First-Person Narratives of California's Early Years, 1849–1900." Provides access to the Library of Congress's American Memory project.
http://lcweb2.loc.gov/ammem/cbhtml/cbhome.html

Centre for Life History Research at the University of Sussex, Brighton, United Kingdom. Supports a variety of life history research and teaching activities. Includes the Mass-Observation Archive of primary sources for social, cultural, and historical research. Sponsors conferences, courses, and a Masters in Life History Research.
http://www.sussex.ac.uk/Units/clhr/

Center for Biographical Research, University of Hawai'i, Manoa. Dedicated to the interdisciplinary study of life writing, particularly biography. Sponsors teaching, scholarship, publication, and outreach activities. Publishes an annual bibliography of scholarship on auto/biography in *Biography: An International Quarterly*.
http://www.hawaii.edu/biograph

"Center for Life Stories Preservation." Links to oral history archive and personal memoirs.
http://www.storypreservation.com/links.html/memoirs.

"First-Person Narratives of the American South." Maintained by the University of North Carolina at Chapel Hill, this site focuses on diaries, autobiographies, and ex-slave narratives written by women, African Americans, enlisted men, laborers, and Native Americans.
http://metalab.unc.edu/docsouth/fpn/fpn.html

"The Fray." An anthology site, one of the oldest on the web, displaying autobiographical writing, with links to the contributors' sites.
http://www.fray.com

"The Genealogy Home Page." Provides links to many other genealogy sites on the Web.
http://www.genhomepage.com/

"My History Is America's History." A National Endowment for the Humanities project that provides resources for collecting family histories, as well as a forum to post one's own family history and read those submitted by other visitors to the site.
http://www.myhistory.org/

"The International Society for Reminiscence and Life Review." A new society with headquarters in the Gerontological Studies Program at the University of Wisconsin—Superior Extension School, its mission is "to further define and develop the interdisciplinary field of reminiscence and life review through discussion and collaboration in practice, research, and education."
http://members.aol.com/johnkunz/soc.htm

"The Mandelbrot Set." A webring for online diaries/journals, listing 35–40 well-designed and interesting sites and providing brief annotations for each.
http://www.jade-leaves.com/mandelbrot_set/sitelist.shtml

"North American Slave Narratives." Maintained by the University of North Carolina at Chapel Hill and funded by the National Endowment for the Humanities, with editorial oversight by William L. Andrews, this site provides access to "narratives of fugitive and former slaves published in broadsides, pamphlets, or book form in English up to 1920 and many of the biographies of fugitive and formaer slaves published in English before 1920."
http://docsouth.unc.edu/neh/neh.html

"Web Autobiography." A listing of sites on autobiography by Professor
    Madeleine Sorapure of the Writing Program at the University of
    California Santa Barbara.
    http://www.writing.ucsb.edu/faculty/sorapure/wa/
    webautobiography.html

List Serve

For people interested in biography, autobiography, and life narrative:
    iaba-l@hawaii.edu. This list serve is moderated by Craig Howes,
    current editor of *Biography* (now housed at the University of
    Hawai'i).

Online Journal Resources

Sites that provide advice and technical assistance for posting one's own
    journal or home page on the Internet, as well as links to the elec-
    tronic diaries posted by others.

"About.com: Personal Web Pages."
    http://personalweb.about.com/internet/personalweb/
"Dear Diary . . ." http://www.deardiary.net/
"Diaries and Journals on the Internet."
    http://www.worldimage.com/diaries/index.html
"Diarists.net." http://www.diarist.net/
"Diaryland." http://www.diaryland.com/
"Open Pages." http://www.hedgehog.net/op/

"How-To" Sites

Sites that offer, usually for a fee, services such as "how-to" manuals, writ-
    ing tips, workshops, and editing services for people who want to
    write their own memoirs.

"Association of Personal Historians." http://www.personalhistorians.org/
"The Center for Journal Therapy." http://www.journaltherapy.com/

"Center for Autobiographic Studies." http://www.storyhelp.com/
"Lifewrite." http://www.lifewrite.com/
"Turning Memories into Memoirs™: Soleil Lifestory Network."
    http://www.turningmemories.com/
"Memoir Makers." http://members.dingoblue.net.au/~memoirs/
    http://members.dingoblue.net.au/~memoirs/

APPENDIX D

Journals

a/b: Auto/Biography Studies. Published biannually. University of North Carolina Department of English, Chapel Hill, North Carolina. Contents of back issues can be accessed via the journal's home page: http://facstaff.uww.edu/hoganj/ab.htm

Auto/Biography. Bulletin of the British Sociological Association Study Group on Auto/Biography. Published biannually. School of Education, University of Exeter, Exeter, United Kingdom.

biography: An Interdisciplinary Quarterly. Published quarterly. Center for Biographical Research, University of Hawai'i, Manoa, Hawai'i. Index is available on the journal's homepage: http://www.hawaii.edu/uhpress/journals/biography

Identity: An International Journal of Theory and Research. Published quarterly starting January 2001. Society for Research on Identity Formation. Published by Lawrence Erlbaum Associates, Mahwah, New Jersey.

Other journals that regularly review studies of life narrative and publish essays in the field include *Prose Studies*, *Narrative*, and *Mosaic*. *Fourth Genre* is a creative nonfiction journal published at Michigan State University.

Notes

1. Life Narrative

1. See Olney, "Some Versions of Memory/Some Versions of Bios," for a parsing of the Greek etymology.

2. See Folkenflik (13) for a translation of this passage from Lejeune's *L'Autobiographie en France*, 14 n. 42, 241.

3. James Olney has similarly opted, in *Memory and Narrative*, for a term more inclusionary than "autobiography" in discussing the writing of Augustine, Rousseau, and Beckett. Interested now in exploring the autobiographical rather than fixing its rules and conventions, Olney employs the term *life-writing* to embrace diverse modes of the autobiographical, observing: "Although I have in the past written frequently about autobiography as a literary genre, I have never been very comfortable doing it. ... I have never met a definition of autobiography that I could really like. ... It strikes me that there has been a gradual alteration—an evolution or devolution as one may prefer—in the nature of life-writing or autobiography over the past sixteen centuries, moving from a focus on 'bios,' or the course of a lifetime, to focus on 'autos,' the self writing and being written; and this shift ... has introduced a number of narrative dilemmas requiring quite different strategies on the writers' part" (xv). We opt for "life narrative" as a similarly wide-ranging term for exploring diverse modes around the autobiographical, but one that signals the exclusion of biography from our investigations.

4. For expanded analyses of the genre of biography and its relationship to other forms of life writing, see Nadel and Backscheider.

5. Though he uses the term *autobiography* in his many studies of life narrative, Lejeune expanded the scope of autobiographical texts beyond traditional works of bourgeois subjects in the nineteenth and twentieth centuries, to include narratives by those who self-publish their life histories in France and those whose personal stories are dictated because they are not authors. See "The Autobiography of Those Who Do Not Write" and "Practice of the Private Journal."

6. Popkin also notes how history, in reconstructing the "big picture" of the past, is modified in the genre he identifies as historians' autobiographies, the life narratives of scholars becoming historians.

7. The Cretan Liar paradox is: all Cretans are liars, says Epidaurus of Crete. See Rosalie L. Colie for a history of self-referential discourse as paradox.

2. Autobiographical Subjects

1. For a genealogy of critical scholarship on memory as a key concept of new historicism, see Kerwin Lee Kline's provocative study.

2. For a discussion of postmemory, the memory of the child of survivors, see Hirsch, who notes that postmemory is distinguished from memory by generational distance and from history by deep personal connection (*Family Frames*, 22).

3. *New York Times*, October 14, 1999, A-19.

4. The hoax alleged by David Stoll in the case of *I, Rigoberta Menchú* is a more complex case of claims and counterclaims about collective testimonio of the Quiché. For a thorough discussion of issues in this ongoing debate, see Pratt, "Mad about Menchú," and Canby.

5. Kelly Oliver distinguishes between subjectivity and subject position in a book that appeared too late to be woven into this discussion. Oliver states, "Subject positions, although mobile, are constituted in our social interactions and our positions within our culture and context. They are determined by history and circumstance.... Subjectivity, on the other hand, is experienced as the sense of agency and response-ability that are constituted in the infinite encounter with otherness, which is fundamentally ethical" (17). Thus, while historical situatedness underlies subject positioning, subjectivity is psychoanalytically driven in familial relations by the subject's original separation and alienation, which some view as traumatic (65). Our experience of subjectivity, however, resides in the tension between subject position and the subjectivity that, although prior to position, is interconnected with it. For Oliver that tension is fundamental to the concept of witnessing (17).

3. Autobiographical Acts

1. This catalog of everyday situations is excerpted from our introduction to *Getting a Life* (2–3).

2. Friedman is interested in the geographics of identity as a contemporary cultural practice in this time of global capitalism. "Rhetorically speaking, geographics involves a shift from the discourses of romanticism to those of post modernity, with a stop in between for the metaphorics of early-twentieth-century modernism, whose emphasis on split selves and fragmentation looks back to the discourse of organic wholeness and forward to the discourse of spatialized flux" (*Mappings*, 19).

3. See our forthcoming collection of essays entitled *Interfaces: Women's Visual and Performance Autobiographies* for extended explorations of autobiographical practices at the intersection of visual and verbal media. Much critical investigation of self-representational practices remains to be done at this intersection of regimes of visuality and textuality.

4. Life Narrative in Historical Perspective

1. See, for example, Richard Bowring on Heian Japan; Georg Misch's discussion of Islamic scholars' autobiographies in *A History of Autobiography*, 962–1006; Tetz Rooke's and Farzaneh Milani's studies of Arab autobiography; and Erwin Panofsky's interesting discussion of tombstone epigraphs in ancient Greece.

2. Georges Gusdorf makes this assertion explicit when he states, "Autobiography becomes possible only under certain metaphysical preconditions.... The curiosity of the individual about himself, the wonder that he feels before the mystery of his own destiny is thus tied to the Copernican Revolution.... It asserts itself only in recent centuries and only on a small part of the map of the world.... The conscious awareness of the singularity of each individual life is the late product of a specific civilization" (29–31). But the assumption that writing autobiography is the mark of attaining individuality and the highest achievement of Western civilization is assumed in the work of such critics as Weintraub and Pascal as well.

3. Only part of Misch's work on autobiography in antiquity has been translated; none of the later books on the Middle Ages and the Renaissance, which were finished by his students from his notes, have been. Although there are three "volumes," each has two parts, comprising six books.

4. See Porter's discussion of "Gibbon's Autobiography: Filling Up the Silent Vacancy" in his forthcoming *Self-Same Songs: Autobiographical Reflections and Performances.*

5. Verene notes that most critics consider Rousseau the "father" of modern autobiography, though both he and Michael Sprinker argue for Vico's importance (59). Mary G. Mason finds the "egoistic secular archetype" of Rousseau's *Confessions* inappropriate as a model for women's autobiography (210).

6. Carretta, the editor of a recent edition of Equiano's narrative, claims that, based on new biographical findings, Equiano may have been born in South Carolina rather than West Africa and that the chronology he gives of his early years is contradicted by factual evidence. Carretta asks whether Olaudah Equiano was "an identity revealed, as the title of the autobiography implies, or an identity assumed by Gustavus Vassa in 1789 for rhetorical (and financial) ends?" (96). And he asserts, "There can be no doubt that Vassa manipulated some of the facts in his autobiography" (103).

7. See William L. Andrews, in *To Tell a Free Story*, for an overview of the origins and development of the genre. His "African-American Autobiography Criticism: Retrospect and Prospect" surveys the development of criticism of the slave narrative. James Olney's essay, "'I Was Born': Slave Narratives, Their Status as Autobiography and as Literature," discusses conventions of the genre. Samira Kawash critiques the notion of "freedom" attained.

8. See John Beverley on testimonio in *Against Literature*. Barbara Harlow, in *Resistance Literature*, offers a comprehensive analysis of how collective testimonial life narratives have intervened in twentieth-century political struggles around the world.

9. The contours of aging are explored by Simone de Beauvoir in *The Coming of Age* and May Sarton in several books. Women's narratives of aging have been studied by Kathleen Woodward, Barbara Frey Waxman, Ruth E. Ray, Margaret Morganroth Gullette, and others.

Appendix C. Internet Resources

1. We are indebted to Professor Madeleine Sorapure of the Writing Program at the University of California, Santa Barbara, for bringing several of the following sites to our attention.

Bibliography

Primary Works

Abbott, Jack Henry. *In the Belly of the Beast: Letters from Prison*. New York: Random House, 1981.

Abelard, Peter, and Héloïse. *The Letters of Abelard and Héloïse*. Translated by Betty Radice. Harmondsworth: Penguin, 1974.

Acker, Kathy. "The Childlike Life of the Black Tarantula by the Black Tarantula." In *Portrait of an Eye: Three Novels*, 1–90. New York: Pantheon Books, 1992.

——. *Kathy Goes to Haiti*. London: Pandora, 1990.

Adams, Henry. *The Education of Henry Adams: An Autobiography*. Boston: Houghton Mifflin, 1918.

Addams, Jane. *Twenty Years at Hull-House: With Autobiographical Notes*. New York: Macmillan, 1910.

Akhmatova, Anna. *A Poem without a Hero*. Translated by Carl R. Proffer. Ann Arbor, Mich.: Ardis, 1973.

Alexie, Sherman. *First Indian on the Moon*. Brooklyn, N.Y.: Hanging Loose Press, 1993.

Allen, Paula Gunn. "The Autobiography of a Confluence." In *I Tell You Now: Autobiographical Essays by Native American Writers*, ed. Brian Swann and Arnold Krupat, 143–54. Lincoln: University of Nebraska Press, 1987.

Ammons, A. R. *Tape for the Turn of the Year*. Ithaca, N.Y.: Cornell University Press, 1965.

Anderson, Laurie. *Stories from the Nerve Bible: A Retrospective, 1972-1992*. New York: Harper Perennial, 1994.

Andrews, William L., ed. *Sisters of the Spirit: Three Black Women's Autobiographies of the Nineteenth Century*. Bloomington: Indiana University Press, 1986.

Angela of Foligno. *Complete Works*. Translated by Paul Lachance. New York: Paulist Press, 1993.

Angelou, Maya. *The Heart of a Woman*. New York: Random House, 1981.

———. *I Know Why the Caged Bird Sings*. New York: Random House, 1969.

Antin, Mary. *The Promised Land*. Boston: Houghton Mifflin, 1912.

Antoni, Janine. *Gnaw*. London: Saatchi Collection, 1992.

Anzaldúa, Gloria. *Borderlands/La Frontera: The New Mestiza*. San Francisco: Spinsters/Aunt Lute, 1987.

Apess, William. "The Experience of Five Christian Indians of the Pequot Tribe." In *On Our Own Ground: The Complete Writings of William Apess, a Pequot*, ed. Barry O'Connell, 117–61. Amherst: University of Massachusetts Press, 1992.

———. "A Son of the Forest." In *On Our Own Ground: The Complete Writings of William Apess, a Pequot*, ed. Barry O'Connell, 1–97. Amherst: University of Massachusetts Press, 1992.

Arnold, Mary Ellicott, and Mabel Reed. *In the Land of the Grasshopper Song: A Story of Two Girls in Indian Country in 1908-1909*. New York: Vantage Press, 1957.

Ashbery, John. *Self-Portrait in a Convex Mirror*. New York: Viking Press, 1975.

Ashbridge, Elizabeth. "Some Account of the Early Life of Elizabeth Ashbridge." In *Journeys in New Worlds: Early American Women's Narratives*, ed. William L. Andrews, 147–80. Madison: University of Wisconsin Press, 1990.

Ashton-Warner, Sylvia. *Teacher*. New York: Simon and Schuster, 1963.

Augustine, Saint, Bishop of Hippo. *The Confessions of St. Augustine*. Translated by Rex Warner. New York: New American Library, 1963.

Aung San Suu Kyi. *Letters from Burma*. London: Penguin Books, 1997.

Baepler, Paul, ed. *White Slaves, African Masters: An Anthology of American Barbary Captivity Narratives*. Chicago: University of Chicago Press, 1999.

Baldwin, James. *Notes of a Native Son*. Boston: Beacon Press, 1957.

Barnes, Mary, and Joseph Berke. *Mary Barnes: Two Accounts of a Journey through Madness*. New York: Harcourt Brace, 1971.

Barnum, P. T. *The Autobiography of P. T. Barnum: Clerk, Merchant, Editor, and Showman, with His Rules for Business and Making a Fortune*. London: Ward and Lock, 1855.

Barthes, Roland. *Camera Lucida: Reflections on Photography*. Translated by Richard Howard. New York: Hill and Wang, 1981.

———. *Roland Barthes*. Translated by Richard Howard. New York: Hill and Wang, 1977.

Beauvoir, Simone de. *The Coming of Age*. Translated by Patrick O'Brian. New York: Putnam, 1972.

Behar, Ruth. *Translated Woman: Crossing the Border with Esperanza's Story*. Boston: Beacon Press, 1993.

Benjamin, Walter. *Berliner Chronik*. Frankfurt am Main: Suhrkamp Verlag 1970.

———. *Berliner Kindheit um Neunzehnhundert*. Frankfurt am Main: Suhrkamp Verlag, 1983.

———. *Gesammelte Schriften*, vol. 6. Edited by Rolf Tiedemann and Hermann Schweppenhuser. Frankfurt am Main: Suhrkamp, 1972–89.

———. *Moscow Diary*. Edited by Gary Smith, translated by Richard Sieburth. Cambridge: Harvard University Press, 1986.

Berkman, Alexander. *Prison Memoirs of an Anarchist*. New York: Mother Earth Publishing Association, 1912.

Beyala, Calixthe. *Your Name Shall Be Tanga*. Translated by Marjolijn de Jager. Oxford: Heinemann Educational Publishers, 1996.

Biko, Steve. *I Write What I Like*. Edited by Aelred Stubbs. New York: Harper and Row, 1978.

———. *Steve Biko: Black Consciousness in South Africa*. Edited by Millard Arnold. New York: Random House, 1978.

Bird, Isabella. *Collected Travel Writings of Isabella Bird*. Bristol, England: Ganesha Publications, 1997.

Black Elk. *Black Elk Speaks: Being the Life Story of a Holy Man of the Ogalala Sioux as Told to John G. Neihardt*. New York: W. Morrow and Co., 1932.

Black Hawk. *Black Hawk: An Autobiography*. Edited by Donald Jackson. Urbana: University of Illinois Press, 1964.

Bok, Edward. *The Americanization of Edward Bok: The Autobiography of a Dutch Boy Fifty Years After*. New York: Scribner's, 1922.

Bornstein, Kate. *Gender Outlaw: On Men, Women, and the Rest of Us*. New York: Routledge, 1994.

Boswell, James. *Boswell on the Grand Tour: Germany and Switzerland, 1764*. Edited by Frederick A. Pottle. London: W. Heinemann, 1953.

———. *Boswell on the Grand Tour: Italy, Corsica, and France, 1765-1766*. Edited by Frank Brady and Frederick A. Pottle. London: W. Heinemann, 1955.

Breytenbach, Breyten. *The True Confessions of an Albino Terrorist*. London: Faber and Faber, 1984.

Brodkey, Harold. *This Wild Darkness: The Story of My Death*. New York: Henry Holt, 1996.

Brontë, Charlotte. *Jane Eyre*. Edited by Margaret Smith. New York: Oxford University Press, 1998.

Browne, Thomas. "Religio Medici." In *Selected Writings*, ed. Geoffrey Keynes, 5–89. Chicago: University of Chicago Press, 1968.

Bugul, Ken (Mariétou M'baye). *The Abandoned Baobab: The Autobiography of a Senegalese Woman*. Translated by Marjolijn De Jager. Brooklyn, N.Y.: Lawrence Hill Books, 1991.

Bunyan, John. *Grace Abounding to the Chief of Sinners*. Edited by Roger Sharrock. Oxford: Clarendon Press, 1962.

——. *The Pilgrim's Progress from This World to That Which Is to Come*. Edited by James Blanton Wharey. Oxford: Clarendon Press, 1960.

Burney, Charles. *Dr. Charles Burney's Continental Travels, 1770-1772*. Edited by Cedric Howard Glover. London: Blackie and Son, 1927.

Burney, Fanny. *The Journals and Letters of Fanny Burney (Madame D'Arblay)*. Vol. 3. Edited by Joyce Hemlow. Oxford: Clarendon Press, 1973.

Burton, Robert. *Anatomy of Melancholy*. Edited by Holbrook Jackson. London: Dent, 1972.

Byerly, Victoria Morris. *Hard Times Cotton Mill Girls: Personal Histories of Womanhood and Poverty in the South*. Ithaca, N.Y.: ILR Press, 1986.

Byron, George Gordon. *Don Juan*. Edited by T. G. Steffan, E. Steffan, and W. W. Pratt. New Haven: Yale University Press, 1982.

Cahun, Claude. *Aveux non avenus*. Paris: Editions de Carrefour, 1930.

Camara, Laye. *The Dark Child*. Translated by James Kirkup and Ernest Jones. New York: Farrar, Straus and Giroux, 1954.

Cantú, Norma Elia. *Canícula: Snapshots of a Girlhood en la Frontera*. Albuquerque: University of New Mexico Press, 1995.

Cardano, Girolamo. *The Book of My Life*. Translated by Jean Stoner. New York: Dover, 1962.

Cardinal, Marie. *The Words to Say It: An Autobiographical Novel*. Cambridge, Mass.: VanVactor and Goodheart, 1983.

Carlyle, Thomas. *Sartor Resartus*. Edited by Archibald MacMechan. Boston: Ginn and Co., 1897.

Carter, Elizabeth. *Letters from Mrs. Elizabeth Carter to Mrs. Montagu Between the Years 1755 to 1800*. New York: AMS Press, 1973.

——. *A Series of Letters Between Mrs. Elizabeth Carter and Miss Catherine Talbot, from the Year 1741 to 1770*. 4 vols. London: F. C. and J. Rivington, 1809.

Casanova, Giacomo. *History of My Life*. 12 vols. Translated by Willard R. Trask. New York: Harcourt, Brace and World, 1966–71.

Casas, Bartolomé de Las. *Witness: Writings of Bartolomé de Las Casas*. Edited and translated by George Sanderlin. Maryknoll, N.Y.: Orbis Books, 1992.

Cavendish, Margaret. *The Life of William Cavendish, Duke of Newcastle, to Which is Added The True Relation of My Birth, Breeding, and Life*. 2nd ed. Edited by C. H. Firth. London: G. Routledge and Sons, 1903.

Cellini, Benvenuto. *Autobiography of Benvenuto Cellini*. Translated by George Bull. Harmondsworth: Penguin Books, 1956.

Charke, Charlotte. *A Narrative of the Life of Mrs. Charlotte Charke (Youngest Daughter of COLLEY CIBBER, Esq.), Written by HERSELF*. Edited by Leonard R. N. Ashley. Gainesville, Fla.: Scholar's Facsimiles and Reprints, 1969.

Chernin, Kim. *In My Mother's House: A Daughter's Story*. New York: Harper and Row, 1983.

Cleaver, Eldridge. *Soul on Ice*. New York: McGraw-Hill, 1968.

Cliff, Michelle. *Abeng: A Novel*. New York: Crossing Press, 1984.

Coetzee, J. M. *Boyhood: Scenes from Provincial Life*. New York: Viking, 1997.

Columbus, Christopher. *The Diario of Christopher Columbus's First Voyage to America, 1492-1493*. Translated by Oliver Dunn and James E. Kelly Jr. Norman: University of Oklahoma Press, 1991.

Condé, Maryse. *Hérémakhonon: A Novel*. Translated by Richard Philcox. Washington, D.C.: Three Continents Press, 1982.

Cortés, Hernán. *Letters from Mexico*. Edited and translated by A. R. Pagden. New York: Grossman Publishers, 1971.

Cowley, Malcolm. *Exile's Return: A Literary Odyssey of the 1920s*. New York: Viking Press, 1956.

Cummings, E. E. *The Enormous Room*. New York: Modern Library, 1934.

Dangarembga, Tsitsi. *Nervous Conditions*. London: Women's Press, 1988.

Danica, Elly. *Don't: A Woman's Word*. San Francisco: Cleis Press, 1988.

Dante Alighieri. *Dante Alighieri's Divine Comedy*. Translated by Mark Musa. Bloomington: Indiana University Press, 1971.

———. *La Vita Nuova (The New Life)*. Translated by Mark Musa. Bloomington: Indiana University Press, 1962.

Day, Dorothy. *The Long Loneliness: The Autobiography of Dorothy Day*. New York: Harper Bros., 1952.

Defoe, Daniel. *A Journal of the Plague Year*. New York: Dutton, 1966.

Delany, Mary. *Letters from Georgian Ireland: The Correspondence of Mary Delany, 1731-68*. Edited by Angélique Day. Belfast: Friar's Bush Press, 1991.

Delbo, Charlotte. *Auschwitz and After*. Translated by Rosette C. Lamont. New Haven: Yale University Press, 1995.

DeQuincey, Thomas. *Confessions of an English Opium Eater*. 1822; Oxford: Woodstock, 1989.

Derounian-Stodola, Kathryn Zabelle, ed. *Women's Indian Captivity Narratives*. New York: Penguin Books, 1998.

Descartes, René. *Discourse on the Method; and, Meditations on First Philosophy*. Edited by David Weissman. New Haven: Yale University Press, 1996.

Diawara, Manthia. *In Search of Africa*. Cambridge: Harvard University Press, 1998.

Dickens, Charles. *David Copperfield*. Edited by Nina Burgis. New York: Oxford University Press, 1981.

Dickinson, Emily. *The Poems of Emily Dickinson*. Cambridge: Belknap Press of Harvard University Press, 1999.

Dillard, Annie. *An American Childhood*. New York: Harper and Row, 1987.

Dinesen, Isak. *Out of Africa*. New York: Random House, 1938.

Donne, John. *Sermons*. New York: Meridian Books, 1958.

Dooley, Thomas A. *The Night They Burned the Mountain*. New York: Farrar, Straus and Cudahy, 1960.

Douglass, Frederick. *Life and Times of Frederick Douglass*. 1892; New York: Collier, 1962.

——. *My Bondage and My Freedom*. 1855; New York: Dover, 1969.

——. *Narrative of the Life of Frederick Douglass, an American Slave*. 1845; New York: Signet, 1968.

Du Bois, W. E. B. *The Autobiography of W.E.B. DuBois: A Soliloquy on Viewing My Life from the Last Decade of Its First Century*. New York: International Publishers, 1968.

Duras, Marguerite. *The Lover*. Translated by Barbara Bray. New York: Pantheon, 1985.

Edwards, Jonathan. "Personal Narrative." In *Selected Writing of Jonathan Edwards*, ed. Harold P. Simonson, 27–44. New York: Ungar Publishing, 1970.

Eiseley, Loren C. *The Star Thrower*. New York: Times Books, 1978.

El Saadawi, Nawal. *A Daughter of Isis: The Autobiography of Nawal El Saadawi*. Translated by Sherif Hetata. London: Zed Books, 1999.

Elaw, Zilpha. "Memoirs of the Life, Religious Experience, Ministerial Travels, and Labors of Mrs. Zilpha Elaw." In *Sisters of the Spirit*, ed. Andrews, 49–160.

Eliot, T. S. *Four Quartets*. New York: Harcourt Brace Jovanovich, 1971.

Emecheta, Buchi. *Head Above Water*. Oxford: Fontana, 1986.

Emerson, Ralph Waldo. *The Journals and Miscellaneous Notebooks of Ralph Waldo Emerson*. 16 vols. Edited by William H. Gilman et al. Cambridge: Belknap Press of Harvard University Press, 1960–82.

Equiano, Olaudah. *Equiano's Travels: His Autobiography; The Interesting Narrative of The Life of Olaudah Equiano, or Gustavus Vassa the African*. Edited by Paul Edwards. London: Heinemann, 1967.

Erasmus, Desiderius. *The Praise of Folly*. Translated by John Wilson. Ann Arbor: University of Michigan Press, 1958.

Erauso, Catalina de. *The Lieutenant Nun: Memoir of a Basque Transvestite in the New World*. Translated by Michele Stepto and Gabriel Stepto. Boston: Beacon Press, 1996.

Fanon, Frantz. *Black Skin, White Masks*. Translated by Charles Lam Markmann. New York: Grove Press, 1967.

Fanshawe, Ann, and Anne Halkett. *The Memoirs of Anne, Lady Halkett, and Ann, Lady Fanshawe*. Edited by John Loftis. New York: Oxford University Press, 1979.

First, Ruth. *117 Days*. New York: Stein and Day, 1965.

Flanagan, Bob. *Bob Flanagan: Super-Masochist*. Edited by Andrea Juno and V. Vale. San Francisco: Re/Search Publications, 1993.

Flynn, Elizabeth Gurley. *I Speak My Own Piece: Autobiography of "The Rebel Girl."* New York: Masses and Mainstream, 1955.

Foote, Julia A. "A Brand Plucked from the Fire." In *Sisters of the Spirit*, ed. Andrews, 161–234.

Fox, George. *The Journal of George Fox*. Cambridge: Cambridge University Press, 1952.

Frank, Anne. *The Diary of a Young Girl*. Translated by B. M. Mooyaart-Doubleday. Garden City, N.Y.: Doubleday, 1952.

Franklin, Benjamin. *The Autobiography of Benjamin Franklin: A Genetic Text*. Edited by J. A. Leo LeMay and P. M. Zall. Knoxville: University of Tennessee Press, 1981.

Franklin, Miles. *My Brilliant Career.* Sydney: Angus and Robertson, 1974.

Fraser, Sylvia. *My Father's House: A Memoir of Incest and Healing.* New York: Harper and Row, 1987.

Frost, Robert. *Collected Poems of Robert Frost.* New York: Henry Holt, 1930.

Fuller, Margaret. *At Home and Abroad, Or Things and Thoughts in America and Europe.* Edited by Arthur B. Fuller. Boston: Crosby, Nichols, 1856.

Gailhard, Jean. *The Compleat Gentleman, or, Directions for the Education of Youth as to Their Breeding at Home and Travelling Abroad.* London: Thomas Newcomb, 1678.

Gandhi, Mahatma K. *An Autobiography, or, The Story of My Experiments with Truth.* 2 vols. Translated by Mahadev Desai. Ahmedabad: Navajivan Publishing House, 1927–29.

Gibbon, Edward. *Memoirs of My Life.* Edited by Georges A. Bonnard. London: Nelson, 1966.

Gilman, Charlotte Perkins. *The Living of Charlotte Perkins Gilman: An Autobiography.* Madison: University of Wisconsin Press, 1990.

Ginibi, Ruby Langford. *Don't Take Your Love to Town.* Edited by Susan Hampton. New York: Penguin, 1988.

Glückel of Hameln. *The Memoirs of Glückel of Hameln.* Translated by Marvin Lowenthal. New York: Schocken Books, 1977.

Goethe, Johann Wolfgang von. *The Auto-Biography of Goethe. Truth and Poetry: From My Own Life.* Translated by John Oxemford. 2 vols. London: Bell and Daldy, 1872.

——. *The Sorrows of Young Werther and Novella.* Translated by Elizabeth Mayer, Louise Brogan, and W. H. Auden. New York: Modern Library, 1993.

——. *Wilhelm Meister's Apprenticeship.* Translated by R. Dillon Boylan. London: G. Bell and Sons, 1898.

Goldman, Emma. *Living My Life.* Edited by Richard and Anna Maria Drinnon. New York: New American Library, 1977.

Gómez-Peña, Guillermo. *A New World Order: Prophecies, Poems, and Loqueras for the End of the Century.* San Francisco: City Lights Books, 1996.

Gordon, Barbara. *I'm Dancing as Fast as I Can.* New York: Harper and Row, 1979.

Gorky, Maxim. *Autobiography of Maxim Gorky: My Childhood. In the World. My Universities.* Translated by Isidor Schneider. New York: Citadel Press, 1949.

Gornick, Vivian. *Fierce Attachments: A Memoir.* Boston: Beacon Press, 1987.

Gosse, Edmund. *Father and Son: A Study of Two Temperaments.* London: W. Heinemann, 1907.

Grealy, Lucy. *Autobiography of a Face*. Boston: Houghton Mifflin, 1994.

Green, Hannah (Joanne Greenberg). *I Never Promised You a Rose Garden*. New York: New American Library, 1964.

Günderrode, Karoline von. "Selected Letters." In *Bitter Healing: German Women Writers from 1700 to 1830, An Anthology*, ed. Jeannine Blackwell and Susanne Zantop, 417–42. Lincoln: University of Nebraska Press, 1990.

Guyon, Jeanne Marie, *Bouvier de La Motte. Madame Guyon, an Autobiography*. Chicago: Moody Press, 1990.

Hadewijch. *The Complete Works*. Translated by Columba Hart. New York: Paulist Press, 1980.

Haizlip, Shirlee Taylor. *The Sweeter the Juice: A Family Memoir in Black and White*. New York: Simon and Schuster, 1994.

Hale, Janet Campbell. *Bloodlines: Odyssey of a Native Daughter*. New York: Random House, 1993.

Halkett, Anne. *The Autobiography of Anne, Lady Halkett*. Edited by John Gough Nichols. Westminster: Camden Society, 1875.

Hamper, Ben. *Rivethead: Tales from the Assembly Line*. New York: Warner Books, 1991.

Harrison, Kathryn. *The Kiss: A Secret Life*. New York: William Morrow, 1998.

Hatoum, Mona. *Mona Hatoum*. London: Phaidon Press, 1997.

Head, Bessie. *A Question of Power*. London: Heinemann Educational, 1974.

Hemingway, Ernest. *A Movable Feast*. New York: Bantam Books, 1965.

Hildegard of Bingen. *Hildegard of Bingen: The Book of the Rewards of Life*. Translated by Bruce W. Hozeski. New York: Garland, 1994.

Hobbes, Thomas. "Considerations upon the Reputation, Loyalty, Manners, and Religion of Thomas Hobbes." In *The English works of Thomas Hobbes of Malmesbury*, ed. Sir William Molesworth. Aalen: Scientia, 1962.

hooks, bell. *Bone Black: Memories of Girlhood*. New York: Henry Holt, 1996.

Hopkins, Gerard Manley. *The Poems of Gerard Manley Hopkins*. Edited by W. H. Gardner and N. H. MacKenzie. 4th ed. London: Oxford, 1967.

Hornbacher, Marya. *Wasted: A Memoir of Anorexia and Bulimia*. New York: Harper Perennial, 1999.

Hurston, Zora Neale. *Dust Tracks on a Road: An Autobiography*. 2nd ed. Edited by Robert Hemenway. Urbana: University of Illinois Press, 1984.

Hutchinson, Lucy. *Memoirs of the Life of Colonel Hutchinson, with the Fragment of an Autobiography by Mrs. Hutchinson*. Edited by James Sutherland. London: Oxford University Press, 1973.

Ignatius of Loyola, Saint. *St. Ignatius' Own Story, As Told to Luis González de*

Cámara. Translated by William J. Young. Chicago: Loyola University Press, 1956.

Jackson, Phil. *Sacred Hoops: Spiritual Lessons of a Hardwood Warrior.* New York: Hyperion, 1995.

Jacobs, Harriet A. *Incidents in the Life of a Slave Girl: Written by Herself.* Edited by Lydia Maria Child and Jean Fagan Yellin. Cambridge: Harvard University Press, 1987.

James, Alice. *The Diary of Alice James.* 1934. Edited by Leon Edel. New York: Dodd, Mead and Co., 1964.

Jemison, Mary. *A Narrative of the Life of Mrs. Mary Jemison.* Edited by June Namias. Norman: University of Oklahoma Press, 1992.

Jesus, Carolina Maria de. *Child of the Dark: The Diary of Carolina Maria de Jesus.* Translated by David St. Clair. New York: E. P. Dutton, 1962.

Johnson, Samuel. *Johnson and Queeney: Letters from Dr. Johnson to Queeney Thrale from the Bowood Papers.* Edited by Marquis of Lansdowne. New York: Random House, 1932.

Johnson, Samuel, and Hester Lynch Piozzi. *The Letters of Samuel Johnson with Mrs. Thrale's Genuine Letters to Him.* Edited by R. W. Chapman. Oxford: Clarendon Press, 1952.

Joslin, Tom (director). *Silverlake Life: The View from Here.* 1993. Distributed by Zeitgeist Films.

Juana Inés de la Cruz, Sor. *A Sor Juana Anthology.* Translated by Alan S. Trueblood. Cambridge: Harvard University Press, 1988.

Julian of Norwich. *The Shewings of Julian of Norwich.* Edited by Georgia Ronan Crampton. Kalamazoo, Mich.: Medieval Institute Publications, 1994.

Kartini, Raden Adjeng. *Letters of a Javanese Princess.* Translated by Agnes Louise Symmers. New York: Norton, 1964.

Kaysen, Susanna. *Girl, Interrupted.* New York: Vintage Books, 1993.

Kemble, Frances Anne. *Journal of a Residence on a Georgian Plantation, 1838-1839.* Edited by John A. Scott. Athens: University of Georgia Press, 1984.

Kempe, Margery. *The Book of Margery Kempe.* Translated by B. A. Windeatt. London: Penguin, 1994.

Kempis, Thomas à. *Imitatio Christi.* Translated by Leo Sherley-Price. Harmondsworth, England: Penguin Books, 1952.

Khaldûn, Ibn. *At-Ta'rîf bi-Ibn Khaldûn wa-rihlatuhû charban wa-sharqan.* Edited by Muḥammad Tâwît aṭ-Ṭânjî. Cairo, n.p., 1370; 1951.

Kingston, Maxine Hong. *The Woman Warrior: Memoirs of a Girlhood among Ghosts*. New York: Vintage, 1976.

Kollontai, Alexandra. *The Autobiography of a Sexually Emancipated Communist Woman*. Edited by Irving Fetscher. Translated by Salvator Attanasio. New York: Schocken, 1975.

Koolmatrie, Wanda. *My Own Sweet Time*. Broome, Australia: Magabala Books, 1994.

Krog, Antjie. *The Country of My Skull*. London: Vintage, 1999.

Labé, Louise. *Louise Labé's Complete Works*. Troy, N.Y.: Whitson Publishing, 1986.

Labumore: Elsie Roughsey. *An Aboriginal Mother Tells of the Old and the New*. Edited by Paul Memmott and Robyn Horsman. Fitzroy, Victoria: McPhee Gribble, 1984.

Lafayette, Madame de [Marie-Madeleine Pioche de La Vergne]. *The Princess of Clèves*. Translated by Nancy Mitford. Harmondsworth, England: Penguin Books, 1978.

Larcom, Lucy. *A New England Girlhood*. Boston: Corinth Books, 1961.

Le Corbusier. *Quando le Cattedrali Erano Bianche*. Translated by Mario Sangiorgio. Faenza: Faenza Editrice, 1975.

Lee, Jarena. "Life and Religious Experience of Jarena Lee." In *Sisters of the Spirit*, ed. Andrews, 25–48.

Leiris, Michel. *Manhood: A Journey from Childhood Into the Fierce Order of Virility*. Translated by Richard Howard. New York: Grossman, 1963.

——. *Scraps*. Vol. 2 of *Rules of the Game*. Translated by Lydia Davis. Baltimore: John Hopkins University Press, 1997.

——. *Scratches*. Vol. 1 of *Rules of the Game*. Translated by Lydia Davis. Baltimore: Johns Hopkins University Press, 1997.

Léry, Jean de. *History of a Voyage to the Land of Brazil, Otherwise Called America*. Translated by Janet Whatley. Berkeley: University of California Press, 1990.

Levi, Primo. *Survival in Auschwitz: The Nazi Assault on Humanity*. Translated by Stuart Woolf. New York: Collier Books, 1993.

Lim, Shirley Geok-lin. *Among the White Moon Faces: An Asian-American Memoir of Homelands*. New York: Feminist Press, 1996.

Lorde, Audre. *a burst of light*. Toronto: Women's Press, 1988.

——. *The Cancer Journals*. Argyle, N.Y.: Spinsters, Inc., 1980.

——. *Zami: A New Spelling of My Name*. Trumansberg, N.Y.: The Crossing Press, 1982.

Louganis, Greg. *Breaking the Surface.* New York: Random House, 1995.

Lowell, Robert. *Life Studies.* New York: Farrar, Straus, and Cudahy, 1959.

——. *Notebook 1967-68.* New York: Farrar, Straus and Giroux, 1969.

Mairs, Nancy. *Waist-High in the World: A Life Among the Nondisabled.* Boston: Beacon Press, 1996.

Malcolm X. *The Autobiography of Malcolm X.* With the assistance of Alex Haley. New York: Grove Press, 1965.

Malraux, André. *Lazarus.* Translated by Terence Kilmartin. New York: Holt, Rinehart and Winston, 1977.

Mandela, Nelson. *No Easy Walk to Freedom: Articles, Speeches, and Trial Addresses.* London: Heinemann, 1973.

——. *The Struggle Is My Life.* New York: Pathfinder Press, 1986.

Martineau, Harriet. *Harriet Martineau's Autobiography.* Edited by Maria Weston Chapman. Boston: James R. Osgood, 1877.

Mathabane, Mark. *Kaffir Boy: The True Story of a Black Youth's Coming of Age in Apartheid South Africa.* New York: Macmillan, 1986.

McCarthy, Mary. *How I Grew.* San Diego: Harcourt, Brace, Jovanovich, 1987.

——. *Memories of a Catholic Girlhood.* New York: Harcourt, Brace, 1957.

McMichael, James. *Four Good Things.* Boston: Houghton Mifflin, 1980.

McNamara, Robert S. *In Retrospect: The Tragedy and Lessons of Vietnam.* New York: Times Books, 1995.

Menchú, Rigoberta. *I, Rigoberta Menchú: An Indian Woman in Guatemala.* Edited by Elisabeth Burgos-Debray. Translated by Ann Wright. London: Verso, 1984.

Merton, Thomas. *The Seven-Storey Mountain.* New York: Harcourt, Brace, 1948.

Mill, John Stuart. *Autobiography.* London: Longmans, Green, Reader, Dyer, 1873.

Miller, Nancy K. *Bequest and Betrayal: Memoirs of a Parent's Death.* New York: Oxford University Press, 1996.

Modjeska, Drucilla. *Poppy.* Sydney: Pan Macmillan, 1997.

Monette, Paul. *Becoming a Man: Half a Life Story.* New York: Harcourt, Brace, Jovanovich, 1992.

——. *On Borrowed Time: An AIDS Memoir.* San Diego: Harcourt, Brace, 1998.

Montagu, Lady Mary Wortley. *The Letters and Works of Lady Mary Wortley Montagu.* Edited by Lord Wharncliffe. New York: AMS Press, 1970.

Montaigne, Michel de. *The Complete Essays of Montaigne.* Translated by Donald M. Frame. Stanford, Calif.: Stanford University Press, 1958.

Montejo, Esteban. *The Autobiography of a Runaway Slave*. Edited by Miguel Barnet. Translated by Jocasta Innes. New York: Pantheon Books, 1968.

Moraga, Cherríe. *Loving in the War Years: Io que nunca pasó sus labios*. Boston: South End Press, 1983.

Moraga, Cherríe, and Gloria Anzaldúa, eds. *This Bridge Called My Back: Writings by Radical Women of Color*. New York: Kitchen Table Press, 1983.

Morgan, Sally. *My Place*. Freemantle, Aus.: Freemantle Arts Press, 1987.

Mother Jones. *The Autobiography of Mother Jones*. Edited by Mary Field Parton. Chicago: Charles H. Kerr, 1925.

Nabokov, Vladimir. *Speak, Memory: A Memoir*. Rev. ed. New York: Putnam, 1966.

Neal, John. *Wandering Recollections of a Somewhat Busy Life: An Autobiography*. Boston: Roberts Brothers, 1869.

Newman, Cardinal John Henry. *Apologia Pro Vita Sua: Being a History of His Religious Opinions*. Edited by Martin J. Svaglic. Oxford: Clarendon Press, 1967.

Nietzsche, Friedrich. *On the Genealogy of Morals and Ecce Homo*. Translated and edited by Walter Kaufmann. New York: Vintage Books, 1967.

Nin, Anaïs. *Incest: From a Journal of Love: The Unexpurgated Diary of Anaïs Nin, 1932-1934*. New York: Harcourt Brace Jovanovich, 1992.

Norris, Kathleen. *Dakota: A Spiritual Geography*. Boston: Houghton Mifflin, 1993.

Novalis (Friedrich von Hardenberg). *Heinrich von Ofterdingen*. Leipzig: Hesse and Becker, 1903.

Nugent, Thomas. *Travels Through Germany: Containing Observations on Customs, Manners, Religion, Government, Commerce, Arts, and Antiquities, with a Particular Account of the Courts of Mecklenburg in a Series of Letters to a Friend*. London: E. and C. Dilly, 1768.

Olds, Sharon. *The Father*. New York: Knopf, 1992.

Ondaatje, Michael. *Running in the Family*. New York: Norton, 1982.

Parkman, Francis. *The California and Oregon Trail: Being Sketches of Prairie and Rocky Mountain Life*. New York: T. Y. Crowell, 1901.

Pascal, Blaise. *Pensés*. Translated by A. J. Krailsheimer. Harmondsworth: Penguin, 1966.

Pepys, Samuel. *Diary and Correspondence of Samuel Pepys, Esq.* 6 vols. London: Bickers and Son, 1875-79.

Petrarch, Francis. "The Ascent of Mount Ventoux." In *Petrarch: A Humanist*

Among Princes. An Anthology of Petrarch's Letters and of Selections from His Other Works, ed. and trans. David Thompson, 27–36. New York: Harper and Row, 1971.

Pilkington, Laetitia. *Memoirs of Mrs. Laetitia Pilkington, 1712-1750, Written by Herself*. London: George Routledge and Sons, 1928.

Plato. *Apology of Socrates*. Translated by Michael C. Stokes. Warminster, England: Arris and Phillips, 1997.

———. *The Symposium*. Translated by Christopher Gill. New York: Penguin Books, 1999.

Plutarch. *Plutarch: The Lives of the Noble Grecians and Romans, the Dryden Translation*. Chicago: Encyclopdia, 1990.

Polo, Marco. *The Travels of Marco Polo, the Venetian*. Translated by William Marsden. Edited by Thomas Wright. New York: AMS Press, 1968.

Pound, Ezra. *The Cantos of Ezra Pound*. London: Faber and Faber, 1954.

Prince, Nancy. *A Narrative of the Life and Travels of Mrs. Nancy Prince*. 2nd ed. Boston: Nancy Prince, 1853.

Proust, Marcel. *The Remembrance of Things Past*. 2 vols. Translated by C. K. Scott Moncrieff. New York: Random House, 1932–34.

Pruitt, Ida. *A Daughter of Han: The Autobiography of a Chinese Working Woman*. Stanford, Calif.: Stanford University Press, 1945.

Reagan, Nancy. *My Turn: The Memoirs of Nancy Reagan*. New York: Random House, 1989.

Rich, Adrienne. *Diving into the Wreck: Poems 1971-72*. New York: Norton, 1973.

Riis, Jacob. *The Making of an American*. New York: Macmillan, 1901.

Rilke, Rainer Maria. *Duino Elegies*. Translated by David Young. New York: Norton, 1978.

———. *The Notebook of Malte Laurids Brigge*. Translated by Stephen Mitchell. New York: Limited Editions Club, 1987

Ringgold, Faith. *Dancing at the Louvre: Faith Ringgold's French Collection and Other Story Quilts*. Berkeley: University of California Press, 1998.

———. *The Change Series: Faith Ringgold's 100-Pound Weight Loss Quilt*. New York: Bernice Steinbaum Gallery, 1987.

Robinson, Mary. *Perdita: The Memoirs of Mary Robinson*. London: Chester Springs Peter Owen, 1994.

Rodman, Dennis. *Bad as I Wanna Be*. New York: Delacorte Press, 1996.

Rodriguez, Richard. *Hunger of Memory: The Education of Richard Rodriguez, an Autobiography*. Boston: D. R. Godine, 1981.

Rogers, Annie G. *A Shining Affliction: A Story of Harm and Healing in Psychotherapy*. New York: Viking, 1995.

Rousseau, Jean-Jacques. *Confessions*. Translated by Angela Scholar. New York: Oxford University Press, 2000.

Rowlandson, Mary. "A True History of the Captivity and Restoration of Mrs. Mary Rowlandson," ed. Amy Schrager Lang. In *Journeys in New Worlds*, ed. William L. Andrews et al., 27–65. Madison: University of Wisconsin Press, 1990.

Ryan, Michael. *Secret Life: An Autobiography*. New York: Pantheon Books, 1995.

Sales, Saint Francis de. *An Introduction to a Devout Life*. 1613; Ilkley, England: Scolar Press, 1976.

Sand, George [Aurore Dudevant Dupin]. *Story of My Life: The Autobiography of George Sand*. A Group Translation. Edited by Thelma Jurgrau. Albany: State University Press of New York, 1991.

Santé, Luc. *The Factory of Facts*. London: Granta, 1999.

Santiago, Esmeralda. *When I Was Puerto Rican*. New York: Vintage, 1993.

Sappho. *Poems and Fragments*. Translated by Mary Barnard. Berkeley: University of California Press, 1958.

Sarrazin, Albertine. "Journal de prison 1959." In *Le Passe-Peine: 1949-1967*, 102–68. Paris: Julliard, 1976.

Sarton, May. *At Eighty-Two: A Journal*. New York: Norton, 1996.

———. *Journal of a Solitude*. New York: Norton, 1973.

Sedaris, David. *Naked*. Boston: Little, Brown, 1997.

Sevigné, Marie de, Rabutin Chantal. *Letters of Madame de Sevigné to Her Daughter and Her Friends*. Translated by Leonard Tancock. Harmondsworth: Penguin, 1982.

Sexton, Anne. *Live or Die*. Boston: Houghton Mifflin, 1966.

Sherman, Cindy. *Cindy Sherman: Retrospective*. New York: Thames and Hudson, 1997.

Sigourney, Lydia H. *Letters of Life*. New York: D. Appleton and Co., 1866.

Silko, Leslie Marmon. *Storyteller*. New York: Seaver Books/Grove Press, 1981.

Smart-Grosvenor, Vertamae. *Vibration Cooking, or the Travel Notes of a Geechee Girl*. New York: Ballantine, 1992.

Smith, John. *The Complete Works of Captain John Smith (1580-1631)*. 3 vols. Edited by Philip L. Barbour. Chapel Hill: University of North Carolina Press, 1986.

Soyinka, Wole. *Aké: The Years of a Childhood*. New York: Random House, 1981.

Spiegelman, Art. *Maus I: A Survivor's Tale: My Father Bleeds History.* New York: Pantheon Books, 1986.

——. *Maus II: A Survivor's Tale: And Here My Troubles Began.* New York: Pantheon Books, 1991.

Staël, Madame de. *Corinne, or Italy.* Translated and edited by Sylvia Raphael. New York: Oxford University Press, 1998.

Stedman, John Gabriel. *Narrative of a Five Years' Expedition Against the Revolted Negroes of Surinam: Transcribed for the First Time from the Original 1790 Manuscript.* Edited by Richard Price and Sally Price. Baltimore: John Hopkins University Press, 1988.

Steedman, Carolyn Kay. *Landscape for a Good Woman.* New Brunswick, N.J.: Rutgers University Press, 1986.

Stein, Gertrude. *The Autobiography of Alice B. Toklas.* New York: Harcourt Brace, 1933.

——. *Everybody's Autobiography.* New York: Random House, 1937.

Stendhal [Henri Brulard]. *The Life of Henry Brulard.* Translated by Jean Stewart and B.C.J.G. Knight. New York: Noonday Press, 1958.

Stevens, Wallace. *Collected Poems.* New York: Knopf, 1954.

Strindberg, August. *The Son of a Servant.* Translated by Claud Field. New York: Putnam's Sons, 1913.

Sui Sin Far. *Mrs. Spring Fragrance and Other Writings.* Edited by Amy Ling and Annette White-Parks. Urbana: University of Illinois Press, 1995.

Sullivan, Louis H. *The Autobiography of an Idea.* New York: Dover, 1956.

Taylor, Sheila Ortiz, and Sandra Ortiz Taylor. *Imaginary Parents: A Family Autobiography.* Albuquerque: University of New Mexico Press, 1996.

Teresa of Avila, Saint. *Interior Castle.* Translated and edited by E. Allison Peers. Garden City, N.Y.: Doubleday, 1961.

——. *The Life of Teresa of Jesus: The Autobiography of St. Teresa of Avila.* Translated by E. Allison Peers. Garden City, N.Y.: Doubleday, 1960.

Terkel, Studs. *Working: People Talk about What They Do All Day and How They Feel about What They Do.* New York: New Press, 1974.

Thoreau, Henry David. *Walden.* Edited by J. Lyndon Shanley. Princeton, N.J.: Princeton University Press, 1971.

Thrale, Hester. *Thraliana; The Diary of Mrs. Hester Lynch Thrale (Later Mrs. Piozzi), 1776-1809.* 2 vols. Edited by Katharine C. Balderston. Oxford: Clarendon Press, 1942.

Timerman, Jacobo. *Prisoner Without a Name, Cell Without a Number.* Translated by Toby Talbot. New York: Knopf, 1981.

Trollope, Frances. *A Visit to Italy.* London: R. Bentley, 1842.

Twain, Mark. *Life on the Mississippi.* New York: Penguin, 1984.

Valéry, Paul. *La Jeune Parque.* Translated by Alistair Elliot. Chester Springs: Defour Editions, 1997.

Varnhagen, Rahel. "Selected Letters," trans. Katharine R. Goodman. In *Bitter Healing: German Women Writers from 1700 to 1830,* ed. Jeannine Blackwell and Susanne Zantop, 408–16. Lincoln: University of Nebraska Press, 1990.

Verghese, Abraham. *My Own Country: A Doctor's Story of a Town and Its People in the Age of AIDS.* New York: Simon and Schuster, 1994.

Vico, Giambattista. *Autobiography of Giambattista Vico.* Translated by Max Harold Fisch and Thomas Goddard Bergin. Ithaca, N.Y.: Cornell University Press, 1944.

Vizenor, Gerald. "Crows Written on the Poplars: Autocritical Autobiographies." In *I Tell You Now: Essays by Native American Writers,* ed. Brian Swann and Arnold Krupat, 99–109. Lincoln: University of Nebraska Press, 1987.

Wakefield, Dan. *Returning: A Spiritual Journey.* New York: Doubleday, 1988.

Warner-Vieyra, Myriam. *Juletane.* Translated by Betty Wilson. London: Heinemann, 1987.

Washington, Booker T. *Up from Slavery.* New York: Doubleday, 1998.

Whitman, Walt. "Song of Myself." In *Leaves of Grass.* New York: Heritage Press, 1950.

——. *Specimen Days.* Vol. 1 of *Prose Works, 1892.* Edited by Floyd Stovall. New York: New York University Press, 1963.

Wideman, John Edgar. *Brothers and Keepers.* New York: Holt, Rinehart and Winston, 1984.

Wiesel, Elie. *Night.* Translated by Stella Rodway. New York: Hill and Wang, 1960.

Wilkomirski, Binjamin. *Fragments: Memories of a Wartime Childhood.* Translated by Carol Brown Janeway. New York: Schocken Books, 1996.

Williams, Donna. *Nobody Nowhere: The Extraordinary Autobiography of an Autistic.* New York: Times Books, 1992.

Williams, Terry Tempest. *Refuge: An Unnatural History of Family and Place.* New York: Vintage Books, 1992.

Wojnarowicz, David. *Close to the Knives: A Memoir of Disintegration.* New York: Vintage Books, 1991.

Wolf, Christa. *Patterns of Childhood.* Translated by Ursula Molinaro and Hedwig Rappolt. New York: Farrar, Straus and Giroux, 1980.

Wollstonecraft, Mary. *A Short Residence in Sweden, Norway, and Denmark.* Edited by Richard Holmes. New York: Penguin, 1987.

——. *A Vindication of the Rights of Woman:* Edited by Miriam Brody. New York: Penguin Books, 1992.

Woodman, Francesca. *Francesca Woodman: Photographic Work.* Wellesley, Mass.: Wellesley College Museum, 1986.

Woolf, Virginia. *Moments of Being: Unpublished Autobiographical Writings.* Edited by Jeanne Schulkind. New York: Harcourt Brace Jovanovich, 1976.

Woolman, John. *The Journal and Major Essays of John Woolman.* Edited by Phillips P. Moulton. New York: Oxford University Press, 1971.

Wordsworth, Dorothy. *Journals of Dorothy Wordsworth.* 2 vols. Edited by Ernest De Selincourt. London: Macmillan, 1941.

Wordsworth, William. *The Prelude; or, Growth of a Poet's Mind.* Edited by Ernest De Selincourt. Oxford: Clarendon Press, 1959.

Wright, Frank Lloyd. *An Autobiography.* New York: Horizon Press, 1977.

Wright, Richard. *Black Boy (American Hunger): A Record of Childhood and Youth.* Restored ed. New York: Harper Collins, 1993.

Wurtzel, Elizabeth. *Prozac Nation: Young and Depressed in America.* Boston: Houghton Mifflin, 1994.

Yearsley, Ann. *Poems: On Several Occasions.* 4th ed. London: G.G.J. and J. Robinson, 1786.

Yeats, W. B. [William Butler]. *Autobiographies: Reveries Over Childhood and Youth and The Trembling of the Veil.* New York: Macmillan, 1927.

——. *A Vision.* London: Macmillan, 1937.

Zitkala-Ša. "Impressions of an Indian Childhood." In *Classic American Autobiographies,* ed. William L. Andrews, 414–32. New York: Mentor, 1992.

Secondary Works

Abbott, H. Porter. *Diary Fiction: Writing as Action.* Ithaca, N.Y.: Cornell University Press, 1984.

——. *The Fiction of Samuel Beckett: Form and Effect.* Berkeley: University of California Press, 1973.

Adams, Timothy Dow. *Light Writing and Life Writing: Photography in Autobiography*. Chapel Hill: University of North Carolina Press, 2000.

———. *Telling Lies in Modern American Autobiography*. Chapel Hill: University of North Carolina Press, 2000.

Alcoff, Linda Martín, and Laura Gray-Rosendale. "Survivor Discourse." In *Getting a Life*, ed. Smith and Watson, 198–225.

Althusser, Louis. *Essays on Ideology*. London: Verso, 1984.

Andrews, William L. "African-American Autobiography Criticism: Retrospect and Prospect." In *American Autobiography*, ed. Eakin, 195–215.

———. *To Tell a Free Story: The First Century of Afro-American Autobiography, 1760-1865*. Urbana: University of Illinois Press, 1986.

Appadurai, Arjun. "Disjuncture and Difference in the Global Cultural Economy." In *Colonial Discourse and Post-Colonial Theory: A Reader*, ed. Patrick Williams and Laura Chrisman, 324–39. New York: Columbia University Press, 1994.

Ashley, Kathleen, Leigh Gilmore, and Gerald Peters, eds. *Autobiography and Postmodernism*. Amherst: University of Massachusetts Press, 1994.

Attridge, Derek, and Rosemary Jolly, eds. *Writing South Africa: Literature, Apartheid, and Democracy, 1970-1995*. Cambridge: Cambridge University Press, 1998.

Backscheider, Paula R. *Reflections on Biography*. Oxford: Oxford University Press, 2001.

Baepler, Paul, ed. Introduction. In *White Slaves, African Masters: An Anthology of American Barbary Captivity Narratives*. Chicago: University of Chicago Press, 1999.

Bakhtin, M. M. [Mikhaolovich Mikhail]. *The Dialogic Imagination: Four Essays*. Edited by Michael Holquist. Translated by Caryl Emerson and Michael Holquist. Austin: University of Texas Press, 1981.

Barrett, Lindon. *Blackness and Value: Seeing Double*. New York: Cambridge University Press, 1999.

Bartkowski, Frances. *Travelers, Immigrants, Inmates: Essays in Estrangement*. Minneapolis: University of Minnesota Press, 1995.

Bataille, Gretchen, and Kathleen Mullen Sands. *American Indian Women Telling Their Lives*. Lincoln: University of Nebraska Press, 1984.

Bauman, H-Dirksen L. "'Voicing' Deaf Identity: Through the 'I's' and Ears of an Other." In *Getting a Life*, ed. Smith and Watson, 47–62.

Beaujour, Michel. *Poetics of the Literary Self-Portrait.* Translated by Yara Milos. New York: New York University Press, 1991.

Belsey, Catherine. "Constructing the Subject: Deconstructing the Text." In *Feminisms: An Anthology of Literary Theory and Criticism,* ed. Robyn R. Warhol and Diane Price Herndl, 657–73. Revised ed. New Brunswick, N.J.: Rutgers University Press, 1997.

Benstock, Shari. "Authorizing the Autobiographical." In *The Private Self: Theory and Practice of Women's Autobiographical Writings,* ed. Benstock, 10–33. Chapel Hill: University of North Carolina Press, 1988.

Bergland, Betty. "Postmodernism and the Autobiographical Subject: Reconstructing the 'Other.'" In *Autobiography and Postmodernism,* ed. Kathleen Ashley, Leigh Gilmore, and Gerald Peters, 130–66. Amherst: University of Massachusetts Press, 1994.

Beverley, John. *Against Literature.* Minneapolis: University of Minnesota Press, 1993.

——. "The Margin at the Center: On 'Testimonio' (Testimonial Narrative)." In *De/Colonizing the Subject,* ed. Smith and Watson, 91–114.

Bhabha, Homi. *The Location of Culture.* London: Rutledge, 1994.

Bjorklund, Diane. *Interpreting the Self: Two Hundred Years of American Autobiography.* Chicago: University of Chicago Press, 1998.

Blackwell, Jeannine, and Susanne Zantop, eds. *Bitter Healing: German Women Writers from 1700 to 1830: An Anthology.* Lincoln: University of Nebraska Press, 1990.

Boelhower, William. "Avant-Garde Autobiography: Deconstructing the Modern Habitat." In *Literary Anthropology: A New Interdisciplinary Approach to People, Signs, and Literature,* ed. Fernando Poyatos, 273–303. Philadelphia: Benjamins, 1988.

——. "The Making of Ethnic Autobiography in the United States." In *American Autobiography,* ed. Eakin, 123–41.

——. *Through a Glass Darkly: Ethnic Semiosis in American Literature.* New York: Oxford University Press, 1987.

Bongie, Chris. *Exotic Memories: Literature, Colonialism, and the Fin de Siècle.* Stanford: Stanford University Press, 1991.

Bottrall, Margaret. *Every Man a Phoenix: Studies in Seventeenth-Century Autobiography.* 1958; Freeport: Books for Libraries Press, 1972.

Bouldrey, Brian. *The Autobiography Box: A Step-by-Step Kit for Examining the Life Worth Living.* San Francisco: Chronicle Books, 2000.

Bowring, Richard. "The Female Hand in Heian Japan: A First Reading." In *The Female Autograph*, ed. Domna C. Stanton, 55–62. New York: New York Literary Forum, 1984.

Branch, Michael P., ed. *Reading the Earth: New Directions in the Study of Literature and Environment*. Moscow: University of Idaho Press, 1998.

Braxton, Joanne. *Black Women Writing Autobiography: A Tradition within a Tradition*. Philadelphia: Temple University Press, 1989.

Brewster, Anne. *Reading Aboriginal Women's Autobiography*. South Melbourne: Sydney University Press, 1996.

Brodkey, Linda. "Writing on the Bias." *College English* 56, no. 5 (Sept. 1994): 524–48.

Broughton, Trev Lynn. *Men of Letters, Writing Lives: Masculinity and Literary Auto/Biography in the Late-Victorian Period*. New York: Routledge, 1999.

Bruner, Jerome. "Life as Narrative." *Social Research* 54 (Spring 1987): 11–32.

Bruss, Elizabeth. *Autobiographical Acts: The Changing Situation of a Literary Genre*. Baltimore: Johns Hopkins University Press, 1976.

——. "Eye for I: Autobiography in Film." In *Autobiography*, ed. Olney, 296–320.

Buckton, Oliver S. *Secret Selves: Confession and Same-Sex Desire in Victorian Autobiography*. Chapel Hill: University of North Carolina Press, 1998.

Buell, Lawrence. "Autobiography in the American Renaissance." In *American Autobiography*, ed. Eakin, 47–69.

——. *The Environmental Imagination: Thoreau, Nature Writing, and the Formation of America*. Cambridge: Harvard University Press, 1995.

Bunkers, Suzanne. "Midwestern Diaries and Journals: What Women Were (Not) Saying in the Late 1800s." In *Studies in Autobiography*, ed. James Olney, 190–210. New York: Oxford University Press, 1988.

Bunkers, Suzanne, and Cynthia A. Huff, eds. *Inscribing the Daily: Critical Essays on Women's Diaries*. Amherst: University of Massachusetts Press, 1996.

Burr, Anna Robeson Brown. *The Autobiography: A Critical and Comparative Study*. Boston: Houghton Mifflin, 1909.

Buss, Helen M. *Mapping Ourselves: Canadian Women's Autobiography in English*. Montreal: McGill-Queen's University Press, 1993.

Butler, Judith. *Bodies That Matter: On the Discursive Limits of "Sex."* New York: Routledge, 1993.

——. *Gender Trouble: Feminism and the Subversion of Identity*. New York: Routledge, 1990.

Canby, Peter. "The Truth about Rigoberta Menchú." *New York Review of Books*, April 8, 1999, 28–33.

Carby, Hazel V. *Reconstructing Womanhood: The Emergence of the Afro-American Woman Novelist*. New York: Oxford University Press, 1987.

Carretta, Vincent. "Olaudah Equiano or Gustavus Vassa? New Light on an Eighteenth-Century Question of Identity." *Slavery and Abolition* 20, no. 3 (December 1999): 96–105.

Caruth, Cathy, ed. *Trauma: Explorations in Memory*. Baltimore: John Hopkins University Press, 1995.

Certeau, Michel de. *The Practice of Everyday Life*. Translated by Steven Rendall. Berkeley: University of California Press, 1984.

Césaire, Aimé. *Discourse on Colonialism*. Translated by Joan Pinkham. New York: Monthly Review Press, 1972.

Chaloupka, William. "(For)Getting a Life: Testimony, Identity, and Power." In *Getting a Life*, ed. Smith and Watson, 369–92.

Chambers, Ross. *Facing It: AIDS Diaries and the Death of the Author*. Ann Arbor: University of Michigan Press, 1998.

Chard, Chloe. *Pleasure and Guilt on the Grand Tour: Travel Writing and Imaginative Geography, 1600-1830*. Manchester, England: Manchester University Press, 1999.

Chen, Xiaomei. *Occidentalism: A Theory of Counter-Discourse in Post-Mao China*. New York: Oxford University Press, 1995.

Chester, Suzanne. "Writing the Subject: Exoticism/Eroticism in Marguerite Duras's *The Lover* and *The Sea Wall*." In *De/Colonizing the Subject*, ed. Smith and Watson, 436–57.

Chow, Rey. *Ethics after Idealism: Theory, Culture, Ethnicity, Reading*. Bloomington: Indiana University Press, 1998.

——. *Women and Chinese Modernity: The Politics of Reading Between West and East*. Minneapolis: University of Minnesota Press, 1991.

——. *Writing Diaspora: Tactics of Intervention in Contemporary Cultural Studies*. Bloomington: Indiana University Press, 1993.

Cockshut, A.O.J. *The Art of Autobiography in Nineteenth- and Twentieth-Century England*. New Haven: Yale University Press, 1984.

Coe, Richard. *When the Grass Was Taller: Autobiography and the Experience of Childhood*. New Haven: Yale University Press, 1984.

Colie, Rosalie L. *Paradoxia Epidemica: The Renaissance Tradition of Paradox*. Princeton: Princeton University Press, 1966.

Cook, Kay K. "Medical Identities: My DNA/Myself." In *Getting a Life*, ed. Smith and Watson, 63–88.

Coullie, Judith Lutge. "(Dis)Locating Selves: Izibongo and Narrative Autobiography in South Africa." In *Oral Literature and Performance in Southern Africa*, ed. Duncan Brown, 61–89. Oxford: Currey, 1999.

——. "The Power to Name the Real: The Politics of the Worker Testimony in South Africa." *Research in African Literatures* 28, no. 2 (Summer 1997): 132–44.

Couser, G. Thomas. *Altered Egos: Authority in American Autobiography*. New York: Oxford University Press, 1989.

——. "Black Elk Speaks with Forked Tongue." In *Studies in Autobiography*, ed. James Olney, 73–88. Oxford: Oxford University Press, 1988.

——. "Making, Taking, and Faking Lives: The Ethics of Collaborative Autobiography." Special issue. *Style on Literary Ethics* (Summer 1998): 334–50.

——. Private correspondence with Julia Watson, June 20, 2000.

——. *Recovering Bodies: Illness, Disability, and Life Writing*. Madison: University of Wisconsin Press, 1997.

Cox, James. *Recovering Literature's Lost Ground: Essays in American Autobiography*. Baton Rouge: Louisiana State University Press, 1989.

Craig, Terrence L. *The Missionary Lives: A Study in Canadian Missionary Biography and Autobiography*. New York: Brill, 1997.

Culley, Margo. *American Women's Autobiography: Fea(s)ts of Memory*. Madison: University of Wisconsin Press, 1992.

——, ed. Introduction. In *A Day at a Time: Diary Literature of American Women from 1764 to the Present*. New York: Feminist Press, 1985.

Dalziell, Rosamund. *Shameful Autobiographies: Shame in Contemporary Australian Autobiographies and Culture*. Melbourne: Melbourne University Press, 2000.

Damasio, Antonio R. *Descartes' Error: Emotion, Reason, and the Human Brain*. New York: Putnam, 1994.

Danahay, Martin. *A Community of One: Masculine Autobiography and Autonomy in Nineteenth-Century Britain*. Albany: State University of New York Press, 1993.

——. "Professional Subjects: Prepackaging the Academic C.V." In *Getting a Life*, ed. Smith and Watson, 351–68.

Davies, Carole Boyce. *Black Women, Writing, and Identity: Migrations of the Subject*. London: Routledge, 1994.

Dekker, Rudolf. *Childhood, Memory, and Autobiography in Holland: From the Golden Age to Romanticism*. New York: St. Martin's Press, 2000.

Delany, Paul. *British Autobiography in the Seventeenth Century.* London: Routledge and Kegan Paul, 1969.

de Lauretis, Teresa. *Alice Doesn't: Feminism, Semiotics, Cinema.* Bloomington: Indiana University Press, 1984.

——. "Eccentric Subjects: Feminist Theory and Historical Consciousness." *Feminist Studies* 16, no. 1 (Spring 1990): 115–50.

de Man, Paul. "Autobiography as De-Facement." *Modern Language Notes* 94, no. 5 (Dec. 1979): 919–30.

Dentith, Simon. "Contemporary Working-Class Autobiography: Politics of Form, Politics of Content." In *Modern Selves: Essays on Modern British and American Autobiography*, ed. Philip Dodd, 60–80. London: Frank Cass, 1986.

Derounian-Stodola, Kathryn Zabelle, and James A. Levernier. *The Indian Captivity Narrative, 1550-1900.* New York: Twayne, 1993.

Derrida, Jacques. *The Ear of the Other: Otobiography, Transference, Translation.* Texts and Discussions with Jacques Derrida. Edited by Christie V. McDonald. Translated by Peggy Kamuf. New York: Schocken Books, 1985.

Dilthey, Wilhelm. *Pattern and Meaning in History: W. Dilthey's Thoughts on History and Society.* Edited by H. P. Rickman. New York: Harper & Row, 1960.

——. *Selected Writings.* Edited and translated by H. P. Rickman. New York: Cambridge University Press, 1976.

Du Bois, W.E.B. *The Souls of Black Folk: Essays and Sketches.* Chicago: A. C. McClurg, 1903.

Eakin, Paul John. *American Autobiography: Retrospect and Prospect.* Madison: University of Wisconsin Press, 1992.

——. *Fictions of Autobiography: Studies in the Art of Self-Invention.* Princeton: Princeton University Press, 1986.

——. *How Our Lives Become Stories: Making Selves.* Ithaca, N.Y.: Cornell University Press, 1999.

——. *Touching the World: Reference in Autobiography.* Princeton: Princeton University Press, 1992.

Eco, Umberto. *The Role of the Reader: Explorations in the Semiotics of Texts.* Bloomington: Indiana University Press, 1979.

Egan, Susanna. *Mirror Talk: Genres of Crisis in Contemporary Autobiography.* Chapel Hill: University of North Carolina Press, 1999.

——. *Patterns of Experience in Autobiography.* Chapel Hill: University of North Carolina Press, 1984.

——. "'Self'-Conscious History: American Autobiography after the Civil War." In *American Autobiography*, ed. Eakin, 70–94.

Emberley, Julia V. *Thresholds of Difference: Feminist Critique, Native Women's Writing, Postcolonial Theory*. Toronto: University of Toronto Press, 1993.

Engel, Susan. *Context Is Everything: The Nature of Memory*. New York: W. H. Freeman, 1999.

Evans, Mary. *Missing Persons: The Impossibility of Auto/biography*. London: Routledge, 1999.

Fabian, Ann. *The Unvarnished Truth: Personal Narratives in Nineteenth-Century America*. Berkeley: University of California Press, 2000.

Felman, Shoshana, and Dori Laub. *Testimony: Crises of Witnessing in Literature, Psychoanalysis, and History*. New York: Routledge, 1992.

Felski, Rita. *Beyond Feminist Aesthetics: Feminist Literature and Social Change*. Boston: Harvard University Press, 1989.

Finke, Laurie. "Mystical Bodies and the Dialogics of Vision." In *Maps of Flesh and Light: The Religious Experience of Medieval Women Mystics*, ed. Ulrike Wiethaus, 28–44. Syracuse, N.Y.: Syracuse University Press, 1993.

Fish, Stanley. "Just Published: Minutiae Without Meaning." *New York Times*, Sept. 7, 1999, A19.

Fisher, Dexter. "The Transformation of Tradition: A Study of Zitkala-S̆a and Mourning Dove, Two Transitional American Indian Writers." In *Critical Essays on Native American Literature*, ed. Andrew Wiget, 202–11. Boston: Hall, 1985.

Fleischman, Suzanne. "Gender, the Personal, and the Voice of Scholarship: A Viewpoint." *Signs* 24, no. 4 (Summer 1998): 975–1016.

Fleishman, Avrom. *Figures of Autobiography: The Language of Self-Writing in Victorian and Modern England*. Berkeley: University of California Press, 1983.

Folkenflik, Robert, ed. "Introduction: The Institution of Autobiography." In *The Culture of Autobiography: Constructions of Self-Representation*, 1–20. Palo Alto: Stanford University Press, 1993.

Foster, Frances Smith. *Witnessing Slavery: The Development of Ante-Bellum Slave Narratives*. Westport, Conn: Greenwood Press, 1979.

Fothergill, Robert A. "One Day at a Time: The Diary as Life Writing." *a/b: Auto/Biography Studies* 10, no. 1 (Spring 1995): 81–91.

——. *Private Chronicles: A Study of English Diaries*. London: Oxford University Press, 1974.

Foucault, Michel. *The History of Sexuality*, vol. 1. Translated by Robert Hurley. New York: Pantheon Books, 1978.

——. "Technologies of the Self." In *Technologies of the Self: A Seminar with Michel Foucault*. Edited by Luther H. Martin, Huck Gutman, and Patrick H. Hutton, 16–49. Amherst: University of Massachusetts Press, 1988.

Franklin, Cynthia G. *Writing Women's Communities: The Politics and Poetics of Contemporary Multi-genre Anthologies*. Madison: University of Wisconsin Press, 1997.

Franklin, H. Bruce. *Prison Literature in America: The Victim as Criminal and Artist*. Westport, Conn.: L. Hill, 1978.

Freud, Sigmund. "Fragment of an Analysis of a Case of Hysteria." In *The Standard Edition of the Complete Psychological Works of Sigmund Freud*, ed. James Strachey, 7:3–122. London: Hogarth Press, 1953.

Friedman, Ellen G. "A Conversation with Kathy Ackerman." *The Review of Contemporary Fiction* 9, no. 3 (Fall 1989): 12–23.

——. "'Now Eat Your Mind': An Introduction to the Works of Kathy Acker." *The Review of Contemporary Fiction* 9, no. 3 (Fall 1989): 37–49.

Friedman, Susan Stanford. *Mappings: Feminism and the Cultural Geographies of Encounter*. Princeton: Princeton University Press, 1998.

——. "Women's Autobiographical Selves: Theory and Practice." In *The Private Self: Theory and Practice of Women's Autobiographical Writings*, ed. Shari Benstock, 34–62. Chapel Hill: University of North Carolina Press, 1988.

Fuderer, Laura Sue. *The Female Bildungsroman in English*. New York: Modern Language Association of America, 1990.

Gagnier, Regenia. *Subjectivities: A History of Self-Representation in Britain, 1832-1920*. New York: Oxford University Press, 1991.

Gates, Henry Louis, Jr. *Bearing Witness: Selections from African-American Autobiography in the Twentieth Century*. New York: Pantheon Books, 1991.

——. *The Signifying Monkey: A Theory of Afro-American Literary Criticism*. New York: Oxford University Press, 1988.

Geesey, Patricia, ed. *Autobiography and African Literature*. Special issue. *Research in African Literatures* 28, no. 2 (Summer 1997).

Gilligan, Carol. *In a Different Voice: Psychological Theory and Women's Development*. Cambridge: Harvard University Press, 1982.

Gilmore, Leigh. *Autobiographics: A Feminist Theory of Women's Self-Representation*. Ithaca, N.Y.: Cornell University Press, 1994.

——. *The Limits of Autobiography: Trauma and Testimony*. Ithaca, N.Y.: Cornell University Press, 2001.

Glissant, Edouard. *Caribbean Discourse: Selected Essays.* Translated by J. Michael Dash. Charlottesville: University Press of Virginia, 1989.

Glotfelty, Cheryll, and Harold Fromm, eds. *The Ecocriticism Reader: Landmarks in Literary Ecology.* Athens: University of Georgia Press, 1996.

Gluck, Sherna Berger, and Daphne Patai, eds. *Women's Words: The Feminist Practice of Oral History.* New York: Routledge, 1991.

Goldman, Anne E. *Take My Word: Autotopographical Innovations of Ethnic American Working Women.* Berkeley: University of California Press, 1996.

Gonzáles, Jennifer A. "Autobiographies." In *Prosthetic Territories: Politics and Hyper-technologies,* ed. Gabriel Brahm Jr. and Mark Driscoll, 133–50. Boulder, Colo.: Westview Press, 1995.

Goodman, Katherine R. *Dis/Closures: Women's Autobiography in Germany between 1790 and 1914.* New York: Peter Lang, 1986.

Green, Barbara. *Spectacular Confessions: Autobiography, Performative Activism, and the Sites of Suffrage.* New York: St. Martin's Press, 1997.

Greenblatt, Stephen. *Renaissance Self-Fashioning: From More to Shakespeare.* Chicago: University of Chicago Press, 1980.

Grewal, Inderpal. *Home and Harem: Nation, Gender, Empire, and the Cultures of Travel.* Durham, N.C.: Duke University Press, 1996.

Grewal, Inderpal, and Caren Kaplan, eds. *Scattered Hegemonies: Postmodernity and Transnational Feminist Practices.* Minneapolis: University of Minnesota Press, 1994.

Grosz, Elizabeth. *Volatile Bodies: Toward a Corporeal Feminism.* Bloomington: Indiana University Press, 1994.

Gullette, Margaret Morganroth. *Declining to Decline: Cultural Combat and the Politics of the Midlife.* Charlottesville: University Press of Virginia, 1997.

Gunn, Janet Varner. *Autobiography: Toward a Poetics of Experience.* Philadelphia: University of Pennsylvania Press, 1982.

Gunning, Sandra. "Reading and Redemption in *Incidents in the Life of a Slave Girl.*" In *Harriet Jacobs and Incidents in the Life of a Slave Girl,* ed. Deborah Garfield and Rafia Zafar, 131–55. New York: Cambridge University Press, 1996.

Gusdorf, Georges. "Conditions and Limits of Autobiography." Translated by James Olney. In *Autobiography,* ed. and trans. Olney, 28–48.

Haaken, Janice. *Pillar of Salt: Gender, Memory, and the Perils of Looking Back.* New Brunswick, N.J.: Rutgers University Press, 1998.

——. "The Recovery of Memory, Fantasy, and Desire: Feminist Approaches to Sexual Abuse and Psychic Trauma." *Signs* 21 (Summer 1996): 1069–94.

Hall, Stuart. "Cultural Identity and Diaspora." In *Colonial Discourse and Post-Colonial Theory: A Reader,* ed. Patrick Williams and Laura Chrisman, 392–403. New York: Columbia University Press, 1994.

Hanley, Christine. *Columbus Dispatch*, Sept. 14, 2000, A-10.

Harlow, Barbara. *Barred: Women, Writing, and Political Detention.* Middletown, Conn.: Wesleyan University Press, 1992.

——. "From a Women's Prison: Third World Women's Narratives of Prison." *Feminist Studies* 12, no. 3 (1986): 501–24.

——. *Resistance Literatures.* New York: Methuen, 1987.

Harris, Jane Gary, ed. *Autobiographical Statements in Twentieth-Century Russian Literature.* Princeton: Princeton University Press, 1990.

Hart, Francis R. "Notes for an Anatomy of Modern Autobiography." *New Literary History* 1 (Spring 1970): 486–511.

Hawkins, Anne Hunsaker. *Reconstructing Illness: Studies in Pathography.* West Lafayette, Ind.: Purdue University Press, 1993.

Hayano, David. "Auto-Ethnography: Paradigms, Problems, and Prospects." *Human Organization* 38, no. 1 (1979): 99–104.

Henderson, Mae Gwendolyn. "Speaking in Tongues: Dialogics, Dialectics, and the Black Woman Writer's Literary Tradition." In *Changing Our Words: Essays on Criticism, Theory, and Writing by Black Women,* ed. Cheryl A. Wall, 116–42. New Brunswick, N.J.: Rutgers University Press, 1989.

Henke, Suzette. *Shattered Subjects: Trauma and Testimony in Women's Life-Writing.* New York: St. Martin's Press, 1998.

Hesford, Wendy S. *Framing Identities: Autobiography and the Politics of Pedagogy.* Minneapolis: University of Minnesota Press, 1999.

Hewitt, Leah D. *Autobiographical Tightropes: Simone de Beauvoir, Nathalie Sarraute, Marguerite Duras, Monique Wittig, and Maryse Condé.* Lincoln: University of Nebraska Press, 1990.

Hirsch, Marianne. *Family Frames: Photography, Narrative, and Postmemory.* Cambridge: Harvard University Press, 1997.

——. "Masking the Subject: Practicing Theory." In *The Point of Theory: Practices in Cultural Analysis,* ed. Mieke Bal and Inge E. Boer, 109–24. New York: Continuum, 1994.

Holman, C. Hugh. Preface to *A Handbook to Literature*, ed. William Flint Thrall and Addison Hibbard. Rev. by C. Hugh Holman, v–vi. New York: Odyssey Press, 1960.

Hooton, Joy. *Stories of Herself When Young: Autobiographies of Childhood by Australian Women*. New York: Oxford University Press. 1990.

Howarth, William L. "Some Principles of Autobiography." In *Autobiography*, ed. Olney, 84–114.

Huff, Cynthia. *British Women's Diaries: A Descriptive Bibliography of Selected Nineteenth-Century Women's Manuscript Diaries*. New York: AMS Press, 1985.

Hughes, Alex. *Heterographies: Sexual Difference in French Autobiography*. Oxford: Berg, 1999.

Hunsacker, Steven V. *Autobiography and National Identity in the Americas*. Charlottesville: University Press of Virginia, 1999.

Ibsen, Kristine. *Women's Spiritual Autobiography in Colonial Spanish America*. Gainesville: University Press of Florida, 1999.

Jackson, David. *Unmasking Masculinity: A Critical Autobiography*. London: Unwin Hyman, 1990.

Jardine, Alice. *Gynesis: Configurations of Women and Modernity*. Ithaca, N.Y.: Cornell University Press, 1985.

Jay, Paul. *Being in the Text: Self-Representation from Wordsworth to Roland Barthes*. Ithaca, N.Y.: Cornell University Press, 1984.

Jelinek, Estelle C., ed. *Women's Autobiography: Essays in Criticism*. Bloomington: Indiana University Press, 1980.

Johnson, Barbara. *The Critical Difference: Essays in the Contemporary Rhetoric of Reading*. Baltimore: John Hopkins University Press, 1980.

Kaminsky, Amy K. *Reading the Body Politic: Feminist Criticism and Latin American Women Writers*. Minneapolis: University of Minnesota Press, 1993.

Kaplan, Caren. *Questions of Travel: Modern Discourses of Displacement*. Durham: Duke University Press, 1996.

——. "Resisting Autobiography: Out-Law Genres and Transnational Feminist Subjects." In *De/Colonizing the Subject*, ed. Smith and Watson, 115–38.

Kawash, Samira. *Dislocating the Color Line: Identity, Hybridity, and Singularity in African-American Narrative*. Stanford: Stanford University Press, 1997.

Kline, Kerwin Lee. "On the Emergence of 'Memory' in Historical Discourse." *Representations* 69 (Winter 2000): 127–50.

Kosta, Barbara. *Recasting Autobiography: Women's Counterfictions in Contemporary German Literature and Film*. Ithaca, N.Y.: Cornell University Press, 1994.

Krailsheimer, A. J. *Studies in Self-Interest: From Descartes to La Bruyère*. Oxford: Clarendon Press, 1962.

Krupat, Arnold. *Ethnocriticism: Ethnography, History, Literature*. Berkeley: University of California Press, 1992.

——. *For Those Who Come After: A Study of Native American Autobiography*. Berkeley: University of California Press, 1985.

——. "Introduction." In *Native American Autobiography: An Anthology*, 3–17. Madison: University of Wisconsin Press, 1994.

Kuhn, Annette. *Family Secrets: Acts of Memory and Imagination*. London: Verso, 1995.

Kuhn, Thomas. *The Structure of Scientific Revolutions*. Chicago: University of Chicago Press, 1970.

Lacan, Jacques. *The Language of the Self: The Function of Language in Psychoanalysis*. Translated by Anthony Wilden. Baltimore: Johns Hopkins University Press, 1968.

Lang, Candace D. "Autobiography in the Aftermath of Romanticism." *Diacritics* 12 (Winter 1982): 2–16.

——. *Irony/Humor: Critical Paradigms*. Baltimore: Johns Hopkins University Press, 1988.

Larson, Wendy. *Literary Authority and the Modern Chinese Writer: Ambivalence and Autobiography*. Durham, N.C.: Duke University Press, 1991.

Lather, Patti, and Chris Smithies. *Troubling the Angels: Women Living with HIV/AIDS*. Boulder, Colo.: Westview Press, 1997.

Leed, Eric J. *The Mind of the Traveler: From Gilgamesh to Global Tourism*. New York: Basic Books, 1991.

Leith, Dick, and George Myerson. *The Power of Address: Explorations in Rhetoric*. London: Routledge, 1989.

Lejeune, Philippe. "The Autobiographical Pact." In *On Autobiography*, ed. Paul John Eakin, trans. Katherine Leary. Minneapolis: University of Minnesota Press, 1989.

——. "The Autobiographical Pact (bis)." In Lejeune, *On Autobiography*, 119–37.

——. *L'Autobiographie en France*. Paris: Colin, 1971.

——. "The Autobiography of Those Who Do Not Write." In Lejeune, *On Autobiography*, 185–215.

———. *On Autobiography*. Edited by Paul John Eakin. Translated by Katherine Leary. Minneapolis: University of Minnesota Press, 1989.

———. "The Practice of the Private Journal: Chronicle of an Investigation (1986–1998)." In *Marginal Voices, Marginal Forms: Diaries in European Literature and History*, ed. Rachel Langford and Russell West, 185–211. Amsterdam: Rodopi, 1999.

Levin, Susan M. *The Romantic Art of Confession: De Quincey, Musset, Sand, Lamb, Hogg, Frémy, Soulié, Janin*. Columbia, S.C.: Camden House, 1998.

Lim, Shirley Geok-lin. *Writing S.E./Asia in English: Against the Grain, Focus on Asian English-Language Literature*. London: Skoob Books, 1994.

Linde, Charlotte. *Life Stories: The Creation of Coherence*. New York: Oxford University Press, 1993.

Ling, Amy. *Between Worlds: Women Writers of Chinese Ancestry*. New York: Pergamon Press, 1990.

Linville, Susan E. *Feminism, Film, Fascism: Women's Auto/Biographical Film in Postwar Germany*. Austin: University of Texas Press, 1998.

Lionnet, Françoise. *Autobiographical Voices: Race, Gender, Self-Portraiture*. Ithaca, N.Y.: Cornell University Press, 1989.

———. "Of Mangoes and Maroons: Language, History, and the Multicultural Subject of Michelle Cliff's *Abeng*." In *De/Colonizing the Subject*, ed. Smith and Watson, 321–45.

———. *Postcolonial Representations: Women, Literature, Identity*. Ithaca, N.Y.: Cornell University Press, 1995.

Lionnet, Françoise, and Ronnie Scharfman, eds. *Post/Colonial Conditions: Exiles, Migrations, and Nomadisms*. 2 vols. New Haven: Yale University Press, 1993.

Lorenz, Dagmar. *Keepers of the Motherland: German Texts by Jewish Women Writers*. Lincoln: University of Nebraska Press, 1997.

Loureiro, Angel G. *The Ethics of Autobiography: Replacing the Subject in Modern Spain*. Nashville: Vanderbilt University Press, 2000.

Lowe, Lisa. *Critical Terrains: French and British Orientalisms*. Ithaca, N.Y.: Cornell University Press, 1991.

———. *Immigrant Acts: On Asian American Cultural Politics*. Durham, N.C.: Duke University Press, 1996.

Lyotard, Jean-François. *The Postmodern Condition: A Report on Knowledge*. Translated by Geoff Bennington and Brian Massumi. Minneapolis: University of Minnesota Press, 1984.

Marcus, Laura. *Auto/Biographical Discourses: Theory, Criticism, Practice*. Manchester: Manchester University Press, 1994.

Martz, Louis Lohr. *The Poetry of Meditation: A Study in English Religious Literature of the Seventeenth Century*. New Haven: Yale University Press, 1954.

Mascuch, Michael. *Origins of the Individual Self: Autobiography and Self-Identity in England, 1591-1791*. Cambridge: Polity Press, 1997.

Mason, Mary G. "Autobiographies of Women Writers." In *Autobiography*, ed. Olney, 207–35.

McKenna, Teresa. *Migrant Song: Politics and Process in Contemporary Chicano Literature*. Austin: University of Texas Press, 1997.

Milani, Farzaneh. *Veils and Words: The Emerging Voices of Iranian Women Writers*. Syracuse: Syracuse University Press, 1992.

Miller, Christopher L. *Theories of Africans: Francophone Literatures and Anthropology in Africa*. Chicago: University of Chicago Press, 1990.

Miller, Nancy K. *Getting Personal*. New York: Routledge, 1991.

——. "Representing Others: Gender and the Subjects of Autobiography." *differences* 6, no. 1 (1994): 1–27.

——. "Writing Fictions: Women's Autobiography in France." In *Life/Lines: Theorizing Women's Autobiography*, ed. Bella Brodzki and Celeste Schenck, 45–61. Ithaca, N.Y.: Cornell University Press, 1988.

Misch, Georg. *A History of Autobiography in Antiquity*. Trans. E. W. Dickes. 2 vols. 1907; London: Routledge & Paul, 1950.

Mitchell, W. J. T. *Picture Theory: Essays on Visual and Verbal Representation*. Chicago: University of Chicago Press, 1994.

Molloy, Sylvia. *Autobiographical Writings in Spanish America: At Face Value*. Cambridge: Cambridge University Press, 1991.

Mostern, Kenneth. *Autobiography and Black Identity Politics: Racialization in Twentieth-Century America*. Cambridge: Cambridge University Press, 1999.

Mouffe, Chantal. "Feminism, Citizenship, and Radical Democratic Politics." In *Feminists Theorize the Political*, ed. Judith Butler and Joan W. Scott, 369–84. New York: Routledge, 1992.

Muske-Dukes, Carol. *Women and Poetry: Truth, Autobiography, and the Shape of the Self*. Ann Arbor: University of Michigan Press, 1997.

Nadel, Ira Bruce. *Biography: Fiction, Fact, and Form*. New York: St. Martin's Press, 1984.

Namias, June. Introduction. In *A Narrative of the Life of Mrs. Mary Jemison*. James E. Seaver. Norman: University of Oklahoma Press, 1992.

Nelson, Katherine. "The Psychological and Social Origins of Autobiographical Memory." *Psychological Science* 4, no. 1 (Jan. 1993): 7–14.

Neuman, Shirley. "Autobiography, Bodies, Manhood." In *Autobiography and Questions of Gender*, ed. Neuman, 137–65. London: Frank Cass, 1991.

———. "Introduction: Reading Canadian Autobiography." In *Canadian Autobiography*, guest ed. Shirley Neuman. Special issue. *Essays on Canadian Writing* 60 (Winter 1996): 1–13.

Nichols, Charles Harold. *Many Thousand Gone: The Ex-Slaves' Account of Their Bondage and Freedom*. Leiden: E. J. Brill, 1963.

Nussbaum, Felicity A. *The Autobiographical Subject*. 2nd ed. Baltimore: Johns Hopkins University Press, 1995.

Oliver, Kelly. *Witnessing: Beyond Recognition*. Minneapolis: University of Minnesota Press, 2001.

Olney, James. "Autobiography and the Cultural Moment." In *Autobiography*, ed. Olney, 3–27.

———. "'I Was Born': Slave Narratives, Their Status as Autobiography and as Literature." In *The Slave's Narrative*, ed. Charles T. Davis and Henry Louis Gates Jr., 148–74. New York: Oxford University Press, 1985.

———. *Memory and Narrative: The Weave of Life-Writing*. Chicago: University of Chicago Press, 1998.

———. *Metaphors of Self: The Meaning of Autobiography*. Princeton: Princeton University Press, 1972.

———. "Some Versions of Memory/Some Versions of Bios: The Ontology of Autobiography." In *Autobiography*, ed. Olney, 236–67.

———. *Tell Me Africa: An Approach to African Literature*. Princeton: Princeton University Press, 1973.

———, ed. *Autobiography: Essays Theoretical and Critical*. Princeton: Princeton University Press, 1980.

Ortner, Sherry B. *Making Gender: The Politics and Erotics of Culture*. Boston: Beacon Press, 1996.

Padilla, Genaro M. *My History, Not Yours: The Formation of Mexican American Autobiography*. Madison: University of Wisconsin Press, 1993.

Panofsky, Erwin. *Tomb Sculpture: Four Lectures on Its Changing Aspects from Ancient Egypt to Bernini*. Edited by H. W. Janson. New York: H. N. Abrams, 1964.

Parati, Graziella. *Public History, Private Stories: Italian Women's Autobiography*. Minneapolis: University of Minnesota Press, 1996.

Pascal, Roy. *Design and Truth in Autobiography.* Cambridge: Harvard University Press, 1960.

Paxton, Nancy. *Writing Under the Raj: Gender, Race, and Rape in the British Colonial Imagination, 1830-1947.* New Brunswick, N.J.: Rutgers University Press, 1999.

Peck, Janice. "The Mediated Talking Cure: Therapeutic Framing of Autobiography on TV Talk Shows." In *Getting a Life*, ed. Smith and Watson, 134–155.

Perreault, Jeanne. *Writing Selves: Contemporary Feminist Autography.* Minneapolis: University of Minnesota Press, 1995.

Peterson, Linda. "Instituting Women's Autobiography: Nineteenth-Century Editors and the Shaping of an Autobiographical Tradition." In *The Culture of Autobiography: Constructions of Self-Representation*, ed. Robert Folkenflik, 80–103. Stanford: Stanford University Press, 1993.

——. *Traditions of Victorian Women's Autobiography: The Poetics and Politics of Life Writing.* Charlottesville: University Press of Virginia, 1999.

——. *Victorian Autobiography: The Tradition of Self-Interpretation.* New Haven: Yale University Press, 1986.

Phillips, Dana. "Ecocriticism, Literary Theory, and the Truth of Ecology." *New Literary History* 30, no. 3 (Summer 1999): 577–602.

Plowman, Andrew. *The Radical Subject: Social Change and the Self in Recent German Autobiography.* Bern: Peter Lang, 1998.

Plummer, Ken. *Telling Sexual Stories: Power, Change and Social Worlds.* London: Routledge, 1995.

Polkey, Pauline, ed. *Women's Lives into Print: The Theory Practice and Writing of Feminist Auto/Biography.* New York: St. Martin's Press, 1999.

Pollock, Griselda. *Differencing the Canon: Feminist Desire and the Writing of Art's Histories.* London: Routledge, 1999.

Popkin, Jeremy D. "Historians on the Autobiographical Frontier." *American Historical Review* 104, no. 3 (June 1999): 725–48.

Porter, Dennis. *Haunted Journeys: Desire and Transgression in European Travel Writing.* Princeton: Princeton University Press, 1991.

Porter, Roger. *Self-Same Songs: Autobiographical Reflections and Performances.* Lincoln: University of Nebraska Press, 2002.

Poster, Mark. *What's the Matter with the Internet?* Minneapolis: University of Minnesota Press, 2001.

Pratt, Mary Louise. *Imperial Eyes: Travel Writing and Transculturation*. London: Routledge, 1992.

——. "Mad about Menchú." *Lingua Franca* 9, no. 8 (Nov. 1999): 22.

——. "'Me llamo Rigoberta Menchú': Auto-Ethnography and the Recoding of Citizenship." In *Teaching and Testimony: Rigoberta Menchú and the North American Classroom*, ed. Allen Carey-Webb and Stephen Benz, 57–72. Albany: State University of New York Press, 1996.

Progoff, Ira. *At a Journal Workshop: Writing to Access the Power of the Unconscious and Evoke Creative Ability*. Los Angeles: J. P. Tarcher, 1992.

Quinby, Lee. "The Subject of Memoirs: *The Woman Warrior*'s Technology of Ideographic Selfhood." In *De/Colonizing the Subject*, ed. Smith and Watson, 297–320.

Raiskin, Judith. *Snow in the Cane Fields: Women's Writing and Creole Subjectivity*. Minneapolis: University of Minnesota Press, 1996.

Rapaport, Herman. "The New Personalism." *Biography* 21, no. 1 (Winter 1998): 36–49.

Ray, Ruth E. *Beyond Nostalgia: Aging and Life-Story Writing*. Charlottesville: University Press of Virginia, 2000.

Raynaud, Claudine. "'A Nutmeg Nestled Inside Its Covering of Mace': Audre Lorde's *Zami*." In *Life/Lines: Theorizing Women's Autobiography*, ed. Bella Brodzki and Celeste Schenck, 221–42. Ithaca, N.Y.: Cornell University Press, 1988.

——. "'Rubbing a Paragraph with a Soft Cloth?' Muted Voices and Editorial Constraints in *Dust Tracks on a Road*." In *De/Colonizing the Subject*, ed. Smith and Watson, 34–64.

Reed-Danahay, Deborah E. *Auto/Ethnography: Rewriting the Self and the Social*. New York: Berg, 1997.

Renza, Louis A. "The Veto of the Imagination: A Theory of Autobiography." In *Autobiography*, ed. Olney, 268–95.

Richter, Gerhard. *Walter Benjamin and the Corpus of Autobiography*. Detroit: Wayne State University Press, 2000.

Rimmon-Kenan, Shlomith. *Narrative Fiction: Contemporary Poetics*. London: Routledge, 1983.

Rodriguez, Barbara. *Autobiographical Inscriptions: Form, Personhood, and the American Woman Writer of Color*. New York: Oxford University Press, 1999.

Rooke, Tetz. *In My Childhood: A Study of Arabic Autobiography*. Stockholm: Stockholm University Press, 1997.

Roorbach, Bill. *Writing Life Stories*. Cincinnati: Writer's Digest, 1999.

Rose, Steven. *The Making of Memory: From Molecules to Mind*. New York: Anchor Books, 1993.

Rowbotham, Sheila. *Woman's Consciousness, Man's World*. Harmondsworth: Penguin, 1973.

Rugg, Linda Haverty. *Picturing Ourselves: Photography and Autobiography*. Chicago: University of Chicago Press, 1997.

Ruoff, A. LaVonne Brown. *American Indian Literatures: An Introduction, Bibliographic Review, and Selected Bibliography*. New York: Modern Language Association of America, 1990.

——. *Literatures of the American Indian*. New York: Chelsea House Publishers, 1991.

Rushdy, Ashraf H. A. *Neo-Slave Narratives: Studies in the Social Logic of a Literary Form*. New York: Oxford University Press, 1999.

Sabbioni, Jennifer, Kay Schaffer, and Sidonie Smith, eds. *Indigenous Australian Voices: A Reader*. New Brunswick, N.J.: Rutgers University Press, 1998.

Said, Edward. *Culture and Imperialism*. New York: Vintage Books, 1994.

Saldívar, José David. *Border Matters: Remapping American Cultural Studies*. Berkeley: University of California Press, 1997.

Saldívar, Ramón. *Chicano Narrative: The Dialectics of Difference*. Madison: University of Wisconsin Press, 1990.

Saldívar-Hull, Sonia. *Feminism on the Border: Chicana Gender Politics and Literature*. Berkeley: University of California Press, 2000.

Sanders, Mark. "Theorizing the Collaborative Self: The Dynamics of Contour and Content in the Dictated Autobiography." *New Literary History* 25 (1994): 445–58.

Sands, Kathleen M. "Indian Women's Personal Narrative: Voices Past and Present." In *American Women's Autobiography: Feas(t)s of Memory*, ed. Margo Culley, 268–94. Madison: University of Wisconsin Press, 1992.

Sartwell, Crispin. *Act Like You Know: African-American Autobiography and White Identity*. Chicago: University of Chicago Press, 1998.

Saussure, Ferdinand de. *Course in General Linguistics*. Edited by Charles Bally, Albert Sechehaye and Albert Riedlinger. Translated by Roy Harris. London: Duckworth, 1983.

Sayre, Robert F. *The Examined Self: Benjamin Franklin, Henry Adams, Henry James*. Madison: University of Wisconsin Press, 1988.

——, ed. *American Lives: An Anthology of Autobiographical Writing*. Madison: University of Wisconsin Press, 1994.

Schacter, Daniel L. *Searching for Memory: The Brain, the Mind, and the Past*. New York: Basic Books, 1996.

Schaffer, Kay. *In the Wake of First Contact: The Eliza Fraser Stories*. Cambridge: Cambridge University Press, 1995.

Scholes, Robert, and Robert Kellogg. *The Nature of Narrative*. New York: Oxford University Press, 1966.

Scott, Joan W. "Experience." In *Feminists Theorize the Political*, ed. Judith Butler and Joan W. Scott, 22–40. New York: Routledge, 1992.

Shea, Daniel B. "The Prehistory of American Autobiography." In *American Autobiography*, ed. Eakin, 25–46.

——. *Spiritual Autobiography in Early America*. Madison: University of Wisconsin Press, 1988.

Sheringham, Michael. *French Autobiography: Devices and Desires*. Oxford: Clarendon Press, 1993.

Shumaker, Wayne. *English Autobiography: Its Emergence, Materials, and Forms*. Berkeley: University of California Press, 1954.

Siegel, Kristi. *Women's Autobiographies, Culture, Feminism*. New York: Peter Lang, 1999.

Siegert, Bernhard. *Relais: Literature as an Epoch of the Postal System*. Translated by Kevin Repp. Stanford: Stanford University Press, 1999.

Sioui, Georges E. *Autohistory: An Essay on the Foundations of a Social Ethic*. Translated by Sheila Fischman. Montreal: McGill-Queen's University Press, 1992.

Smith, Paul. *Discerning the Subject*. Minneapolis: University of Minnesota Press, 1988.

Smith, Sidonie. *Moving Lives: Twentieth-Century Women's Travel Writing*. Minneapolis: University of Minnesota Press, 2001.

——. "Performativity, Autobiographical Practice, Resistance." *a/b: Auto/Biography Studies* 10, no. 1 (Spring 1995): 17–33.

——. *A Poetics of Women's Autobiography: Marginality and the Fictions of Self-Representation*. Bloomington: Indiana University Press, 1987.

——. *Subjectivity, Identity, and the Body: Women's Autobiographical Practices in the Twentieth Century*. Bloomington: Indiana University Press, 1993.

Smith, Sidonie, and Julia Watson, eds. *De/Colonizing the Subject: The Politics of Gender in Women's Autobiography*. Minneapolis: University of Minnesota Press, 1992.

———. *Getting a Life: Everyday Uses of Autobiography*. Minneapolis: University of Minnesota Press, 1996.

———. *Interfaces: Women's Visual and Performance Autobiographies*. Ann Arbor: University of Michigan Press, forthcoming.

———. *Women, Autobiography, Theory: A Reader*. Madison: University of Wisconsin Press, 1998.

Smith, Valerie. *Self-Discovery and Authority in Afro-American Narrative*. Cambridge: Harvard University Press, 1987.

Sodhi, Meena. *Indian English Writing: The Autobiographical Mode*. New Delhi: Creative Books, 1999.

Sollors, Werner. *Beyond Ethnicity: Consent and Descent in American Culture*. New York: Oxford University Press, 1986.

———. *Neither Black Nor White Yet Both: Thematic Explorations of Interracial Literature*. New York: Oxford University Press, 1977.

Southey, Robert. "Portugueze Literature." *Quarterly Review* 1 (1809).

Spacks, Patricia Ann Meyer. *Imagining a Self: Autobiography and Novel in Eighteenth-Century England*. Cambridge: Harvard University Press, 1976.

Spender, Stephen. "Confessions and Autobiography." In *Autobiography*, ed. Olney, 115–22.

Spengemann, William C. *The Forms of Autobiography: Episodes in the History of a Literary Genre*. New Haven: Yale University Press, 1980.

Spivak, Gayatri Chakravorty. "Lives." In *Confessions of the Critics: North American Critics' Autobiographical Moves*, ed. H. Aram Veeser, 205–18. New York: Routledge, 1996.

Sprinker, Michael. "Fictions of the Self: The End of Autobiography." In *Autobiography*, ed. Olney, 321–42.

Stanley, Liz. *The Auto/Biographical I: The Theory and Practice of Feminist Auto/Biography*. Manchester: Manchester University Press, 1992.

Stanton, Domna C. "Autogynography: Is the Subject Different?" In *The Female Autograph*, ed. Domna C. Stanton, 3–20. New York: New York Literary Forum, 1984.

———, ed. *The Female Autograph*. New York: New York Literary Forum, 1984.

Starobinski, Jean. "The Style of Autobiography." In *Autobiography*, ed. Olney, 73–83.

Stepto, Robert B. *From Behind the Veil: A Study of Afro-American Narrative.* Champaign-Urbana: University of Illinois Press, 1979.

Stoll, David. *Rigoberta Menchú and the Story of All Poor Guatemalans.* Boulder, Colo.: Westview Press, 1999.

Stone, Albert E. *Autobiographical Occasions and Original Acts: Versions of American Identity from Henry Adams to Nate Shaw.* Philadelphia: University of Pennsylvania Press, 1982.

——. "Modern American Autobiography: Texts and Transactions." In *American Autobiography*, ed. Eakin, 95–120.

Strathern, Marilyn. "The Limits of Auto-Anthropology." In *Anthropology at Home*, ed. Anthony Jackson, 16–37. London: Tavistock Publications, 1987.

Sturrock, John. "The New Model Autobiographer." *New Literary History* 9, no. 1 (Autumn 1977): 51–63.

Suleri, Sara. *The Rhetoric of English India.* Chicago: University of Chicago Press, 1992.

Swindells, Julia. *The Uses of Autobiography.* London: Taylor and Francis, 1995.

Tambling, Jeremy. *Confession: Sexuality, Sin, the Subject.* Manchester: Manchester University Press, 1990.

Thomson, Rosemarie Garland. *Extraordinary Bodies: Figuring Physical Disability in American Culture and Literature.* New York: Columbia University Press, 1997.

——. *Freakery: Cultural Spectacles of the Extraordinary Body.* New York: New York University Press, 1996.

Van Den Abbeele, Georges. *Travel as Metaphor: From Montaigne to Rousseau.* Minneapolis: University of Minnesota Press, 1992.

Veeser, H. Aram, ed. *Confessions of the Critics: North American Critics' Autobiographical Moves.* New York: Routledge, 1996.

Verene, Donald Phillip. *The New Art of Autobiography: An Essay on the Life of Giambattista Vico Written by Himself.* Oxford: Clarendon Press, 1991.

Warhol, Robyn, and Helena Michie. "Twelve-Step Teleology: Narratives of Recovery/Recovery as Narrative." In *Getting a Life*, ed. Smith and Watson, 327–50.

Watson, C. W. *Of Self and Nation: Autobiography and the Representation of Modern Indonesia.* Honolulu: University of Hawai'i Press, 2000.

Watson, Julia. "Ordering the Family: Genealogy as Autobiographical Pedigree." In *Getting a Life*, ed. Smith and Watson, 297–323.

———. "Unspeakable Differences: The Politics of Gender in Lesbian and Heterosexual Women's Autobiographies." In *De/Colonizing the Subject*, ed. Smith and Watson, 139–68.

Watson, Martha. *Lives of Their Own: Rhetorical Dimensions in Autobiographies of Women Activists*. Columbia: University of South Carolina Press, 1999.

Waxman, Barbara Frey. *To Live in the Center of the Moment: Literary Autobiographies of Aging*. Charlottesville: University Press of Virginia, 1997.

Weintraub, Karl Joachim. *The Value of the Individual: Self and Circumstance in Autobiography*. Chicago: University of Chicago Press, 1978.

Whitlock, Gillian. *The Intimate Empire: Reading Women's Autobiography*. London: Cassell, 2000.

Wimsatt, W. K. "The Intentional Fallacy." In Wimsatt, *The Verbal Icon: Studies in the Meaning of Poetry*, 3–18. Lexington: University of Kentucky Press, 1954.

Wimsatt, W. K., Jr., and Cleanth Brooks. *Literary Criticism: A Short History*. New York: Knopf, 1957.

Wingrove, Elizabeth. "Interpellating Sex." *Signs* 24, no. 4 (Summer 1999): 869–93.

Wong, Hertha D. Sweet. "First-Person Plural: Subjectivity and Community in Native American Women's Autobiography." In *Women, Autobiography, Theory*, ed. Smith and Watson, 168–78.

———. *Sending My Heart Back Across the Years: Tradition and Innovation in Native American Autobiography*. New York: Oxford University Press, 1992.

Wong, Sau-Ling Cynthia. "Immigrant Autobiography: Some Questions of Definition and Approach." In *American Autobiography*, ed. Eakin, 142–70.

———. *Reading Asian American Literature: From Necessity to Extravagance*. Princeton: Princeton University Press, 1993.

Woodhull, Winifred. *Transfigurations of the Maghreb: Feminism, Decolonization, and Literatures in France*. Minneapolis: University of Minnesota Press, 1993.

Woodward, Kathleen. *Aging and Its Discontents: Freud and Other Fictions*. Bloomington: Indiana University Press, 1991.

———, ed. *Figuring Age: Women, Bodies, Generations*. Bloomington: Indiana University Press, 1999.

Woolf, Virginia. *A Room of One's Own*. London: Hogarth Press, 1929.

Wu, Pei-Yi. *The Confucian's Progress: Autobiographical Writings in Traditional China*. Princeton: Princeton University Press, 1990.

Yates, Frances A. *The Art of Memory*. Chicago: University of Chicago Press, 1966.

Ziegenmeyer, Nancy, and Larkin Warren. *Taking Back My Life*. New York: Summit, 1992.

Index

Sidonie Smith is professor of English and women's studies at the University of Michigan. She has coedited three collections with Julia Watson: *Women, Autobiography, Theory: A Reader; Getting a Life: Everyday Uses of Autobiography* (Minnesota, 1996); and *De/Colonizing the Subject: The Politics of Gender in Women's Autobiography* (Minnesota, 1992). Her other publications include *Moving Lives: Twentieth-Century Women's Travel Writing* (Minnesota, 2001); *Indigenous Australian Voices: A Reader* (coedited with Jennifer Sabbioni and Kay Schaffer); *Writing New Identities: Gender, Nation, and Immigration in Contemporary Europe* (coedited with Gisela Brinker-Gabler; Minnesota, 1997); *Subjectivity, Identity, and the Body: Women's Autobiographical Practices in the Twentieth Century; A Poetics of Women's Autobiography: Marginality and the Fictions of Women's Self-Representation;* and *Where I'm Bound: Patterns of Slavery and Freedom in Black American Autobiography*. Her current project is on autobiography, human rights, and social change (with Kay Schaffer).

Julia Watson is associate professor of comparative studies of literature and culture at The Ohio State University. With Sidonie Smith, she has coedited three collections of essays: *De/Colonizing the Subject: The Politics of Gender in Women's Autobiography* (Minnesota, 1992); *Getting a Life: Everyday Uses of Autobiography* (Minnesota, 1996); and *Women, Autobiography, Theory: A Reader*. She has published several essays on autobiography, postcolonial writing, and feminist theory, and is working on a book on autoethnographic reading practices.